# The Book of Garden Flowers

. . . . *Flowers are here*
*Of loveliest colours and of sweetest smell.*

Christopher North.

# THE BOOK OF
# GARDEN FLOWERS

*by*

G. A. R. PHILLIPS

*With 80 Plates in Colour by*

JOAN LUPTON

A DESCRIPTIVE GUIDE TO
BOTH ANNUALS AND PERENNIALS
OF WHICH 320 VARIETIES ARE
ILLUSTRATED IN COLOUR

FREDERICK WARNE & CO. LTD.
LONDON AND NEW YORK

# CONTENTS

# PREFACE

THE object of this book is to provide an easy medium for the choice and identification of certain garden plants. Only those that may be admitted to the mixed flower border have been included. This has necessitated the inclusion of the more familiar favourites and, in addition, some of the lesser known but equally deserving genera have been described.

There are two sections. The first deals with plants of a perennial character, but does not confine itself to orthodox herbaceous perennials, viz. those plants that die down to ground-level each autumn and break into new growth and flower the following year. If such a limit were imposed there would be, indeed, a most unnecessary curtailment of the scope of the flower border. In order to give the widest possible choice within the range of two hundred subjects, bulbous plants, both hardy and half-hardy, have been included. Admittance has also been given to certain shrubby subjects of a dwarf or easily controlled character; these provide a permanent framework, as it were, upon which to build the border. Roses have been omitted, for these could only be dealt with adequately in a separate volume. The same remark applies to the alpine kingdom.

In the second section, attention has been concentrated on annuals to sow in their flowering positions, annuals to sow in heat and transplant to outdoor flowering positions, biennials, and perennials best treated as annuals or biennials. The list in this section has been limited to one hundred and twenty subjects and could be enlarged considerably. As, however, this book is intended to deal with the better known flowering plants only, it has been decided not to exceed this limitation.

In the descriptions of the various plants technical terms have been avoided so far as this is possible, and, to aid the reader, there is a full and illustrated Glossary of botanical terms. The nomenclature of L. H. Bailey's *Manual of Cultivated Plants*, 2nd ed. (1949), has generally though not always been followed. Line drawings of the various forms of inflorescence have not been given for there is, indeed, so much variation in flower and foliage that the only really satisfactory source of identification is by illustration. It is here that the coloured drawings of the various genera, carried out so admirably by Miss Joan Lupton, will prove to be

7

invaluable. Each drawing may be taken as a reliable guide to the plant it represents.

In addition to information concerning the habitat of each subject, its colour and habit, details have been given briefly concerning the particular cultural requirements of each, and suggestions have been made for its use in the flower garden. Methods of propagation have been given and also the season of flowering.

The genera have been arranged in alphabetical order of their botanical names in each section.

These details have been amplified in a general way in the introductory portion of each section, for it is thought that the reader, in addition to being able to recognize the various plants, will also have a flower garden where he or she may wish to cultivate a number of these plants for their own enjoyment.

I should not like this book to go forth among the flower lovers for whom it has been written without expressing my deep appreciation of the co-operation of Messrs. Frederick Warne & Co. Ltd., in the matters of format and general arrangement, of the very accurate and charming way in which Miss Joan Lupton has performed the important work of illustration, and to my old friend Mr. A. J. Macself for reading through the manuscript of the second section.

G. A. R. PHILLIPS

Stratford-upon-Avon

# THE BOOK OF GARDEN FLOWERS

## SECTION I—PERENNIALS

### PLANTING AND CULTIVATION

AROUND the question of planting much controversy has raged among gardeners, but all accept certain rules concerning this very important operation. The time for planting is controlled by the nature of the soil and climatic conditions. Where the soil is of a light and well-drained character certain advantages attend autumn planting if it can be completed not later than the end of October; this will enable the plants to become established before the dormant season and they will have the advantage of starting renewed life the following spring as established plants. The growth will be stronger, the flowers of better quality, and they will have longer stems than those planted in the spring. Where, however, the soil is heavy and retentive of water during winter, it is unsafe to plant until new growth appears in February or March. The plants will require a summer in which to become established and should provide a brave display the following year.

Whilst a certain amount of latitude is permissible in deciding whether to plant in the autumn or spring, so far as herbaceous perennials and shrubs are concerned, there are others that must only be planted at certain seasons of the year if unsatisfactory results are to be avoided. The Eremurus must be planted at some time between mid-September and late October, for only during that period are the tubers really dormant. Daffodils, Tulips, Bulbous Iris, Scillas, Chionodoxa, Snowdrops, Crocus and, in fact, all spring-flowering bulbs should be planted as early as possible in the late summer or autumn. On the other hand, the half-hardy bulbous subjects must not be planted in the open earlier than mid-March; these comprise Gladioli, Tigridia, Watsonia and Calochortus. If required for some colour scheme, rather earlier than their normal season of flowering, the corms may be potted in late autumn and brought on in gentle heat for planting out-of-doors in April or May. If a greenhouse is available they may be transferred to larger pots and brought into flower under glass some weeks earlier than out-of-doors. Outdoor Chrysanthemums are usually supplied as rooted cuttings from the propagation boxes or grown on in pots; these will have been hardened off by

9

the time they are supplied in April and may be planted out-of-doors immediately. Dahlias are supplied in the form of tubers or as green plants. The tubers should be stored in boxes of dry soil or sand in a place where there is no risk of exposure to frost, potted into suitably sized pots and brought into a cold frame in March, giving night protection from frost and admitting air daily when growth appears. They must not be planted out in the open until all risk of frost has vanished, usually in late May or early June. Green plants supplied in a properly hardened-off condition at the proper time for planting are often preferred to tubers as they require very much less attention and skill. They will, of course, require to be lifted, in company with the other half-hardy bulbous subjects mentioned, as soon after the first autumnal frost as is possible.

The choice of site is important and, except where special conditions are recommended, this should be in that part of the garden enjoying maximum sunshine and providing adequate protection from the prevailing wind. Such protection is especially important for tall plants such as Delphiniums, Sunflowers, Crambe, etc., as even the most sturdy support will be insufficient against winds of gale force.

Preparation of the soil is very important, for upon it ultimate success or failure will depend. Where the soil is light and, in consequence, well drained, some form of moisture-retentive humus will be necessary. In these days of mechanized agriculture, farmyard manure has become an extremely scarce commodity in many localities, making it necessary to find some other medium to take its place. Granulated peat, supplied in bales, is an excellent substitute, being a great moisture conserver. The peat will be perfectly dry when received; it should be broken into fine particles and then thoroughly soaked with rain water for preference, otherwise tap water may be used. This is very important for, if buried in a dry condition, the peat will remain dry and create drought conditions at the roots of the plants. Before drenching, fertility may be achieved by adding one six-inch pot full of bone meal or fish manure or a mixture of both to each full barrow load of peat and well mixed. This peat mixture should be buried about nine inches deep so as to form a permanent sponge that will provide the necessary moisture for the roots should a drought occur during the summer.

The best system of digging is to employ that method known as bastard trenching. This consists of excavating a trench to the depth of the fertile soil but without digging out any of the subsoil.

The excavated soil is taken to that point where the digging is to terminate and deposited there so that it can be used to fill in the final trench. Soil is turned over into the trench that has been excavated, and this will range from one to two spade's depth, the peat compost being spread over the first spade depth so that it will lie at approximately nine inches below the surface. Before filling in, the subsoil should be loosened with a digging fork. Such preparation should be carried out in the autumn or winter to allow the soil to settle properly before planting is attempted.

Heavy soils may be treated in a similar way and, if very heavy and retentive of moisture, the introduction of coarse sand, grit or even pea gravel mixed with the top foot of soil will help to achieve the necessary porosity. In such soils manure from horses that have been bedded on straw will be the most serviceable. If this digging can be completed in the autumn and the surface left in a rough condition for pulverization by exposure to the weather so much the better. The desirable fine surface can be encouraged by a dressing of basic slag.

All soils should be tested for lime deficiency, which is more likely to occur in light sandy soils than in heavy loam. If the plants to be grown are lime lovers, lime may be applied imme- diately after digging so that it may be washed in by the rains. A mild form of lime, such as chalk or hydrated lime, is best for light soils and a stronger type, such as burnt lime, for heavy.

Staking will require attention as the plants of tall or medium height develop. Except for plants of a bushy habit such as Dahlias, that form a main central stem, single stakes in them- selves are useless and create an ugly trussed-up appearance, utterly destroying the true habit of growth of a plant. For plants of a spreading nature, such as Michaelmas Daisies, Heleniums, Gypsophila and most composites, short twiggy peasticks are unrivalled, and if placed in position before growth is very high the plants will grow into these supports and find strength enough to weather very strong gales. Delphiniums, the tall Rudbeckias and Sunflowers, are best supported with a stout bamboo cane five or six feet long of which at least one foot is thrust in the ground. Each individual stem is tied to the cane with green twist or split rings. If the canes are painted green they will be very inconspicuous.

The remainder of the maintenance consists in keeping the weeds under control, watering only if a prolonged drought renders this necessary, and giving protection from slugs and other pests by the application of a suitable pest-destroyer. It is important that if watering is practised it should be continued with regularity whenever the weather is dry, otherwise the roots will be attracted to the surface and suffer from drought if the life-preserving moisture is absent. It is better not to water at all than to water at spasmodic intervals.

## PROPAGATION

Most amateur gardeners will want to try their hand at increasing their stock of different plants. So far as herbaceous perennials are concerned, there are three main methods of propagation, viz. by seed-raising, division of the root-stock and rooting of cuttings (stem or root). Seed provides the most natural method of propagation, and seedlings are often more robust than plants raised by either of the other methods. It should be known, however, that whereas seedlings of species come fairly true to type, those raised from garden forms often manifest great variety in colour and habit. To obtain true stock of such varieties one or the other of the vegetative methods must be employed.

The life of a seed can vary considerably. Delphinium seed sown as soon as ripe will give practically 100 per cent germination; if sown a year later this will probably be reduced to 50 per cent or even as low as 25 per cent. Seed of Dictamnus if sown in late summer as soon as ripe will germinate satisfactorily in the following spring, but if kept until the spring before being sown it will not germinate until a year later, and may not germinate at all. Foxglove seed has given a full percentage of germination when sown five or more years after harvesting. These examples will give some idea of the variation in the longevity of the germinating capacity of seeds. It is best to sow as soon as ripe or, at the latest, in the spring following. For convenience seeds are sown in boxes about three inches deep or in earthenware pots or pans. The best compost consists of one part of sandy loam, one part of granulated peat or leafmould and two parts of coarse river sand. The seeds should be scattered evenly and not thickly over the surface and then covered with a thin layer of sand and the whole made firm by a short board made to fit into the box. Water with a hand syringe and then cover with a pane of glass which, in turn, is covered with newspaper or some other opaque material. In the course of germination the compost should be kept in a moist but not a wet condition. As soon as germination has taken place, all covering should be removed, otherwise the seedlings will become drawn and weakly in their struggle to find light. As soon as the first pair of true leaves appear the seedlings may be carefully lifted and pricked off into similar boxes or frames containing a compost consisting of one part sandy loam, one part peat or leafmould and one part of coarse sand. Here they may be left during the winter, taking care, where the genus is perfectly hardy, to admit full air to prevent damping off. In the spring, when growth has reached an inch or so high, plant in the positions where they are to flower. Seed sown in spring requires similar treatment and, as the seedlings will not suffer a dormant period until the following winter, they may be planted in their permanent positions as soon as large enough.

Division of the root-stock is the simplest and most easily performed method of vegetative propagation. As soon as growth is about an inch high in February or March the whole is lifted, the soil washed off by immersion in a bucket of water and the individual crowns, each with a piece of root attached, broken from the remainder, planted out where they are to flower and shaded with pots or boxes for about a week to prevent wilting whilst they recover. There are certain exceptions to this rule. Bearded Irises are best lifted and the rhizomes cut into pieces, each containing two or three eyes or growths, and planted out immediately, giving a top dressing of lime to maintain a healthy condition. Herbaceous Peonies are treated likewise in September or October, but the dressing of lime is not necessary in this instance.

Cuttings provide the best method of large-scale propagation, and this method is favoured by most professional horticulturists. Top (or stem) cuttings are taken in late winter or early spring just as new growth has reached an inch or so high; this method is particularly useful for Delphiniums, Lupins, Michaelmas Daisies and similar plants. Cuttings are taken with a heel of the parent crown. They are carefully trimmed so as to remove any rough edges where water may lodge and cause decay. These are inserted in pots, boxes or frames containing a compost similar to that recommended for seed sowing, taking care that there is a little sand at the base of each. They must be shaded for a fortnight or more until callusing has taken place, and from then onwards the shading may be removed except when there is particularly warm sunshine liable to cause wilting. Watering is most important, and if the cuttings are over-watered it is very probable they will decay before being able to callus. The water required by an unrooted cutting should be just sufficient to maintain it in a fresh condition and, until roots have been formed to suck in a greater quantity of water, this should be given very sparingly and then only by means of a fine spray from a syringe. As soon as the cuttings have produced sufficient roots to enable them to be lifted with a soil ball held together by a mass of fibrous roots, they may be planted out in their flowering positions.

Root cuttings may be taken in late summer, early autumn or in winter. The plants are lifted and the strongest roots cut away. These are cut into pieces of about an inch long and then inserted in the usual sandy compost, taking care that they are in a vertical position about a quarter of an inch below the surface and the uppermost portion comprising that which would normally be nearest the parent root. If there is any doubt in regard to the latter question, place in a horizontal position about half an inch below the surface. These must be watered sparingly and may be planted out when they have developed sufficient root and top growth.

Bulbous subjects are usually propagated by means of offsets, removed and planted out when the parent bulbs are lifted as the foliage ripens. Plants with corms, such as Gladioli, will often produce a mass of small cormlets, the size of a pea or less, at the base of the corm; these may be sown at the normal planting time to develop into flowering size corms in two or three years' time. Lilies may be propagated by means of bulbils, produced in the leaf axials of some species and hybrids, and from scales removed immediately after flowering and placed in pure sand until small bulblets have formed. The last-named method requires some experience and is best left in the hands of the professional grower.

Cuttings of the shrubs included in this book are best taken in late July or August of half-ripened wood, cut at a node or leaf joint and rooted in a sandy compost as recommended for certain herbaceous perennials. They should not be planted out until the following spring.

## PLANNING THE FLOWER BORDER

To obtain the best results in a flower border a full knowledge of the plants to be employed is necessary. Height, habit, season of flowering, colour and the best position, whether in sun or shade, are all vitally important.

Assuming that the soil has been prepared in accordance with the recommendations already given, the border may be planned. First make a list of the various plants required, taking care that there is an even balance between the various heights and seasons of flowering. Allow for not less than three plants of one variety to form a group, and write wooden garden labels for each group. Place these in the positions that the plants are to occupy, and only when one is perfectly satisfied that height, season and colour accord harmoniously should planting be done. The tall plants will naturally dominate the back of the border, grouped in triangular fashion thus ∴ or ∵ starting at one end with a late-flowering plant such as a tall Michaelmas Daisy, following on with an earlier flowering one such as a Delphinium, and then a mid-season one such as Heliopsis, then back to a late-flowering plant such as Sunflower (Helianthus). This process is repeated, taking care that there is a good proportion of the most important subjects such as Delphiniums, *Anchusa azurea*, *A. italica*, Mulleins, Monks-hoods, tall Heleniums and Michaelmas Daisies. Plan to terminate, as at the beginning, with a Michaelmas Daisy.

In the middle section start and end with some plant that flowers over a long season such as Catananche, Scabiosa or Gaillardia which will be placed before the Michaelmas Daisies. In front of the Delphinium a group of the late-flowering *Kniphofia erecta* will help to obscure the flowerless gap in late summer; before the group of Heliopsis arrange a group of Lupins well back in the middle section to allow the planting of Phlox in front. There are many plants of the family Compositae suitable for the middle section, and care must be taken not to use them too freely and obtain a rather flat effect. This is where plants such as Salvia, *Delphinium belladonna*, Kniphofias and Gladioli are valuable. To achieve a double-season effect from one area of ground, Gladioli may be interplanted among Bearded Irises. Many of the stem-rooting Lilies find their ideal position among plants like Peonies, *Aster amellus*, the dwarf Solidagos and similar plants, whose foliage shades the ground above the roots arising from the stem of the Lily between the bulb and ground-level; to such roots the hot sun can prove fatal. Further double-season effects may be obtained by interplanting May-flowering Tulips among groups of late-flowering subjects such as the New Dwarf Asters, *Gypsophila paniculata*, etc., to provide a colourful display before there is much of interest in bloom among herbaceous perennials.

The front portion of the border must be treated in a similar manner, keeping mainly to dwarf plants but allowing dwarf Kniphofias, *Gladiolus primulinus* and other slender subjects that bear their flowers in a short spike, to break any tendency towards flatness. The lovely varieties of the dwarf *Tulipa kaufmanniana* are never seen to such advantage as when planted to the fore of a border with a ground covering of Thyme. Narcissi may be used with discretion, but are seen at their best when naturalized in bold drifts in turf at the margins of a lawn or coppice: it will not be wise to cut the foliage with a lawn-mower, so the grass must be allowed to grow until the foliage has withered in July, when it may be kept under control by means of a scythe.

Colour harmony is important and many bold effects can be obtained by those who have an eye for colour. Yellow Lupins planted near to deep blue Irises, the scarlet *Lychnis chalcedonica* near to the white clouds of *Gypsophila paniculata* "Bristol Fairy", pink Pyrethrums at the back of a group of the rich blue *Anchusa caespitosa*, *Salvia superba* in association with the bronze-red Helenium "Moerheim Beauty", are examples of the many varied schemes that may be achieved. Other examples are: varieties of *Lobelia cardinalis* as a foreground to tall purple Michaelmas Daisies and the soft effect of pale pink Hollyhocks, *Eryngium amethystinum*, *Gypsophila paniculata florepleno* (not "Bristol Fairy"), *Scabiosa caucasica* "Clive Greaves" with a front planting of *Sedum spectabile* "Brilliant" and *Physostegia virginiana* "Vivid" with perhaps a bush or so of Cotton Lavender (*Santolina chamaecyparissus*).

Borders of special colouring are often favoured so that there is the Blue Border, with flowers of varying shades of blue colouring predominating and a few pale pink and white flowers placed as foils. The Grey Border will contain such subjects as *Stachys lanata*, Lavender, *Cineraria maritima* (a grey foliaged biennial), the shrubby *Senecio grayi*, Santolina of sorts, *Nepeta mussini* or *N. faassenii* and others with grey or glaucous foliage. The White Border has found support now that there is not that unreasonable dislike for white flowers that existed for some years; here the pure white of many species of Lilium, white-flowered Peonies, Phloxes, Delphiniums, Lupins, Michaelmas Daisies (double for preference so that there will be no yellow centres), Gypsophila, Cimicifuga and white Chrysanthemums, all against a background of green foliage, give a wonderfully cool effect on a sweltering day in high summer. Similarly there can be borders where pink, yellow and orange flowers predominate.

Where space permits, borders can be arranged to provide displays for certain seasons of the year only. In such borders it is not difficult to obtain a bold display of colour over a short period with very few apparent gaps and without the necessity to camouflage them. The Spring Border will extend from April to June and contain most of the bulbous subjects of that period interplanted with the herbaceous perennials that provide the grand finale in June; among the latter will be Iris, Peonies, Lupins Delphiniums, Eremuri, Pyrethrums, all well calculated to provide a bold display of great beauty. The Summer Border will last throughout July and August when the mainstay will be the Phloxes, Heleniums, Rudbeckias, Kniphofias, Gladioli, *Aster frikartii*, Lythrum, Sidalcea, *Scabiosa caucasica*, Gypsophila, Catananche and suchlike. In the Late Summer or Autumn Border the Michaelmas Daisies in great variety, Lobelias of the Cardinalis group, late-flowering Kniphofias, Crinums, Solidagos, Helianthus, and Chrysanthemums of the Korean and *Rubellum* groups. Hollyhocks will give a most delightful picture in the waning days that herald the resting season for most plants.

The scope for floral effects is endless, and therein lies the great fascination of the flower garden. Gone are the days of the artificial and stereotyped effects of the carpet bedding, none of which ever fitted well into the British landscape. Thanks to the great apostles of the more natural form of gardening, the late William Robinson and Gertrude Jekyll, the gardens of our land are richer today than ever before. Although there is the wealth of the flora of the whole temperate world to draw upon, garden lovers will do well not to forget those lovely gems of a past age, particularly the old garden Pinks, the double Primroses, and the old English garden Roses that have been threatened with extinction from an ill-deserved neglect that, fortunately, is passing to an age of greater enlightenment.

## PERENNIALS FOR SPECIAL PURPOSES

Few gardens are so happily situated that their conditions of climate and soil enable all perennials to be grown without special selection. Some gardens have soil of a sandy and porous nature that cannot hold moisture for any length of time, and it soon becomes sun-baked and dry. On low-lying ground, however, waterlogging in winter may be common and the soil is never without moisture even during the most prolonged drought. There are also those gardens situated in woodland where tall forest trees continually cast their shadows; in the hands of the skilled garden craftsman some of the most charming natural effects may be achieved. But to attempt them is no work for the beginner. Considerable skill is necessary in the planting of such a garden where, among other plants, perennials suitable for such woodland conditions are particularly valuable.

The enormous advance in the art of floral arrangement has

opened up new opportunities for the use of cut flowers, and many perennials that were hitherto regarded purely as garden plants are now employed in many pleasing ensembles in the home.

For the guidance of those who are as yet insufficiently experienced to select perennials for these special requirements the following lists have been compiled.

### PERENNIALS FOR DRY AND SUN-BAKED SOILS

*Achillea ptarmica*
*Alstromeria* species
*Alyssum saxatile*
*Amaryllis belladonna*
*Arabis caucasica (A. albida)*
*Armeria* species
*Begonia* species
*Calochortus* species
*Catananche caerulea*
*Centranthus ruber*
*Crinum powellii*
*Dahlia* species
*Echinacea purpurea*
*Eryngium giganteum*

*Iris* (bearded) species
*Linaria* species
*Nepeta* species
*Oenothera missouriensis*
*Penstemon* species
*Phygelius capensis*
*Salvia superba*
*Saponaria officinalis*
*Sedum* species
*Stachys lanata*
*Thymus* species
*Tigridia* species
*Zauschneria californica*

### PERENNIALS FOR WET SOILS

*Aconitum* species
*Astilbe* species
*Epilobium* species
*Hosta* species
*Iris kaempferi*
*Iris sibirica*
*Lobelia syphilitica*
*Lythrum* species
*Malva moschata*
*Mimulus* species

*Myosotis* species
*Podophyllum emodi*
*Polygonum* species
*Primula japonica*
*Primula pulverulenta*
*Rodgersia pinnata*
*Senecio clivorum*
*Solidago* species
*Spiraea* species
*Trollius* species

### PERENNIALS FOR WOODLAND

*Achillea millefolium* var.
*Anemone hybrida*
*Astilbe* species
*Astrantia maxima*
*Cimicifuga* species
*Dicentra spectabilis*

*Epilobium* species
*Epimedium* species
*Geranium* species
*Hosta* species
*Iris* species
*Linaria* species

### PERENNIALS FOR WOODLAND (*cont.*)

*Lysimachia* species
*Macleaya cordata*
*Mertensia* species
*Oenothera* species
*Podophyllum* species
*Polygonatum multiflorum*
*Polygonum* species
*Primula* species
*Pulmonaria* species
*Tiarella cordifolia*
*Trillium* species
*Vinca* species

### PERENNIALS FOR CUT FLOWERS

*Acanthus mollis latifolius*
*Achillea eupatorium*
*Alstromeria* species
*Agapanthus africanus*
*Allium* species
*Amaryllis belladonna*
*Anthemis tinctoria*
*Aster* species
*Calochortus* species
*Campanula* species
*Catananche caerulea*
*Chrysanthemum* species
*Coreopsis* species
*Crinum powellii*
*Crocosmia* species
*Dahlia* species
*Delphinium* species
F *Dianthus* species
*Dicentra spectabilis*
*Dierama pulcherrima*
*Echinops ritro*
*Eryngium* species
*Gaillardia* species
*Galtonia candicans*
*Gerbera jamesonii*
*Gladiolus* species
*Gypsophila paniculata*
*Helenium* species
*Helianthus* species
*Heliopsis* species
*Helleborus* species
*Heuchera* species
*Hosta* species (foliage)
*Incarvillea* species
F *Iris* species
*Kniphofia* species
*Lavatera* species
*Liatris pycnostachya*
F *Lilium* species
*Limonium latifolium*
*Lupinus polyphyllus*
*Lychnis* species
*Lythrum* species
*Macleaya cordata* (flower and
F *Narcissus* species          foliage)
*Nerine bowdenii*
*Ornithogalum* species
F *Paeonia* species
*Papaver* species
*Penstemon* species
*Phlox* species
*Scabiosa caucasica*
*Tulipa* species
*Verbena* species
*Veronica* species
*Watsonia beatricis* and others

Those marked F are noted for fragrance.

# DESCRIPTION OF SPECIES

## Bear's Breech (Plate 1)

Family *ACANTHACEAE*        *Acanthus mollis latifolius*

Mostly natives of southern Europe, the genus *Acanthus* comprises several species, *A. mollis latifolius* being the most noteworthy. Full exposure to sun, and a rich but light and well-drained soil, are essential. Excessive moisture is fatal.

The foliage is large, spiny and elegantly laciniated. Flower spikes are about one and a half feet in length, the whole plant being three to four feet high. The individual flowers, an inch across, are hooded, and purple and white. They are effective at the back of the herbaceous border with flowers of contrasting colours. As a single specimen on the outskirts of shrubberies the Acanthus is striking, and should be left for many years undisturbed, for only then does it attain full beauty.

Propagation is by seed, division in spring or early autumn, and by root cuttings.

The flowering period is in late July and August.

## Yarrow: Milfoil (Plate 1)

Family *COMPOSITAE*        *Achillea* species

A genus widely spread throughout the northern hemisphere (including dwarf varieties). Grows in any well-drained soil in full sun, and may be left undisturbed for several years.

The three most useful species for herbaceous borders are: *A. millefolium* (Milfoil), two to three feet in height with finely cut foliage and clustered heads two inches across of pink (cherry-red or purple in the forms "Cerise Queen" and "Kelway"), and white; *A. filipendulina* (syn. *A. eupatorium*), Caucasus, reaching four or five feet high with flat clustered heads of yellow flowers, five inches across; *A. ptarmica* (Sneezewort) reaching two to three feet high with serrated leaves and white flowers borne in loose corymbs, especially the double forms "Perry's White", "The Pearl" and "Boule de Neige". For the front and centre of herbaceous borders Achilleas may be considered among the more

Pl. 1.

20

1. Bear's Breech (*Acanthus mollis latifolius*), p. 20.  2. Yarrow (*Achillea filipendulina*), p. 20.
3. Monkshood (*Aconitum napellus*), p. 21.    4. African Lily (*Agapanthus africanus*), p. 21.

1. Brittonastrum (*Agastache mexicanum*), p. 22.  2. Garlic (*Allium albopilosum*), p. 22.
3. Peruvian Lily (*Alstromeria aurantiaca*), p. 23.  4. Yellow Alyssum (*Alyssum saxatile*), p. 24.

21

indispensable perennials and, in addition, are much used for floral decorations.

Propagation is by seed, division in spring or early autumn, and by cuttings, division being the most favoured.

The flowering season extends from June until September.

## Monkshood (Plate 1)

Family *RANUNCULACEAE*                    *Aconitum* species

Ornamental herbaceous perennials of tall stature native to Europe, temperate Asia and North America. The roots and foliage of certain species yield drugs valued for medicinal purposes; all are reputed to be poisonous.

For herbaceous borders certain species only are important. *A. napellus* is the best known with three to four feet erect stems clothed with leaves divided to the base and cleft into linear lobes; the blue flowers are borne in racemes and have the upper sepal formed into a hood or helmet. Rather similar to this but more branched and later flowering are *A. × cammarum* "Sparks' variety" with dark purple flowers, and *A. × cammarum bicolor* (syn. *A. bicolor*) with white and purple flowers. *A. vulparis* (*A. lycoctonum* of gardens) is three to six feet high, has yellow flowers with a longer and narrower head; *A. carmichaelii wilsonii*, a late-flowering species, attains a height of five feet, bearing racemes of rich blue hooded flowers; there is an improved form known as "Barker's variety". At the back of herbaceous borders the Aconitums are effective and should be contrasted with other flowers of complementary colours, such as the yellow Rudbeckias, white *Chrysanthemum maximum*. They are easily cultivated in any moderately rich, well-drained garden soil.

Propagation is by seeds sown as soon as ripe or by division in early autumn or spring.

The flowering season is in June and July for *A. napellus*, June to September for *A. vulpartis*, August for *A. × cammarum*, and September for *A. carmichaelii wilsonii*.

## African Lily (Plate 1)

Family *LILIACEAE*                    *Agapanthus africanus*

Also known as *A. umbellatus* and Lily-of-the-Nile, although it is a native of Cape Colony. The foliage is abundant, long, thick and narrow, rising from two to three feet and bright green. The flowers, about an inch across, are borne in large umbels on leafless stems to a height of three or more feet, as many as twenty or thirty flowers composing a single umbel. The colour is pale to deep blue, according to the variety, and there is a form *giganteus* that has stems of over four feet. There is also a white flowered form.

*A. africanus* and its forms are hardy out-of-doors only in the milder parts of Britain, particularly in the west and south-west. Its variety *mooreanus*, with short and upright foliage and dark blue flowers as large as the type, is more hardy and may be grown in most gardens given a southern aspect. The position must be in full sun, and a rich soil that has been prepared by the introduction of a quantity of farm-yard manure is necessary to grow these plants satisfactorily. They make excellent tub plants.

Propagation is usually practised by division of the roots in spring and rarely by seed.

The flowering season is in July and August.

## Brittonastrum (Plate 2)

Family *LABIATAE*                                    *Agastache mexicanum*

A hardy herbaceous perennial from Mexico that was introduced as recently as 1943 and is also known as *Brittonastrum mexicanum*. It closely resembles a Bergamot (*Monarda didyma*) in general appearance and habit with flowers of vivid purplish rose borne in dense terminal spikes. Its height is two to three feet, and a group of these plants in the herbaceous border provides an arresting array of colour. In addition it is a useful cut flower and is best used alone for vases, its particular shade being difficult to blend satisfactorily with other colours indoors, although it is at home with other plants in the border other than those of pink or red colouring.

Easily grown in any good garden soil provided there is adequate drainage, and may be allowed to remain undisturbed for a number of years to form large clumps when the effect *en masse* can be fully appreciated.

Propagation is by division or from seed, the seedling being very true to type and showing little variation.

The flowering season is in July and August.

## Garlic: Onion (Plate 2)

Family *LILIACEAE*                                    *Allium* species

Allium is the ancient Latin name for garlic and comprises a genus of bulbous plants distributed over Europe, North Africa,

Abyssinia, Asia, North America and Mexico. The onion, leek, garlic, chive and shallot are all members of this genus. Although possessing the characteristic pungent odour, there are a number of species that are eminently suitable for inclusion in planting schemes. *A. albopilosum* has violet heads eight inches across borne on one-foot stems; *A. moly*, umbels of bright yellow star-shaped flowers, on one-foot stems; *A. caeruleum*, sky-blue umbels on one- to two-feet stems; and *A. stipitatum* and *A. giganteum*, large umbels of lilac, borne on three- to four-feet stems; *A. tubero-sum*, with white flowers from August to October on stems to one and a half feet, can be used for edging. Alliums grow freely in any ordinary garden soil that is well drained and fully exposed to the sun. The bulbs should be planted to a depth equal to three times their own diameter and a foot apart. Apart from their value as border plants they are excellent for naturalizing in grass-land, provided the grass has not to be mown in summer. Plant in autumn.

Propagation is by offsets taken from bulbs at the time of planting or by seed sown in spring in a light and gritty soil.

The flowering season extends from May until October, according to the species.

## Peruvian Lily (Plate 2)

Family *AMARYLLIDACEAE*                    *Alstromeria* species

A race of colourful lily-like perennials, natives of tropical and subtropical South America, of which a number of species are hardy in Britain. Although sun lovers, the more robust species grow well under semi-shaded conditions.

*A. aurantiaca, Chile*, has given rise to a number of improved garden forms all producing heads of bright orange flowers, two inches or more across, shaped like lilies and borne on two- to three-feet stems. *A. lutea* is a robust species with yellow flowers, and *A. chilensis* varies from pale pink to bright red, but is not so hardy as the former. *A. puctulla* (syn. *psittacina*) has tubular flowers of red margined green and is as easy to grow as *A. aurantiaca*. The most recent introduction is *A. ligtu* var. *angus-tifolia*, and its hybrids produce large heads of flowers of charac-teristic lily-like form, varying in colour from cream to rich peach, apricot, salmon and rose. *A. haemantha* has smaller flowers of deep red.

Alstromerias are easily grown in a deep sandy soil and the roots should be planted six to nine inches below the surface. They require three years in which to become established, and are better allowed to remain undisturbed. Plant in October or early spring.

Propagation is by root division in the case of the *aurantiaca* group, and by seed with the remainder.

The flowering season is in July.

## Yellow Alyssum (Plate 2)

Family *CRUCIFERAE*                                    *Alyssum saxatile*

A plant that has for many years been a great favourite in gardens where several forms are cultivated, the original species being a native of Europe. The habit of the plants is either branching and inclined to a semi-prostrate habit or tufted, and they are particularly useful for furnishing the front of herbaceous borders or to provide bright splashes of colour in rock gardens.

*A. saxatile* is the species most commonly used in the front of borders and attains a foot high, bearing masses of small golden yellow flowers borne in clusters. The various forms of this species include var. *compactum*, a plant of tufted habit, var. *pleniflorum*, a form with double flowers, rather more effective than the original species, var. *variegatum*, a most effective form with variegated foliage, and var. *citrinum* with paler sulphur-yellow flowers. One of the easiest plants in cultivation, Alyssum should be planted in the early spring in any good garden soil that is well drained.

Propagation is by division of the roots, cuttings or by seed.

The flowering season is in late May and June.

## Belladonna Lily (Plate 3)

Family *AMARYLLIDACEAE*                          *Amaryllis belladonna*

A plant that was introduced to our gardens from Cape Colony as long ago as 1712. The bulbs produce deep green leaves, strap-shaped and up to one and a half feet long. The flower stems reach about the same height and bear from five to twelve large funnel-shaped flowers, not unlike some species of lilies; these are soft rose in colour and delightfully perfumed.

There are various forms of the Belladonna Lily, each varying slightly in the tone of the flowers and also in size, the Kew variety being the best of all. The bulbs require to be planted nine inches deep in autumn in a well-drained soil that has been enriched with leafmould or granulated peat. The position should face south and be protected from cold winds. Where the winter is severe a protective litter of bracken should be placed over the position where the bulbs are planted. When once the bulbs are established it is not wise to disturb them for at least five years, when they may be lifted and transplanted if desired as soon as the foliage ripens. During growth a mulch of farm-yard manure is beneficial.

Propagation is by means of offsets removed when the bulbs have been lifted and ripened.

The flowering season is in August and September.

This plant is also called *Callicrore rosea* and *Brunsvigia rosea*.

## Alkanet (Plate 3)

Family *BORAGINACEAE*                                    *Anchusa* species

One of the loveliest of all blue-flowered perennials and a native of the Mediterranean region containing species of both tall and dwarf stature and a number of garden origin.

*A. italica* (syn. *A. azurea*) reaches a height of from three to five feet with ovate-lanceolate foliage of rough shining appearance; it is best known by its garden forms "Dropmore" variety, "Pride of Dover", "Opal" and "Morning Glory", the latter being the tallest. The flowers are round, less than an inch across, of varying shades of blue and borne on many laterals branching from the main stem. *A. caespitosa*, a native of Crete and the most recent introduction, is one to one and a half feet high and produces masses of brilliant blue flowers, white centred, over a long period. A related plant, *Brunnera macrophylla*, often known as *A. myositidiflora*, has broad rounded foliage, attains a height of one to one and a half feet, and bears in April and May many clustered heads of small blue flowers like Forget-me-nots. The coarseness of the roots of the *italica* varieties makes a well-drained soil imperative, a wet soil causing decay. *A. myosotidiflora* and *A. caespitosa* also prefer well-drained soils and all are sun lovers.

Propagate *italica* varieties from root cuttings, *A. caespitosa* from crown cuttings, *Brunnera macrophylla* (*A. myosotidiflora*) from seed or by division. Seedlings show some variation.

The flowering season is from spring to early summer.

## Windflower (Plate 3)

Family *RANUNCULACEAE*                                    *Anemone* species

A large genus that is chiefly found in north temperate and mountainous regions. Apart from many dwarf species that are eminently suitable for rock gardens or for naturalizing in woodland, there are others that have particular value in herbaceous borders. Renowned for the brilliancy of its colouring, *A. fulgens*, a hybrid of *A. pavonia* and *A. hortensis*, is also noteworthy as having given rise to the famous St. Brigid strain with a colour range that varies from white to shades of pink, crimson, purple and almost blue, excellent alike for border effect or for cutting, with flowers three or more inches across. The leaves are lobed and irregularly cut, and the flowers reach a height of a foot when well grown in a rich soil. *A.* × *hybrida*, often known as *A. japonica*, is of herbaceous habit with elegantly cut foliage and branching stems, bearing large flowers, three inches across, of white, pink or purple in late summer.

Anemones will grow well in either semi-shade or in sun, but a rich sandy loam, into which leafmould has been introduced, is necessary for the best results.

Propagation is by seed for the St. Brigid Anemones, by division for *A.* × *fulgens*, and by division or root cuttings for *A.* × *hybrida*.

The flowering season extends throughout the greater part of the year for the St. Brigid varieties, and in late summer for *A.* × *hybrida*.

(*A. sulphurea*, i.e. *Pulsatilla sulphurea*, usually difficult; hence should be omitted.)

## Chamomile (Plate 3)

Family *COMPOSITAE*                                    *Anthemis tinctoria*

A perennial species of a genus that inhabits the temperate regions of the Old World. Many flower heads are borne on branching stems that attain a height of two or three feet, the white, cream or yellow rays spreading from a central yellow disc. Also known as the Yellow Marguerite.

The species is not now widely grown, having been superseded by the varieties of garden origin that have originated from it with flowers up to three inches across, notably "Perry's variety", golden yellow, "Grallagh Gold", an even deeper yellow, "Wargrave variety", cream. *A. sancti-johannis* with orange-yellow flowers is a closely related species which hybridizes with *A. tinctoria* in gardens. The foliage is finely cut and aromatic when crushed. Valuable plants for the fore portion of the central section of herbaceous borders where they contrast well with flowers of purple or blue colouring. Very hardy and becoming established over a period of many years. Much valued as a decorative cut flower. Grows in full sun in any good porous soil.

Propagation may be performed by means of seed, division of established clumps and by cuttings in early spring.

The flowering season extends from June until late summer.

## St. Bernard's Lily (Plate 4)

Family *LILIACEAE*                                    *Anthericum liliago*

A genus of over fifty species that find their homes in Africa and occasionally in the western hemisphere. The roots are rhizomatous and the inflorescence comprises racemes of small, white flowers not unlike some lilies in form. The foliage is narrow, upright and rushlike.

*A. liliago* will attain a height of two to three feet with an open raceme of white flowers, an inch or less in diameter. Its form var. *major* is larger in every way and is to be preferred to the type. *A. racemosum* is very similar but rather more branched and smaller in every way. *A. liliastrum* (which is sometimes called *Paradisa liliastrum*, and *Liliastrum album*), is a related plant sometimes known as St. Bruno's Lily. The three species mentioned will thrive in any good, well-drained garden soil and will benefit from a covering of decayed farm-yard manure in winter. Their place is towards the front of the border, where they will develop into tufts as they become established. Water liberally during dry weather.

Propagation is either naturally by stolons, by seed, or by division in late winter.

The flowering season is in early summer.

## Antholyza (Plate 4)

Family *IRIDACEAE*                                    *Antholyza* species

*Antholyza aethiopica* (syn. *Chasmanthe aethiopica*) is quite hardy in the milder localities of Britain. The corms resemble those of the Gladiolus and the foliage is also similar with branched spikes of brightly coloured reddish-orange funnel-shaped flowers on stems three to four feet high overtopping the foliage.

The name *Antholyza* properly belongs to *A. ringens*, a Cape species rarely cultivated and probably not hardy. The species usually called an *Antholyza* in gardens is *Curtonus paniculatus* (syn. *A. paniculata*), which is *A. aethiopica*; reaches three feet and bears spikes of red and yellow flowers.

A rich loamy soil that is well drained is necessary for best cultivation and the corms should be planted in early March, lifted and stored during the autumn and winter with frost protection.

Propagation is by means of division of the corms and also by cormlets that form at the base of the corms. Seed is also sometimes used.

The flowering season is from June to August.

## Columbine (Plate 4)

Family *RANUNCULACEAE*          *Aquilegia* various garden forms

An old garden favourite, *A. vulgaris*, the common Columbine, is native to Europe. The newer forms have originated from the fusion of the qualities of various species that are native to North America and parts of Asia, notably Siberia and Japan. The plants form compact clumps with foliage of fernlike aspect and stems of varying height, carrying branching stems bearing singly many flowers, two or more inches across, and noteworthy on account of their long spurs. Long-spurred hybrids (*A.* ×*cultorum*) are the most usually planted, although the red and yellow species (*A. californica*, *A. canadensis* and *A. skinneri* as well as the soft golden yellow *A. chrysantha* and the blue *A. caerulea*) are well worth attention. A hybrid, "Crimson Star", is a dwarf form with red and white flowers, reaching about a foot in height. Other species and strains will vary in height from one and a half to three feet. The colour range extends from pale cream to shades of red and almost orange and brilliant blue. At the front of the border the Columbine should be massed for effect, and so long as the soil is reasonably fertile it will give a good account of itself.

Propagation is by seed sown as soon as ripe to produce plants that will flower in the following year.

The flowering season is in May and June.

## Rock Cress (Plate 4)

Family *CRUCIFERAE*                    *Arabis albida*

The genus comprises many species native to Europe and America of which a number are alpine. The flowers are small and borne on stems, a few inches high, in terminal racemes over a considerable period of time. The plants are leafy and of tuft-like growth, but inclined to become straggling if not cut back annually.

*A. albida* (syn. *A. caucasica*), the White Arabis, provides masses of small white flowers of single form, but is not often grown today,

*Pl.* 3.

28

1. Belladonna Lily (*Amaryllis belladonna*), p. 24.
2. Alkanet (*Anchusa* species), p. 25.
3. Windflower (*Anemone fulgens*), p. 25.
4. Chamomile (*Anthemis tinctoria*), p. 26.

*Pl.* 4.
1. St. Bernard's Lily (*Anthericum liliago*), p. 27.    2. Antholyza (*Antholyza aethiopica*), p. 27.
3. Columbine (*Aquilegia × cultorum*), p. 28.    4. Rock Cress (*Arabis albida*), p. 28.

having given place in public favour to the double white form (var. *flore-pleno*) which gives a more substantial effect. The fragrant flowers are useful to form carpets at the front of herbaceous borders for early bulbous subjects, and being of a neutral colour may be used in combination with all shades. There is also a pink flowered form of hybrid origin: *A. × arendsii* ("Rosabella"), but its place is rather in the rock garden than the perennial border. One of the easiest plants to cultivate, the Arabis will grow in any reasonably well-drained soil in either partial shade or in full sun.

Propagation is by means of division, seed or cuttings.

The flowering season extends from March to May.

## Thrift (Plate 5)

Family *PLUMBAGINACEAE* *Armeria maritima*

Also known as the Sea Pink, the genus has its various species in Europe, western Asia, North Africa and North America. The species most used in gardens is *A. maritima*, the Common Thrift, and a native of the coastal regions of North America and Europe. The leaves are short, narrow and form a moss-like tuft from which rise many slender and upright stems to a height of a few inches, bearing tightly clustered heads of small flowers that vary from white to pale pink in the native state but in rich pink and reddish purple tones in varieties of garden origin. "Bees Ruby" is a hybrid of uncertain origin with stems fully a foot high and bearing large heads of ruby-red flowers; it is, in every way, a giant form of Thrift and most useful for planting in the front of the border. *A. latifolia*, six to twelve inches, is a crimson-flowered species from Portugal.

In cultivation Armerias demand full sun and ample drainage, it being wise, except in the most porous soils, to incorporate plenty of coarse grit into the soil around the roots.

Propagate by seed or division of the roots in early spring.

The flowering season extends from late May until early July.

## Wormwood (Plate 5)

Family *COMPOSITAE* *Artemisia* species

Known variously as Lad's Love, Old Woman, Old Man, Tarragon, Wormwood and Southern Wood, the Artemesias are mostly natives of the northern hemisphere and most frequently found in arid regions. The dissected leaves are alternate and the flower-heads inconspicuous. An exception to this last rule is *A. lactiflora,* China, which reaches a height of five feet with woody stems, bearing plumes of small milky-white flowers in late summer; it is valuable among the late Michaelmas Daisies and also to contrast with the vivid autumnal tints of Vines, Maples and other subjects noted for their rich autumnal colouring. The silvery foliage of *A. palmeri, A. ludoviciana* (syn. *A. stelleriana*) and *A. abrotanum* is valuable for its softening effect with stronger colours and its harmony with soft pinks, blues and white. *A. absinthium,* the true Wormwood, is shrubby in habit and is used in medicine as well as in the manufacture of the liqueur, absinthe. In cultivation no particular care is necessary, for all grow well in almost any garden.

Propagate by division.

The flowering season is immaterial, except in the case of *A. lactiflora* which blooms in September, as foliage is the main attraction.

# Milkweed (Plate 5)

Family *ASCLEPIADACEAE*                    *Asclepias* species

Perennials of considerable attraction both in the border and as cut flowers, being natives of North America. In *A. tuberosa* the leaves are alternate, long and narrow, and each stem bears several flower-heads of small closely clustered flowers of brilliant orange to a height of two to three feet. The roots are tuberous and require to be planted in a partially shaded position where the soil has been enriched with leafmould. Under such conditions it will require a year or so for the plants to become established, and they are best allowed to remain undisturbed indefinitely. There is an even brighter form than *A. tuberosa* in the variety "Vermilion". Another species, *A. incarnata,* with opposite leaves, is occasionally seen in gardens where its flowers, borne in loose umbels and of a rather dull red-purple hue, are an attraction for bees. It is a native of swamps and therefore grows well in moist soil. Others are *A. purpurea,* three to four feet, with lilac flowers, and *A. speciosa,* two to three feet, with fragrant purplish flowers. A characteristic of the genus is its curious habit of producing its pollen in a waxy mass (technically a pollinium), which is removed in its entirety by insects.

Propagation is by seed sown as soon as ripe, requiring three years before the resultant progeny attain the flowering stage.

The flowering season is in July and August.

## Asphodel (Plate 5)

Family *LILIACEAE*          *Asphodelus* and *Asphodeline* species

A race of stately herbaceous perennials to which is closely allied the Asphodeline, the main difference being that whereas Asphodelus bears its flowers on naked stems those of the Asphodeline are leafy. Natives mostly of southern Europe, the genus also contains a number of annuals that require greenhouse culture. The flower spikes of *Asphodelus ramosus* reach a height of between three and five feet, bearing wide open small lily-like flowers of pure white. *A. acaulis*, twelve to eighteen inches, is a pink flowering species. *Asphodeline liburnica* (syn. *Asphodelus capillaris* and *A. creticus*) carries spikes of yellow flowers striped with green, whilst *A. lutea* has deep yellow flowers and its form *A. lutea sibirica* has paler flowers. There is also a double-flowered form.

In the garden these plants are seen to best advantage if planted near to water, or before the less strong growing shrubs, whose foliage provides an admirable background. In association, too, with brightly coloured perennials the effect can be most pleasing. To obtain the best results a deep rich soil is necessary and a position in sun or partial shade.

Propagation is by division of the roots in early spring, or by seed.

The flowering period is in late April and May.

## Star-wort: Michaelmas Daisy (Plate 6)

Family *COMPOSITAE*                                    *Aster* species

Comprises a number of brightly coloured species of North American origin and many varieties of garden origin possessing considerable value for effect in the herbaceous border. *A. subcaeruleus* bears bright lavender-blue flowers, each three inches across, with a central orange disc on two-feet stems in June; *A. yunnanense* blooms at the same time and is of similar habit, having heliotrope flowers. *Solidaster luteus* (syn. *A. hybridus luteus*, *Asterago lutea*), a bigeneric hybrid from a cross between the white-flowered one- to two-foot high *Aster ptarmicoides* and a Solidago, has masses of bright yellow flowers in summer. The Michaelmas Daisies comprise the many varied and beautiful garden varieties of *A. amellus*, *A. novae-angliae*, *A. novi-belgii* and the new dwarf hybrids, all September flowering. These species vary in height from two feet in the case of *A. amellus* and from three to five feet in the case of the *novae-angliae* and *novi-belgii* groups, and the colour range varies from white to shades of pink, purple, blue, violet and intermediate shades. The flowers vary from less than an inch to three inches across. *A. cordifolius* is tall and bears masses of small flowers of various shades. *A. tradescanlii* likewise has small but very abundant flowers. *A. × frikartii* has large violet-blue flowers.

Grows well in any normal soil, given full sun.

Propagation is by means of division in early spring.

The flowering season extends from June to October, according to the species.

## Goat's Beard (Plate 6)

Family *SAXIFRAGACEAE*                    *Astilbe* species

Comprises about fourteen species inhabiting moist places in eastern Asia and eastern North America and eminently suitable for colourful effect in the garden. The plants are mostly of tall habit, with elegant fern-like foliage and small flowers, varying from white to shades of pink, salmon, purple and red, borne in dense spikes that form feathery panicles.

The present race of garden varieties is believed to have originated from crosses between *A. astilboides* and *A. thunbergii*, with probably the occasional use of *A. rutilans* and *A. carminia* as well as *A. japonica* and *A. davidii*, a species of tall habit with crimson magenta flowers and violet filaments and deep blue anthers. For the middle portion of the border and on the banks of ponds or streams as well as in sparse woodland where the soil is never really dry, the Astilbes are to be seen under the most suitable conditions. *A. simplicifolia*, *A. × crispa* and *A. × humilis* are attractive miniatures valuable for rock gardens.

Propagate by division or seeds.

The flowering season is from July until late August.

## Masterwort (Plate 6)

Family *UMBELLIFERAE*        *Astrantia major and A. maxima*

Six species of Astrantia are known in Europe and western Asia, and all are characterized by their flowers being borne in leafy umbels and varying in colour from white and blush to rose. The palmate foliage is lobed or dissected and the height of the plant is one to two feet, being of neat habit. *A. major* has flowers of white or blush, but the related *A. maxima* (syn. *A. helleborifolia*, *A. carniolica rosea*) with rich pink flower-heads, rather more than

Pl. 5.

1. Thrift (*Armeria maritima*), p. 29.
3. Milkweed (*Asclepias tuberosa*), p. 30.

2. Wormwood (*Artemisia lactiflora*), p. 29.
4. Asphodel (*Asphodelus liburnica*), p. 31.

*Pl. 6.*
  1. Star-wort (*Aster amellus*), p. 31.
  3. Masterwort (*Astrantia maxima*), p. 32.
  2. Goat's Beard (*Astilbe hybrid*), p. 32.
  4. Rock Cress (*Aubrietia deltoidea*), p. 33.

an inch across, is preferable. Seedlings show considerable variation and it is possible to select quite a number of pleasing colours
from among them. The leaves have a disconcerting resemblance
to those of ground elder.

Easily cultivated, the Astrantia, like so many perennials, will
give the best results if given a soil that has been well enriched
with farm-yard manure. It is particularly at home in moist places,
provided it is not allowed to become submerged. Planting may be
carried out in early autumn or, in the case of seedlings, in early
spring.

Propagation may be by division of the roots in early spring or
by seed.

The flowering season is in June and early July.

## Rock Cress (Plate 6)

Family *CRUCIFERAE*                                  *Aubrietia deltoidea*

A colourful and almost evergreen race of trailing plants of the
eastern Mediterranean region from Sicily to Persia. The name is
derived from that of Claude Aubriet, a French natural history
painter. The best-known species is *A. deltoidea*, but the garden
forms are of mixed origin. They have small spoon-shaped foliage,
toothed and greyish green in colour, with single flowers, half an
inch across, varying in shade, among garden forms, from pale
pink to lavender, purple and crimson. There are also double
forms of garden origin and a form with variegated foliage.

The Aubrietias are useful for furnishing the front of the
herbaceous border, particularly where there is an edging of rock
stone which the trailing growths will cover quickly with a close
carpet followed, in season, by masses of brightly coloured flowers.
They are valuable also for providing bold patches of colour in the
rock garden. It is wise to cut back after flowering in order to
maintain a neat and tidy habit of growth. They can be grown
successfully in any well-drained soil in full sun and are usually
planted from pots in early March.

Propagate from cuttings for preference, by division or by seed.

The flowering season is in spring and early summer.

## False Indigo (Plate 7)

Family *LEGUMINOSAE*                                  *Baptisia australis*

Baptisia is a North American genus comprising twenty-five or
more species of which *B. australis* is alone deemed worthy of

3

garden cultivation. The leaves are short stalked, with three obovate leaflets. The flower spike reaches a height of four to six feet and bears lupin-like flowers of a rich indigo blue in long racemes. *B. tinctoria* has yellow flowers, *B. alba* white, and *B. leucantha* cream flowers. The plant will grow well in any good garden soil, but prefers a position in full sun or partial shade and a liberal quantity of leafmould or peat should there be a deficiency of humus. The time for planting is in either October or March, and the plants may remain undisturbed for a number of years. The Baptisia will best be given a place in the natural or wild garden where its vigorous habit should enable it to become suited to the conditions.

Propagation is by division in the spring, or from seed.

The flowering season is in June and July.

## Begonia (Plate 7)

Family *BEGONIACEAE*                           *Begonia tuberhybrida*

A name given to the tuberous Begonias of garden origin that have been derived from such species as *B. boliviensis*, *B. clarkei*, *B. davisii*, *B. pearcei*, *B. rosiflora*, *B. veitchii* and others from the tropics that are used for outdoor planting in summer. The exotic double forms are best suited for greenhouse culture owing to their flowers becoming weighed down by rain and spoiled. The single forms, however, with both plain and crisped petals are useful and colourful subjects for summer bedding, and comprise a very wide range of colours from white and shades of yellow to pink, salmon, orange, scarlet, crimson. The tubers may be potted in March, using a rich compost containing leafmould, old manure, coarse sand and loam. These are grown on in a cool greenhouse where frost can be excluded and are planted out-of-doors in early June. The soil should have been well enriched by the previous incorporation of old manure and the position should enjoy full sun. Perfect drainage is essential.

Propagation is by means of seed or cuttings.

The flowering season is in summer.

## Daisy (Plate 7)

Family *COMPOSITAE*                                 *Bellis perennis*

A native of Europe and the Mediterranean region and one of the popular favourites of British gardens. The present garden forms with double flowers originated from the wild daisy of our meadows. The leaves are strap-shaped, widening towards the end, and form a basal tuft. The flowers are freely borne on six-inch stems and attain a diameter up to two inches, varying in colour from white to shades of pink and red. An old favourite is the Hen and Chickens Daisy, so called from its curious habit of producing secondary and smaller flowers from the scales when the main flowers are fully developed. This old-fashioned plant, together with others of the genus, is seen to best effect when massed in generous batches of one colour. "Rob Roy" is a brilliant red form. They are of the simplest culture, requiring a good normal garden soil, well drained and exposed to the sun or in partial shade, and planting may be carried out in late summer or in February or March.

Propagation is effected by division of selected forms in spring or from seed.

The flowering season is in spring and early summer.

## Rockfoil (Plate 7)

Family *SAXIFRAGACEAE*                    *Bergenia cordifolia*

Known also as *Megasea cordifolia* and one of a large genus comprising mostly plants for the rock garden. The plant is from Siberia and has large dark, glossy green foliage, heart-shaped and produced in profusion. The flowers are three-quarters of an inch or more across, of a variable shade of rose pink and borne on thick, fleshy stems from one to one and a half feet high, and barely rising above the foliage. There are a number of varieties of garden origin. Will grow in any position but, being early flowering, one that faces due south or is protected somewhat from wintry weather is preferable.

Propagate by division of the root or from seed.

The flowering season for *Bergenia cordifolia* is in early spring.

## False Chamomile (Plate 8)

Family *COMPOSITAE*                      *Boltonia* species

A race of perennials comprising about five known species that find their homes in the United States of America and eastern Asia. The plants are usually tall and branching, with leafy stems and alternate foliage. The flowers closely resemble the Michaelmas Daisies in form and size, and the genus deserves more attention in gardens, where it is comparatively rare. *B. asteroides*, a native

of Panama to Illinois, has branching stems, four to five feet,
bearing flowers whose rays vary from white to violet and purple.
The most attractive species is *B. latisquama*, two to eight feet,
with larger flowers and rays of a pleasing bluish-violet tone.
There is also a dwarf form, *B. l. nana*, only two to three feet high,
with pinkish rays and branching from the base.

Of the easiest culture, Boltonias need little attention beyond
ordinary maintenance when once they become established and are
admirable plants for the back of the border, except the dwarf
form, which associates well with yellow or orange-coloured late
perennials.

Propagation is by means of division or seed, which may show
some variation.

The flowering season is in September and October.

## Yellow Ox-eye (Plate 8)

Family *COMPOSITAE*                           *Buphthalmum* species

This genus does not possess a popular name; its scientific name
is derived from a Greek word meaning "ox-eye". It comprises
several species found in Europe and western Asia which are
showy in the herbaceous border. The height of an established
plant varies from three to five feet, with entire alternate foliage
and flower-heads of large size with long yellow rays. Three
species are known in gardens, viz. *B. speciosissimum*, *B. salici-
folium* and *B. speciosum*, the finest of all, with largest flowers most
effective in the mass.

Easily cultivated, provided there is adequate drainage, and
worthy of a place towards the back of the middle portion of the
herbaceous border, where it associates well with Salvias or other
blue-flowered perennials of similar height.

Propagation may be effected by means of division of established clumps as soon as growth begins in late winter or from seed
sown as soon as ripe.

The flowering season is from July onwards.

## Mariposa Lily (Plate 8)

Family *LILIACEAE*                             *Calochortus* species

Known also as Star Tulip, Butterfly Tulip and Globe Tulip,
a genus of cormous plants from western America. There are about

*Pl. 7.*

36
1. False Indigo (*Baptisia australis*), p. 33.
2. Begonia (*Begonia tuberhybrida*), p. 34.
3. Daisy (*Bellis perennis*), p. 34.
4. Rockfoil (*Bergenia cordifolia*), p. 35.

*Pl.* 8.    37
1. False Chamomile (*Boltonia asteroides*), p. 35.    2. Yellow Ox-eye (*Buphthal mum* species), p. 36.
3. Mariposa Lily (*Calochortus luteus*), p. 36.    4. Quamash (*Camassia esculenta*), p. 37.

fifty species with narrow foliage and stems, somewhat branched, bearing on long stems flowers varying in colour from white to yellow and bluish-purple, and from one and a half to three inches across. The perianth consists of three inner and three outer segments, the latter being sepal-like and somewhat narrow; the inner segments are bearded on the inside and are broader and larger than the outer ones. A selection of attractive species would include *C. benthamii*, six to eight inches high, with canary yellow flowers; *C. elegans*, eight inches high, with greenish-white flowers and a purple base, its variety *amoenus* having attractive pink flowers; *C. lilacinus*, six to eight inches high, with up to ten flowers of pale purplish pink, borne on branching stems, one bulb often throwing as many as a dozen stems. In cultivation a light and porous soil is necessary, and a position in full sun with ample moisture during growth but protection from winter rains. The corms require to be thoroughly ripened by placing lights over them or by lifting.

Propagation is by means of seeds or from bulbils produced on the upper part of the stems.

The flowering season is in summer.

# Quamash (Plate 8)

Family *LILIACEAE*                        *Camassia* species

A small genus of plants with bulbs, native to North America and related to the Scillas and Ornithogalums. The leaves are strap-shaped with loose racemes of star-shaped flowers that open from the base upwards and varying from one to two inches across. *C. cusicki*, from Oregon and California, has rosettes of broad greyish-green leaves, three to four feet high, with racemes of large delicate blue flowers. *C. esculenta* (*Quamash*), which ranges from British Columbia to California, has channelled leaves a foot long and flower stems, two to three feet high, with many bright blue flowers. *C. leichtlini* reaches a height of three to four feet with racemes of creamy white flowers; its var. *atroviolaces* has purple flowers. Camassias grow well in any well-drained garden soil into which leafmould has been introduced, and prefer a position that is warm and sheltered.

Propagate by lifting the bulbs when the foliage has ripened and removing the offsets and replanting in September.

The flowering season is from May to July.

## Bellflower (Plate 9)

Family *CAMPANULACEAE*            *Campanula* species

A very large genus of herbaceous perennials, annuals and biennials, varying greatly in habit and stature and widely spread over nearly all the northern hemisphere; there are many species in the Mediterranean region. The greater number are eminently suitable for rock gardens, being of dwarf habit. Those of sufficient vigour and possessing a habit suiting them to herbaceous borders comprise *C. persicifolia*, with leafy stems clothed with short narrow foliage, rising to three feet and bearing large bell-shaped flowers, two or more inches across, of lavender or white in double or single form; *C. lactiflora* with branching stems up to four feet, bearing panicles of blue or white flowers less than an inch across; *C. latifolia*, up to five feet with racemes of larger, violet-purple flowers, its form *burghaltii* being pale blue; *C. glomerata* and its vars. *dahurica* and *pusilla*, with clustered heads of deep purple flowers on one and a half feet stems; *C. pyramidalis*, the Chimney Campanula, has stately spikes up to six feet densely clothed with open bells of blue or white; *C. grandis*, up to one and a half feet, with stems bearing closely arranged wide-open flowers of deep blue and two inches across.

Easily cultivated in a medium, well-drained soil in full sun and perfectly hardy.

Propagate by means of division of the roots in early spring or from seed.

The flowering season is in June and July, according to species.

## Blue Spiraea: Moustache Plant (Plate 9)

Family *VERBENACEAE*            *Caryopteris* species

Natives of China and Japan and comprising both species and forms of garden origin. The plant is shrubby with lance-shaped and toothed foliage, green with a reverse of silvery grey. The flowers are small, tubular, with a beautifully fringed lip, of variable tones of violet-blue and borne in short racemes at the ends of the stems. *C. incana* (syn. *C. mastacanthus*) is medium voilet-blue, but the hybrid *C. × clandonensis* has deeper coloured flowers and enjoys a greater popularity. The plant may grow four to eight feet in height and should be pruned back severely each spring as the leaf-buds begin to swell. Hardy in most parts of Britain, they prefer a rich well-drained soil and a position in full sun. A severe winter may cut the plant to ground-level, but the new growth will develop and flower in the same year. Effective in the herbaceous border planted to contrast with the late-flowering Kniphofias, Lobelia Cardinalis and dwarf pink Michaelmas Daisies.

Propagation is effected by root division in March to April, cuttings of half-ripened wood in summer, or from seed.

The flowering season is in late summer and autumn.

## Cupid's Dart (Plate 9)

Family *COMPOSITAE*                              *Catananche caerulea*

The name originates from a Greek word referring to its ancient use in making love philters. It is native to the Mediterranean region and valuable in borders for its long season of flowering and also as a cut flower. The foliage is lanceolate and tomentose. The stems up to two feet, bearing daisy-like flat heads with wide blue rays, not unlike Cornflowers. The form *C. caerulea major* has double flowers, three inches across, and is preferable to the type. The best white form is "Perry's White", snow white; and *C. c. bicolor* has flowers of lavender and white. In the middle of the border their long season of flowering makes them particularly valuable.

Will grow easily in any good garden soil that has been well cultivated and enriched with rotted organic manure. Plant in early autumn or late winter, and allow to remain undisturbed for a number of years.

. Propagation is effected by root division, by root cuttings and from seed which will probably show some variation from type.

The flowering season extends from June to early September.

## Balm of Gilead (Plate 9)

Family *LABIATAE*     *Cedronella triphylla* (syn. *C. canariensis*)

A perennial shrub, three feet, allied to Dracocephalum, and native to the Canary Islands, having oblong or lanceolate foliage, aromatic when crushed. The flowers are borne in loose whorls and are purple or white in colour with corollas about one inch long. It is related to *Agastache* (*Brittonastrum*) dealt with already.

It requires a sheltered and sunny position in a soil that is rich and well drained. In localities where severe winters are common it is wise to afford some protection in the form of bracken placed loosely over the plants during the coldest weather. Early spring is the best time for planting.

Propagation is by means of cuttings in spring or summer; they may also be raised from seed.

The flowering season extends from June to October.

## Cornflower (Plate 10)

Family *COMPOSITAE*                    *Centaurea* species

The genus consists of many annual and perennial species distributed throughout Europe, Asia, North Africa and a few in North America and Chile. Possessing alternate leaves and flowers, mostly blue, white or pink in colour, the best species are invaluable for border planting. *C. montana*, Caucasus, is of dwarf, somewhat sprawling, habit, two to three feet; has leafy stems and coarse flowers of blue, rose or white in May, and three or more inches across. *C. steenbergii* bears its large deep-pink two-inch flowers centred with white on two-feet stems, and *C. macrocephala*, Caucasus, is the most spectacular with huge yellow flower-balls, rather like those of the thistle in form, borne on leafy four-feet stems. *C. babylonica*, Levant, and *C. ruthenica*, Caucasus, also have yellow flowers, grow four to seven feet, and are attractive also for their ornamental foliage. *C. dealbata*, two feet, with silvery-pink flowers and beautiful foliage, is a lovely showy species from the Caucasus. The yellow flowered species associate well with blue Delphiniums.

Easily grown in any good garden soil in full sun and perfectly hardy. May be allowed to remain undisturbed for many years.

Propagate from seed or by division of the roots.

The flowering season extends from May until summer, according to species.

## Red Valerian (Plate 10)

Family *VALERIANACEAE*                    *Centranthus* species

Some species are native to the Mediterranean region, but those usually seen in gardens are European. The foliage is lanceolate, smooth and glaucous, and the habit of the plant is compact. The flowers are small and borne in umbels about two inches across at the end of the eighteen-inch stems. They vary in colour from crimson to white, and are produced freely. *C. ruber* and its white variety *albus* are the species most commonly found in gardens, and have been known in Britain for many years. *C. angustifolius* reaches two feet with clear rose or white flowers of similar form. Both species are fragrant. These are the main perennial species suitable for herbaceous borders where they should occupy a mid-position.

Cultivation is easy for the Valerian grows in any soil and often naturalizes itself in the crevices of old walls and masses of the red form are commonly seen on railway embankments in the western counties.

Propagation is by means of division or seeds.

The flowering season extends through the whole summer.

## Giant Scabious (Plate 10)

Family *DIPSACEAE*                            *Cephalaria gigantea*

A plant common to parts of Russia and Asia Minor and a valuable subject for the back of herbaceous borders, *C. gigantea* (also known as *C. tatarica* and *C. elata*) has pinnate foliage and tall stems branching up to six feet and bearing flat, scabious-like flowers of creamy-yellow about four inches in diameter, sometimes larger. The flower stems appear rather naked, and it is necessary for best effect to display them against the background of a hedge or wall. The plant is also effective when brought a little towards the middle of the border, where it helps to break any tendency towards flatness.

In cultivation the Cephalaria offers no difficulty, and may be grown in any well-drained soil, where it will thrive and become established sufficiently well to remain in one position for several years. It is often appreciated as a cut flower, especially as a foil to blue forms of *Scabiosa caucasica*.

Propagation may easily be carried out by either division in the spring or from seed sown as soon as ripe.

The flowering season is in July and August.

## Snow-in-Summer (Plate 10)

Family *CARYOPHYLLACEAE*                     *Cerastium tomentosum*

One of a genus of world-wide distribution and a native of Europe. This is a perennial of a very dwarf and creeping habit, with narrow oblong greyish and woolly leaves in great profusion, reaching a height of six inches. The flowers are small, pure white, and borne with great freedom, forming a snowy carpet valuable as a groundwork for spring bulbous subjects. It is also popular for use as an edging to pathways and will clamber over rocks freely.

Usually planted from pots in spring, but may be transplanted from the open ground if the operation is carried out carefully. Will grow in any well-drained soil that possesses a reasonable proportion of humus, and prefers a position in full sun. Best allowed to remain as a permanent plantation at the front of herbaceous borders, at the top of retaining walls and as an edging.

Propagation may be effected either by division of the root or from cuttings taken immediately the flowering season has passed. The flowering season is in spring and early summer.

## Lead-wort (Plate 11)

Family *PLUMBAGINACEAE*        *Ceratostigma plumbaginoides*
                                                      (syn. *Plumbago larpentae*)

A native of China and one of the loveliest of all blue-flowered plants. Of sub-shrubby habit, maintaining a shrubby character in mild climates, but being cut to ground-level by severe frost and renewing its growth in spring to flower on the current season's growth. Neat, alternate leaves, with flowers three-quarters of an inch diameter borne in umbels, and of a lovely clear blue similar in hue to the familiar greenhouse plumbago. When well grown the plant will develop a bushy habit up to one to one and a half feet. A fine plant for the front of herbaceous borders, where it associates well with pink and yellow flowered perennials of similar height.

Should be planted in full sun in a good well-drained peaty soil with, if possible, a southern or western exposure. When established is best allowed to remain undisturbed, being impatient of transplanting except in a very young stage of growth.

Propagation is effected by means of cuttings taken of nearly ripe wood in cold frame in July or August, or from seed.

The flowering season is in late summer.

## Wallflower (Plate 11)

Family *CRUCIFERAE*                                    *Cheiranthus* species

Old favourites in British gardens and natives of southern Europe. In addition to the familiar biennial forms so popular for spring bedding, there are perennial forms that should be included in the flower garden. All have the typical lance-shaped foliage. Not the least among these is the double-flowered form of *C. cheiri*, known as Harpur Crewe, with spikes of small fragrant flowers in March and April; it is of shrubby habit and forms a neat, rounded bush. *C. semperflorens* (syn. *C. mutabilis*), of Morocco, is a very variable species, producing a wide range of colour among its seedlings which may vary from mauve and pink to yellow and russet shades. It reaches a height of one foot and requires a sunny position. For the front of the border *C. alpinus* is useful where its clear yellow flowers on six-inch stems will appear from late March until June. It is lovely in contrast with pale blue Violas.

Propagation is from cuttings taken after flowering or from seed, which may show considerable variation.

The flowering period is in spring.

## Glory-of-the-Snow (Plate 11)

Family *LILIACEAE*                    *Chionodoxa* species

A charming bulbous genus from the high altitudes of Crete and Asia Minor. The blooms appear as the snow melts, hence their common name. The chief species is *C. luciliae*, with star-shaped six-petalled flowers, three-quarters of an inch across, of brilliant blue shading to a white centre, several flowers borne on each stem to a height of about six inches. *C. gigantea* has flowers twice the size of the type, whilst *C. sardensis* has gentian blue flowers without the white centre, *C. grandiflora* has violet flowers, and *C. nana* white and lilac. There is also a white form. Planted in the front of herbaceous borders, in rock gardens and naturalized in the wild garden in bold drifts, Chionodoxa give an enchanting effect early in the year.

The bulbs require to be planted in early autumn, and will succeed in any well-drained soil. They may be left to establish themselves in large colonies, provided they are given a light mulch of sifted manure each autumn.

Propagation is effected by offsets and seed.

The flowering season is in February.

## Chrysanthemum (Plate 11)

Family *COMPOSITAE*                    *Chrysanthemum* species

An important genus containing a number of species, and their forms valuable alike for the garden or for cutting and all native to the Old World, particularly China. *C. maximum*, the Shasta Daisy, has toothed leaves and three- to four-feet stems, bearing mostly single flowers of white ray petals, up to six inches in diameter, with a central yellow disc; modern developments include both double and anemone-centred forms. *C. morifolium* (*indicum*) is a parent of the popular garden chrysanthemum and comprises both double and single forms of a very wide range of colour. The Korean Chrysanthemums have mostly single flowers borne profusely on two- to three-feet stems and comprising almost every colour except blue. *C. rubellum* (syn. *Chrysobottonia pulcherrima*) is an attractive plant with single rose flowers. There is a dwarf group of compact and free-flowering habit with single and double flowers, known as the Cushion Chrysanthemum. The Pompon varieties have small fully double, rounded flowers, about two inches wide borne on branching stems two feet high.

Will grow in a rich soil that has been well enriched with humus and a position in full sun.

Propagation may be effected by division of the root in spring, cuttings or seed.

The flowering season of *C. maximum* varieties is in summer, the remainder in late summer and early autumn.

## Golden Knee (Plate 12)

Family *COMPOSITAE*                          *Chrysogonum virginianum*

This native of the south-eastern states of North America, although not of first importance, is useful as a border plant. Of a dwarf, prostrating habit, up to one foot high, the plant has leafy stems and small star-shaped flowers of bright yellow produced with great freedom. As a carpeter to taller perennials and also for bulbous subjects, such as Tulips and Gladioli, the Chrysognum is particularly useful.

As a plant that is not particular in the matter of soil, able to grow in almost any situation providing there is some drainage, it is very useful for covering barren spaces where other plants would not grow so freely.

Propagation is readily achieved by dividing creeping root-stocks and runners in March.

The flowering season is from early spring until well into autumn.

## Chicory (Plate 12)

Family *COMPOSITAE*                          *Cichorium intybus*

Although a native of the Mediterranean region, where it grows freely in stony soil at the roadside at variable altitudes and inhabits chalk cliffs, Chicory, or Succory, also grows wild in Europe and Britain. The foliage is broadly oblong and hairy, clothing branching wand-like stems which reach a height of from

*Pl.* 9.

1. Bellflower (*Campanula persicifolia*), p. 38.  2. Blue Spiraea (*Caryopteris incana*), p. 38.
3. Cupid's Dart (*Catananche caerulea*), p. 39.  4. Balm of Gilead (*Cedronella triphylla*), p. 39.

*Pl* 10.                                                                        45
1. Cornflower (*Centaurea montana*), p. 40.                  2. Red Valerian (*Centranthus ruber*), p. 40.
3. Giant Scabious (*Cephalaria gigantea*), p. 41.    4. Snow-in-summer (*Cerastium tomentosum*), p. 41.

three to four feet, and bear flowers one and a half inches or more across, of a bright azure blue close to the stem. Although a wild plant, its floral colour alone commends Chicory for the flower garden, where a few plants massed together cannot be other than pleasing. For cutting, too, they have a definite decorative value. There are white and pink forms.

It is easy to cultivate, may be grown in any soil, and in sun or partial shade. It is particularly useful for filling in odd corners where it would be difficult to grow other plants.

Propagation is effected most readily by means of seed.

The flowering season is from July to October.

## Snake Root: Bugbane (Plate 12)

Family *RANUNCULACEAE*                *Cimicifuga* species

A genus of perennials, natives of North America. *C. americana* is a plant of moist woodland, having large foliage and slender stems three to four feet high, bearing many small white flowers in an elongated raceme. *C. racemosa* and its form *dissecta* have creamy-white flowers and three to five feet stems. *C. simplex*, three feet, native to Kamtschatka, is also favoured in gardens, having parted foliage and erect racemes of small white flowers; "Elstead" is a charming variety, four to five feet high, with pendulous creamy-white flower spikes. In association with blue Michaelmas Daisies of tall stature or with the later Kniphofias of scarlet colouring the Cimicifugas, especially *C. simplex*, are particularly effective. They are also useful as a cut flower in an autumnal floral ensemble.

In cultivation they prefer a moist soil rich in humus and a shady situation. Under such conditions they will become established and may be allowed to remain in one position for many years. They are excellent plants for woodland.

Propagation is effected by division of the root in spring, or from seed.

The flowering season is in late summer and early autumn.

## Clematis (Plate 12)

Family *RANUNCULACEAE*            *Clematis* various species

Apart from the well-known climbing forms there are several Clematis of herbaceous habit, mostly natives of Asia and valuable for use in herbaceous borders. *C. heracleaefolia* is of strong and upright growth, with large bright green leaves, ovate and rounded at the base, slightly hairy and toothed. The flowers are borne in corymbs and comprise four light blue sepals that become reflexed. The best form is *C. h.* var. *davidiana*, which reaches a height of three feet and may need support; the flowers are borne in clustered heads of six to twelve, are of a brighter blue than the type and are fragrant. *C. campanile* is a hybrid, growing four feet high, with fragrant flowers of pale azure blue, and *C. integrifolia* is a native of southern Europe, two feet high, with blue and silver flowers. *C. recta* is of tufted habit, with pinnate leaves and many flowers one inch across, white, fragrant, and borne in branching terminal panicles up to three feet.

A light, rich loam, dressed with lime, is best for Clematis, and perfect drainage is essential. Support in the form of short twiggy peasticks is necessary to keep the plants tidy.

Propagation is by seed, stem cuttings and by division.

The flowering season is from June to August for *C. recta*; August to September for the others.

## Bell-wort (Plate 13)

Family *CAMPANULACEAE*                *Codonopsis* species

The genus comprises a number of perennial species of twining or prostrate growth from the Himalayas, of which three are particularly useful for herbaceous borders, being similar to some Campanulas. *C. clematidea* (syn. *Glosocomia clematidea*) has small ovate leaves up to three-quarters of an inch long and bell-shaped pale blue flowers, one and a quarter inches long, attractively veined and spotted with yellow and white inside, produced on long terminal penduncles, and grows three feet high. *C. ovata*, often confused with the foregoing species, has blue flowers, but grows only one foot high. Common species in gardens is *C. clematidea*, often confused with *C. ovata*. *C. rotundifolia* is eighteen inches tall, with blue- and yellow-throated flowers and attractive interior markings.

A well-drained sandy soil and full exposure to the sun are essentials to successful cultivation, and an excellent position is at the top of a retaining wall, where the flowers, being in an elevated position, are seen to best advantage.

Propagation is best achieved by sowing seed as soon as ripe, wintering in a cold frame and planting out in spring.

The flowering season is in June.

## Autumn Crocus (Plate 13)

Family *LILIACEAE* *Colchicum* species

C. *autumnale*, the Autumn Crocus, is also known as Meadow Saffron, and the source of a narcotic poison. This attractive little plant is a native of Europe, and is common in Britain. It produces its bright purple cup-shaped flowers, similar in form to the crocus but unrelated, naked from the earth to a height of six to nine inches in autumn. The large lance-shaped leaves appear in spring and summer long after the flowers have faded. C. *bornmuelleri*, a plant from Asia Minor, has pretty flowers of rosy lilac during the same season, and C. *speciosum* produces flowers varying from clear rose to deep crimson-purple, each with a white throat. There is also a rare white-flowered form. Colchicums grow well in a rich, moist soil that is well drained. Naturalized in shrubberies, and at the front of herbaceous borders companioned with the drawf blue Michaelmas Daisies, they are effective. Plant not later than August.

Propagation is by separating the corms as soon as the leaves have died down in July.

The flowering season is from August to October.

## Lily-of-the-Valley (Plate 13)

Family *LILIACEAE* *Convallaria majalis*

A native of Asia and Europe and occasionally found in England and one of the most delightful of plants. The leaves and flowers grow from a creeping rootstock, the foliage being lance-shaped and deep green in colour, rising to six inches or more. The flowers are bell-shaped, a quarter of an inch in diameter, pure white and deliciously fragrant and are carried on stalks, six to twelves inches high, from ten to twenty on each. They are followed by red berries in autumn. There are a number of forms, the most noteworthy being Fortin's Giant, with larger flowers than the type. There is also var. *rosea*, a form with white flowers flushed with pink, and var. *prolificans* which grows tall.

A well-drained rich loam containing coarse sand and a position in partial shade will grow them to perfection. September and October are the best months for planting. They should be allowed to form large clumps and, in the initial planting, should be placed four inches apart. When gathering the flowers give the stalks a sharp upward jerk and leave at least one leaf to each plant.

Propagate by division of the rootstocks when clumps become overcrowded in September.

The flowering season is May and June.

## Coreopsis (Plate 13)

Family *COMPOSITAE*                                    *Coreopsis* species

Natives of North America and one of the most popular perennials, especially for cutting. *C. grandiflora* has lance-shaped leaves and slender branching stems two to three feet high, bearing flowers two and a half inches across and broadly winged, bright yellow in colour. Perry's variety is a double form. *C. pubescens superba* has an arresting crimson central blotch to each flower. *C. lanceolata* resembles a dwarf form of *C. grandiflora*. *C. verticillata* has fine feathery foliage surmounted by small yellow flowers. There is an improved form with larger flowers known as *C. v. grandiflora*; the height does not exceed a foot. *C. rosea*, a foot high, bears pale rose flowers. Towards the front of herbaceous borders near to purple or dark blue perennials of similar height the Coreopsis is seen to best advantage.

Plant in spring in well-drained rich soil and allow to become established. Of the easiest culture.

Propagation is by division or seed.

The flowering season is in late July and August.

## Crown Vetch (Plate 14)

Family *LEGUMINOSAE*                                 *Coronilla iberica*

A European plant and a member of a genus that finds its home in the Mediterranean countries and the Canary Islands. Of a rather straggling habit of growth this plant produces typical leguminous foliage and many pea-shaped flowers in dense umbels, about half an inch in length and bright yellow in summer. Its long-flowering period makes it useful for planting to trail over the margins of paved pathways and to provide a foreground in the herbaceous border to such subjects as *Salvia patens*, *Anchusa caespitosa* and other dwarf perennials with light to medium blue flowers. Easily grown in any soil that possesses reasonable drainage and enjoys a good sun exposure. Planting may be carried out in either early autumn or in February or March.

Propagation is effected by division of the root as soon as growth appears in late winter or from seed sown as soon as ripe or in late winter.

The flowering season is from June to October.

*Pl.* 11.

48

1. Lead-wort (*Ceratostigma plumbaginoides*), p. 42.   2. Wallflower (*Cheiranthus cheiri* var.), p. 42.
3. Glory-of-the-snow (*Chionodoxa luciliae*), p. 43.   4. Chrysanthemum (*Chrysanthemum mori-folium*), p. 43.

*Pl.* 12.                                                                                               49

1. Golden Knee (*Chrysognum virginianum*), p. 44.    2. Chicory (*Cichorium intybus*), p. 44.
3. Snake Root (*Cimicifuga racemosa*), p. 45.    4. Clematis (*Clematis heracleaefolia*), p. 45.

## Fumitory (Plate 14)

Family *FUMARIACEAE*                                    *Corydalis* species

A genus containing both perennial and annual forms native to
Europe, China or Canada. The plants are well worth attention if
only on account of their attractive fern-like foliage, which makes
a pleasing carpet of restful green. The flowers are small, four-
petalled and borne in a cluster at the end of the short stems.
*C. allenii*, rose; *C. thalictrifolia*, yellow, with foliage resembling
Thalictrum, and tuberous roots; and *C. lutea*, a rather rampant
spreading growth with finely divided leaves and pale yellow
flowers are all of prostrate or semi-prostrate habit. *C. nobilis* is
of erect habit, has fern-like foliage and flowers of white tipped
with yellow, each being about an inch in length, and *C. lede-
bouriana*, purple flowers. For shaded or sunny positions, especially where a wall or hedge will provide some winter protection
to the foliage, the Fumitories will flourish but, owing to their
spreading nature, should be used with discretion in borders and
rock gardens.

Propagate by division or seed sown in the positions where the
plants are to grow.

The flowering season extends through the greater part of spring
and summer.

## Crambe: Flowering Seakale (Plate 14)

Family *CRUCIFERAE*                                    *Crambe cordifolia*

A native of the Caucasus, this plant gives the impression of
being a gigantic Gypsophila. The foliage is large and heart-
shaped and the white flowers, small but produced in great
quantities, form massive branching panicles up to a height of
five or six feet. The plant is not long lived in many climates, the
seedlings making only foliage for the first two years after sowing
and flowering in the third year, and then often becoming weakly
and perishing. *C. maritima* is the Sea Kale useful for its glaucous
foliage and esteemed as a vegetable. For the back of the herbaceous border as a background to the most brightly coloured
perennials of medium or tall stature, *C. cordifolia* is excellent and
it is also very effective, where space permits, massed in the wild
garden. The plant grows best on a chalky or gravelly soil, and
appears to resent root disturbance when once established.

Propagate from seed which is best sown as soon as ripe in pots
and planted out in the spring in their permanent positions.

The flowering season is in June.

4

## Cape Lily (Plate 14)

Family *AMARYLLIDACEAE*                    *Crinum longifolium*

This attractive lily-like plant, often known as *C. capense*, finds its home throughout the whole of South Africa and is the hardiest of the many species. The plant is bulbous, its bulbs being three or four inches in diameter. The leaves are strap-shaped, up to three feet long and three inches across and greyish-green in colour. The flowers, funnel-shaped and wide open at the mouth, are three to four inches long and the segments an inch across, the colour being white flushed red on the exterior, and borne on stems about one foot high and pedicels two inches long, from six to twelve on each stem. The best garden forms originating from crosses between this species and *C. moorei*, a pink-coloured species, are *C. powellii*, medium rose-pink, and borne on two-feet stems, and its white form *C. p. album* and a deeper coloured form, *C. p. rubrum*. A soil comprising a mixture of loam, peat, leafmould and coarse sand is necessary for cultivation. Good draining and ample moisture during growth are essential, drier conditions being preferable when the plants are dormant. The protection of a wall, nearby shrubs or a covering of bracken during winter is advisable in all but the mildest climates.

Propagate by means of offsets or seed sown as soon as ripe. The flowering season is in summer.

## Crocosmia (Plate 15)

Family *IRIDACEAE*                    *Crocosmia crocosmiflora*

A hybrid of garden origin the result of a cross between the South African *C. pottsii* and *C. aurea*; often known as Mont-bretia. The foliage is sword-like, similar to that of the Gladiolus but narrower. The flowers are funnel-shaped and borne on branching leafy stems to a height of two or three feet. The species is known mostly by its many beautiful varieties of garden origin, some having flowers up to three inches across and varying in colour from lemon yellow to orange, golden yellow and shades of scarlet and crimson; the Earlham strain is one of the most note-worthy. *C. tritonia pottsii* reaches up to four feet with bright yellow flowers, and *Tritonia rosea* has attractive small pink flowers spotted yellow at the base. May be grown in a well-drained rich soil containing ample humus, and the addition of well-decayed farm-yard manure will add to the size of the

Pl. 13.

50

1. Bellwort (*Codonopsis clematidea*), p. 46.     2. Autumn Crocus (*Colchicum bornmuelleri*), p. 47.
3. Lily-of-the-valley (*Convallaria majalis*), p. 47.     4. Coreopsis (*Coreopsis grandiflora*), p. 48.

*Pl.* 14.

5

1. Crown Vetch (*Coronilla iberica*), p. 48.
3. Crambe (*Crambe cordifolia*), p. 49.

2. Fumitory (*Corydalis lutea*), p. 49.
4. Cape Lily (*Crinum logifolium*), p. 50.

individual flowers. Plant in March and lift in October and store under frost-proof conditions during autumn and winter.

Propagate in February by detaching the stolons, potting in a leafy compost and planting in the open ground in May.

The flowering season is in late summer.

## Crocus (Plate 15)

Family *IRIDACEAE* *Crocus* various species

A genus of probably one hundred species from the Mediterranean region and extending to south-west Asia. The foliage is narrow, channelled, erect and grass-like, the flowers being funnel-shaped and borne on long slender tubes that rise from amid the foliage; when expanded they vary from one to two inches across, sometimes a little more. Among the spring-flowering species mention can be made of *C. balansae*, the only orange-yellow March flowering form; *C. tommasinianus*, pale lavender; *C. susianus*, rich yellow in mid-winter; *C. biflorus*, the Scotch Crocus, varying from white to lavender. Among those that bloom in autumn: *C. clusii*, from Spain and pale to deep purple; *C. longiflorus*, with fragrant flowers or rosy lilac with yellow base; and *C. nudiflorus*, clear violet, blooming in autumn before the foliage, which appears in spring, are noteworthy, but there are many others of garden value. Plant in late summer or early autumn in well-drained soil in sunny positions.

Propagate by lifting and separating the corms after they have been well established, or from seed.

The flowering season is from February to April for spring flowering and from September to December for autumn flowering forms.

## Sowbread (Plate 15)

Family *PRIMULACEAE* *Cyclamen* species

This genus is native to Central and southern Europe and countries bordering the Mediterranean, where their corms are devoured by wild boar, hence the common name. It includes both tender and hardy species. Of the hardy species the following are noteworthy. *C. orbiculatum*, from the Caucasus and Asia Minor, reaches three inches high, having rounded leaves, which in var. *coum* are plain green with purple reverse; the flowers are of typical cyclamen form, small, and vary from purple-rose to white, appearing from

December to March. *C. europaeum* has marbled foliage with purplish-red fragrant flowers; blooms from June to October. *C.
ibericum* (syn. *C. vernum*), Caucasus, has foliage zoned with white
and purple flowers in late winter, while *C. atkinsi* is a hybrid
between *C. orbiculatum coum* and *C. ibericum*, similar to the last
named but with larger foliage and flowers appearing in spring.
*C. neapolitanum* has green or sometimes parti-coloured foliage and
flowers on stems up to three inches high and pink or white in
colour in August and September. Cyclamen are shade lovers, and
the corms should be planted in a leafy soil, leaving the top portion
just above ground-level; perfect drainage is essential and the introduction of limestone rubble is beneficial. Plant from June to
November, and bed the base of each tuber in sand.

Propagation is from seed, or by cutting the old corms to pieces,
each with an eye.

The flowering season varies according to the species as detailed
above.

## Dahlia (Plate 15)

Family *COMPOSITAE*                 *Dahlia pinnata* and *D. juarezii*

An important race of tuberous-rooted perennials, closely related
to Cosmos and Coreopsis and found native in Mexico and Guatemala. *D. pinnata*, also known as *D. variabilis* and *D. rosea*, is a
very variable species, probably of hybrid origin, and has been
used to a considerable extent in the evolution of the modern
varieties of garden origin. The cactus varieties that have raised
the genus to such eminence are derived from *D. juarezii*. From
these and possibly other species have arisen the present garden
forms known variously as cactus, semi-cactus, pompon, decorative, collarette, etc. The plants vary in height from a foot to five
or even six feet, with very leafy stems and foliage of rounded
form and slightly serrated at the margin. The flowers vary greatly
in size from two inches in diameter in the case of pompon varieties
to as much as fifteen inches in the case of large decorative
varieties. They are mostly double in form, although some have
single or semi-double flowers. Dahlias will grow in any rich soil
in full sun and with perfect drainage. Being only half hardy, it is
necessary to lift the tubers after the first autumnal frost, dry and
store in frost-proof conditions.

Propagation is by means of division of the tubers or of cuttings
taken from tubers started into growth in February in heat, and
rooted under glass.

The flowering season is from July until September.

## Larkspur (Plate 16)

Family *RANUNCULACEAE*                    *Delphinium* species

An important race of hardy plants that find their homes widely distributed over the northern hemisphere, comprising both annual and perennial species. The foliage is elegantly lobed and divided and the flowers borne in spikes on branching stems of various heights. *D. elatum*, reaching a height of three to six feet, has spurred flowers of blue, an inch or less across and, with *D. cheilanthum* and *D. formosum*, is believed to have been the main influence in the evolution of the present-day magnificent garden varieties. Its form *belladonna* is a dwarf branching plant with florets of blue. *D. cardinale*, from California, has scarlet florets on three- to four-feet stems; *D. nudicaule*, from the same habitat, is of similar colour but with partly closed florets on one and a half feet stems; *D. macrocentron*, from East Africa, has greenish-blue florets shaded yellow, up to three feet; and the Syrian *D. sulphureum* has yellow florets on three- to four-feet spikes. There are many other species. For gardens the varieties of *elatum* type are most used, and require a deep, rich, well-manured soil in sun or partial shade, good drainage, and ample moisture during growth.

Propagate by means of division, cuttings or seed.

The flowering season is in June and July and again in late summer.

## Pink (Plate 16)

Family *CARYOPHYLLACEAE*                    *Dianthus* species

An important race of perennials and a few annuals native to southern Europe, northern Africa and one or two from North America. *D. caryophyllus* is the Carnation, Clove-Pink, Picotee and Grenadine. The foliage varies in thickness and sometimes is as fine as coarse grass, is narrow and pointed, glaucous green in colour. The flower stems vary from a foot high in the case of Pinks to three feet for Carnations. The fragrant flowers are borne on the terminals of the stems in small quantities. Carnations are usually grown under glass, except Border Carnations, which may be grown out-of-doors, but these are hardly suitable for herbaceous borders. The Pinks comprise such groups as the *allwoodii*, *herbertii*, *winteri*, all good garden plants, about a foot high and free flowering. Varieties of the laced type, also "Mrs. Sinkins" and "Inchmery", whose parentage is difficult to trace

are old favourites. Given a warm soil, perfect drainage and old
mortar rubble in the soil, Pinks will be among the most satisfactory of garden plants.

Propagation is by means of cuttings, layering and seed.

The flowering season extends throughout the summer, provided
flowers are removed regularly as they fade.

## Bleeding Heart (Plate 16)

Family *FUMARIACEAE*                                *Dicentra* species

Natives of North America or eastern Asia. The perennial
species of this genus now in cultivation are the old garden
favourite *D. spectabilis*, from Siberia and Japan, at one time
known as *dielytra* with elegant, finely cut foliage and bearing
on two-feet arching stems pendent flowers, heart-shaped, deep
rose with inner petals or white that protrude conspicuously.
There is also a white-flowered form. *D. eximia* and *D. formosa*
have finer foliage with smaller flowers of rose. *D. chrysantha*,
known as Golden Eardrops, reaches a height of three feet and
bears golden yellow flowers; rather a rarity. A rich light soil in
partial shade will suit these easily grown plants admirably and
a large established clump is most attractive. *D. spectabilis*,
although long cultivated in Britain, is used more often for forcing
in January than as a garden plant.

Propagation is by means of division of the roots when growth
appears, or root cuttings.

The flowering season is in spring.

## Burning Bush (Plate 16)

Family *RUTACEAE*                                *Dictamnus albus*

One species alone is known with variations and native to the
region from South Europe to North China. The old garden
favourite *D. albus*, once known as *D. fraxinella*, has glossy,
leathery foliage with three-feet stems, bearing terminal racemes
of fragrant flowers, somewhat like the Peruvian Lily (q.v.)
in form but rather smaller, and white in colour. Its var.
*purpureus* has larger flowers suffused purple, var. *ruber* has rosy
purple flowers with deeper coloured veins, and var. *caucasicus*
has flowers double the size of the type. The whole plant has the
strong aroma of lemon and on a sultry evening will ignite if a
lighted match is held beneath the flowers. A good strong loam
is best for these plants, and a position in full sun where it will

*Pl.* 15.

54
1. Crocosmia (*Crocosmia crocosmiflora*), p. 50.
2. Crocus (*Crocus vernus*), p. 51.
3. Sowbread (*Cyclamen neapolitanum*), p. 52.
4. Dahlia (*Dahlia × juarezii*), p. 52.

Pl. 16.
1. Larkspur (*Delphinium elatum*), p. 53.
2. Pink (*Dianthus* species), p. 5
3. Bleeding Heart (*Dicentra spectabilis*), p. 54.
4. Burning Bush (*Dictamnus albus* var. *ruber*)
p. 54.

become one of the most permanent of perennials, having been known to outlive several generations.

Propagate by seed sown immediately when ripe, its powers of germination waning very rapidly if stored for later sowing.

The flowering season is in early summer.

## Wand-flower (Plate 17)

Family *IRIDACEAE*                    *Dierama pulcherrima*

A bulbous-rooted plant, allied to Sparaxis, and native to South Africa. The foliage is sword-shaped and the stems are tough but slender, bearing along the upper portion many pendulous funnel-shaped flowers, varying in colour from white to shades of pink and purple, some being effectively striped. The individual flowers are about one and a half inches in length and are attached to the stem by means of fine pedicels. The height varies from four to six or more feet, and the gracefully arching stems make it one of the most graceful of all perennials. It requires a well-drained light, sandy loam, and the presence of leafmould is beneficial. Planted in bold groups among the later flowering perennials, Dieramas will lend an air of distinction to any border. They are particularly lovely by the side of ponds and streams. Except in the most severe climates the plants may be left out-of-doors in winter, it being advisable in hard weather to provide a top covering of bracken. In very exposed localities the plants should be lifted in the autumn and stored away from frost in boxes of sandy soil. It is not advisable to disturb established plants.

Propagation is from seed or by offsets from old bulbs, though it is inadvisable to disturb well-established plants.

The flowering season is from July to September.

## American Cowslip (Plate 17)

Family *PRIMULACEAE*                    *Dodecatheon meadia*

One of a number of species found in the woodlands and prairies of North America and a distinctive, attractive and rather uncommon plant. The rounded, strap-like, oblong foliage forms a rather flat rosette from which rise leafless stalks, slender and reaching a height of one to one and a half feet. The flowers are borne at the end of the stem in a bunch of a dozen or more on short arching or semi-erect pedicels. They are not unlike Cyclamen in form with a long and pointed style, of rose colour with reddish-yellow stamens and a yellow circle to the corolla. Of its various forms var. *splendidum* is crimson with a yellow zone; **var.** *giganteum* is a giant form and contains a white form; var. *elegans* is smaller than the type with darker coloured flowers in a greater quantity.

A well-drained soil, rich in leafmould and enjoying partial shade, is ideal for these plants whose requirements suggest the cultivated margins of streams and ponds or the open parts of woodland where they will not become smothered with strong weeds.

Propagate by division in early spring, or by seeds which are slow in producing flowering plants.

The flowering season is in May and June.

## Leopard's Bane (Plate 17)

Family *COMPOSITAE*                    *Doronicum plantagineum*

The genus contains over twenty species native to Europe and temperate Asia, the one named above being the most worthy for garden cultivation. The leaves are oval and toothed with leafy stems, two feet high and bearing yellow, daisy-like flowers, three inches across. The form *D. p. excelsum* has flowers an inch larger and is more robust in growth, often attaining five feet. This and the type are the ones most usually favoured in cultivation, being superior to the other known species. They are much valued as cut flowers. The plant demands little from its cultivator provided the soil is given moderate cultivation, is well drained and enjoys a certain amount of sun. It is said that the species in question lends itself to forcing, but little appears to have been attempted in this direction. It associates well with the earliest blue-flowered perennials.

Propagation is effected by division of the root in October or when growth begins.

The flowering season is from April to early June.

## Dragon's Head (Plate 17)

Family *LABIATAE*                    *Dracocephalum* species

A genus reaching its greatest development in Asia, with a few species in Europe and North America. The leaves may be entire and toothed as in *D. ruyschiana* or deeply cut. The flowers occur in whorls, crowded together into spikes or heads, on erect stems springing from a somewhat woody base. *D. ruyschiana*, native to the Alps, grows twelve to eighteen inches high, and has flowers of purplish-blue. Var. *japonicum* has white flowers, shaded with blue, and is sometimes preferred to the type. *D. grandiflorum* is a dwarf of six to nine inches from Siberia, having blue flowers, two inches long. Others are *D. austriacum*, a blue-flowering species of Central Europe, twelve to eighteen inches high; and *D. speciosum*, which comes from the Himalaya and carries its whorls of blue-lilac flowers on eighteen-inch stems.

Dracocephalums are among the most effective of border perennials and are useful for breaking up the flatness of the central portion where there are often too many composites.

Propagation may be done by division of the roots in October or March; by cuttings of young shoots in April to May—under handlights; or by seeds sown in April.

The flowering season is from June to September.

## Purple Cone-flower (Plate 18)

Family *COMPOSITAE*                    *Echinacea purpurea*

At one time known as *Rudbeckia purpurea*, to which family it is related, this species is a native of North America. The foliage is dark green, ovate and serrated, the stems reach a height of two feet, bearing singly rayed flowers of varying tones of purple with a central cone of dark brown. The type has the defect of its ray petals being very reflexed, but this has been remedied in such varieties of garden origin as The King and Abendsonne, whose petals lie perfectly horizontally to the central cone and are often three or four inches across. The height of garden varieties varies from two to four feet. Planted in bold groups, the Echinaceas provide a rich colour at a time when there is usually a plethora of yellow and orange in the border.

A rich, warm and well-drained soil is necessary for good cultivation, and the plants resist drought conditions extremely well.

Propagation is best effected by means of root cuttings taken early in the year.

The flowering season is from July until September.

## Globe Thistle (Plate 18)

Family *COMPOSITAE*                    *Echinops* species

The genus includes perennial species native chiefly to the Mediterranean region and the Middle East. They are rather coarse, erect-growing plants with decorative, bristly pinnate foliage of prickly lobes and teeth. The flower-heads are round, prickly and thistle-like in appearance. *E. ritro* has heads of steely-blue flowers on three-feet stems; *E. bannaticus* (syn. *E. ruthenicus*) has greyish-blue heads on two- to three-feet stems; *E. nivalis* is of the same height as *E. ritro* and has white heads; *E. giganteus* and *E. sphaerocephalus* have large heads of white and reach as high as four to five feet. Among the most cherished of herbaceous perennials these plants provide soft colours that are valuable for toning down the more garish flowers. They are splendid in association with pink Hollyhocks and *Gypsophila paniculata*, Flamingo. As cut flowers they lend themselves to many effective arrangements. They are easily grown in any good, well-drained soil in full sun or partial shade.

Propagation is by means of root cuttings.

The flowering season extends from July to September.

## Willow Herb (Plate 18)

Family *ONAGRACEAE*                    *Epilobium angustifolium* and
                                                          *hirsutum*

The genus is widely distributed throughout the temperate regions and contains a number of species of garden value of shrubby and herbaceous character. There are many that are unworthy of note as garden plants but two are attractive. *E. angustifolium* is a native of British woodland and can attain a height of four feet or more with spikes of deep rose; there is also a white form. It is a rampant plant that is not suitable for herbaceous borders owing to its habit of overspreading its allotted space by means of underground runners that spread with considerable rapidity. At the same time in shade and beneath the drip of trees it is excellent and associates well with the Foxglove. *E. hirsutum*, known as "Codlins and Cream", four feet, is rather stouter in growth but should be grown in woodland and by the margins of streams and ponds; it has a variegated form. There are dwarfer and more refined species suitable for rock gardens.

Propagate by division in spring, or from seed.

The flowering season is in July.

## Barren-wort (Plate 18)

Family *BERBERIDACEAE*        *Epimedium pinnatum colchicum*

Twenty species are known, all natives of the northern hemisphere, one in north-west Africa. *E. pinnatum colchicum*, the most

*Pl.* 17.                                                                 58

1. Wand-flower (*Dierama pulcherrima*), p. 55.   2. American Cowslip (*Dodecatheon meadia*), p. 55.
3. Leopard's Bane (*Doronicum plantagineum*), p. 56.   4. Dragon's Head (*Dracocephalum ruyschiana*), p. 56.

*Pl.* 18.
1. Purple Cone-flower (*Echinacea purpurea*), p. 57.   2. Globe Thistle (*Echinops ritro*), p. 57.
3. Willow Herb (*Epilobium angustifolium*), p. 58.   4. Barren-wort (*Epimedium*), p. 58.

useful species for herbaceous borders, is a native of Persia and the Caucasus, having compound foliage with heart-shaped leaflets and leafless flower-stems to one and a half feet high, with clusters of fragile, bright yellow flowers in a slender raceme. There are other species and hybrids with white and rose and sulphur flowers, but none is so suited to the herbaceous border as *E. pinna'um colchicum.* The plant is practically evergreen, the old foliage remaining in condition until the new leaves appear in spring. It is unwise to remove this foliage as it protects the young growth in spring. The young foliage is often suffused with tender shades of rose. A position where a generous quantity of peat has been incorporated into the soil is necessary for successful cultivation, and a site in partial shade is advisable. Its creeping stems that travel just beneath the soil demand an adequate supply of humus.

Propagate by means of division in spring.

The flowering season is in early summer.

## Winter Aconite (Plate 19)

Family *RANUNCULACEAE*          *Eranthis hyemalis*

A dwarf perennial with a tuberous rootstock native to Europe, with related species in Asia. The leaves are divided with a row immediately beneath the five- to eight-sepalled yellow flowers, borne on six-inch stems and not unlike the buttercup, an inch or more across. *E. hyemalis* grows well in any well-drained soil and appreciates the presence of a little leafmould or peat. Among shrubs, in woodland, naturalized in short turf and at the front of herbaceous borders it will be among the first of plants to show its flowers in the New Year, and they have been known to appear above snow-covered earth. When planted in autumn it is well to allow the roots to remain undisturbed for a number of years when the flowers will form an effective carpet of golden yellow. It is well to plant thickly, three or four inches apart and about the same depth.

Propagate by lifting the tubers when dormant in summer, dividing and replanting; seed sown as soon as ripe will remain dormant until the following spring. Two attractive hybrids with larger flowers, named *E.* × *tubergenii* and *E.* "Guinea Gold", have been raised in Holland.

The flowering season is from January to March.

## Foxtail Lily (Plate 19)

Family *LILIACEAE* *Eremurus* species

Imposing and attractive perennials with tuberous roots from central and southern Asia, including Persia, Turkestan and Siberia. The foliage is long and linear, springing from the central crown of a fleshy rootstock that, in shape, may be said to resemble a wheel without the rim. The flowers are borne on leafless stems that vary in height according to the species. *E. himalaicus* is majestic and imposing with leaves a foot long and stems that can attain a height of seven feet or more; the flower-spike is from three to four feet long and comprises star-shaped flowers, over an inch across, of pure white. *E. robustus* has leaves three feet long, stems and flower-spikes of eight to ten feet, with rosy-pink flowers of two inches across. *E. bungei* has narrow greyish-green foliage a foot long, with flower-spikes that vary in height from two to three feet, the upper portion being well furnished with flowers, an inch across, of bright yellow.

Planting may be done only in September or October when the roots are dormant, keeping the crown level with the surface of the soil and protecting in winter by a covering of bracken. Good drainage is essential.

Propagate by division in September, or by means of seed.

The flowering season is in May and June.

## Flea-bane (Plate 19)

Family *COMPOSITAE* *Erigeron* species

A genus of plants not unlike dwarf Michaelmas Daisies, comprising both herbaceous and alpine species, widely distributed throughout the world. *E. speciosus*, from the western coast of North America, has a dwarf habit with short, narrow foliage and daisy-like flowers on one-and-a-half- to two-feet stems, of purplish lilac, about two inches across, with a yellowish disc at the centre. *E. macranthus*, of similar but rather neater habit, reaches a foot high and bears freely large purple flowers, yellow centred. *E. mucronatus* (syn. *Vittadenia triloba*) is of compact habit, nine inches high, and bears masses of pink flowers over a long period that fade to white. There are a number of improved forms of garden origin. A normal garden soil that is well drained and a position towards the front of the border in full sun will grow these easily cultivated plants to perfection. The flowers are useful for floral arrangements.

Propagation is easily effected by division of the roots in late summer or in March.

The flowering season is in June and July.

## Sea Holly (Plate 19)

Family *UMBELLIFERAE*                              *Eryngium* species

A race of perennials mostly to be found in Europe and the Mediterranean region and others widely distributed in temperate regions. The blue-green foliage is deeply lobed and spiny with branching leafy stems and flower-heads similar in form to those of the Teazel, enclosed in finely cut spiny bracts. The foliage varies in size considerably, according to the species. *E. amethystinum*, Europe, reaches a height of one and a half feet with flower-heads of metallic blue; *E. giganteum*, America, reaches three to four feet and has larger heads of a less brilliant colour and is often grown as a biennial; *E. oliverianum*, Orient, is two to four feet in height with highly coloured blue flower-heads; *E. alpinum*, Europe, reaches one to two feet and possesses heads of bright metallic blue. *E. pandanifolium*, from Monte Video, is a gigantic blue-flowered species, from ten to fifteen feet high. Valuable for long effect in the border, the flowers are good for cutting and may be dried and treated as everlastings. The Eryngiums are easily grown in any well-drained soil and are particularly suited to maritime localities and chalky soils.

Propagation is by means of division, root cuttings and seed.

The flowering season is from July to September.

## Dog's-Tooth Violet (Plate 20)

Family *LILIACEAE*                              *Erythronium* various species

With the exception of two species these charming bulbous subjects are native to North America. The foliage is oblong and pointed, green and sometimes attractively mottled. The stem is slender, leafless and carries flowers either singly or several to a stem. The perianth of the flower is often recurved and comprises six divisions. *E. dens-canis* is the only European species, with six-inch stems, bearing singly rosy-purple flowers over an inch across which may vary to white, flesh colour in the various forms. A moist peaty soil fully exposed to the sun is necessary for its cultivation. *E. americanum*, with mottled foliage, has one-inch flowers, pale yellow on stems nine inches high. *E. oregonum*, often known as *E. giganteum*, is pure white with a ring of orange-red and a diameter of three inches. *E. grandiflorum* will carry as many as five flowers on one stem, of a bright golden yellow and three inches across. There are a number of other species. Plant from September to November in a gritty soil rich in humus, and cover the bulbs with twice their own depth of soil. Give an annual mulch of well-decayed manure in winter. Allow to remain undisturbed for several years.

Propagate by division of the bulbs, which may be lifted when dormant.

The flowering period is in spring.

## Spurge (Plate 20)

Family *EUPHORBIACEAE*                    *Euphorbia* species

A genus of plants of variable habit, containing hardy and tender species and occurring in most temperate and tropical countries. A few only are worthy of attention for garden planting. *E. epithymoides* and *E. polychroma* form rounded clumps to the height of one foot with oblong leaves of deep green enclosing an inflorescence of yellow flowers, and are among the best species for planting at the front of the border. *E. pilosa* reaches one and a half feet, with oblong leaves of golden yellow in its best form var. *major*. *E. wulfenii* is a curiously attractive plant up to three feet, and forms a clump, bearing in great density narrow leaves of glaucous green, the inflorescence being yellowish, small and bunched. Many of the species possess poisonous sap, so that care is advisable when handling them. At the front of herbaceous borders or in rock gardens the dwarfer forms are effective, *E. wulfenii* being particularly effective towards the front of the shrubbery. Any well-drained soil in full sun or partial shade is suitable.

Propagate from cuttings or seed.

The flowering season is spring or summer.

## Dropwort: Queen of the Meadow (Plate 20)

Family *ROSACEAE*                         *Filipendula* species

A genus of hardy herbaceous perennials native chiefly to Europe and Asia. *F. vulgaris pleniflora* (syn. *F. hexapetala flore-pleno*, *Spiraea filipendula flore-pleno*) is the double form of *F. vulgaris*, Dropwort. It is an elegant plant with mostly radical, fern-like leaves, long and narrow, from among which rise

*Pl.* 19.
1. Winter Aconite (*Eranthis hyemalis*), p. 59.     2. Foxtail Lily (*Eremurus bungei*), p. 60.
3. Flea-bane (*Erigeron speciosus*), p. 60.     4. Sea Holly (*Eryngium amethystinum*), p. 61.

*Pl.* 20.
  1. Dog's-Tooth Violet (*Erythronium*), p. 61.
  3. Dropwort (*Filipendula rubra*), p. 62.
  2. Spurge (*Euphorbia polychroma*), p. 62.
  4. Fritillary (*Fritillaria imperialis*), p. 63.

slender stems of one to two feet that carry branching sprays of small double creamy-white flowers. *F. ulmaria* (syn. *Spiraea ulmaria*), the Queen of the Meadow or Meadowsweet, native to Britain, Europe and many parts of Asia, has large, elm-like, lobed leaves, three-feet stems, bearing creamy-white, sweetly scented flowers in long feathery plumes. Var. *flore-pleno* has double flowers and is even more attractive, and var. *aurea* has golden variegated foliage, while var. *variegata* has foliage tinted white and green. *F. palmata* (syn. *F. purpurea*) has leaves the shape of the palm of the hand and carries spreading plumes of deep purplish-pink flowers on three-feet stems. It has a white form, var. *alba*. *F. rubra* (syn. *Spiraea lobata*) has large palmate leaves and peach-pink flowers on three-feet stems. Its var. *venusta* has flowers of deeper pink, and var. *magnifica* with the deepest pink flowers is all the more impressive, since it grows four to five feet high. These plants, so suitable for the flower border, are related but distinct from the shrubs of the genus *Spiraea*. They will grow in ordinary soils, though *F. ulmaria* appreciates a well-manured one or the waterside.

Propagate by division in spring.

The flowering season is June to August.

## Fritillary (Plate 20)

Family *LILIACEAE*                                          *Fritillaria* species

A genus of bulbous plants of variable characteristics native to Europe, Asia and North America. The plants have stems furnished sparsely or generously with narrow alternate or whorled leaves. The flowers resemble lilies except that they are bell rather than funnel-shaped. The old Crown Imperial, *F. imperialis*, Orient, has a stem up to three feet high, leafy at the top, beneath which is a dense cluster of large pendulous bell-shaped flowers the size of Tulips, which vary in colour from yellow to shades of orange and red, all more or less evil-smelling, but very handsome and reminiscent of old-world gardens. The seed-pods alter their position and become vertical when ripening. *F. meleagris*, the Snake's Head, reaches only one to one and a half feet and may be found growing in moist meadows in certain localities of England. The drooping flowers are solitary, one and a half inches deep, with a yellowish ground effectively marked with light or dark purple; there are also white, rose and purple forms. There are many other species. A deep, rich and sandy loam will grow these bulbs to perfection.

Propagate by means of offsets taken in late summer when transplanting.

The flowering season is in April and May.

## Lady's Ear Drops (Plate 21)

Family *ONAGRACEAE*                              *Fuchsia* species

A colourful genus, comprising about a hundred species mostly native to tropical America, with a few in New Zealand. Shrubby plants with opposite, oval leaves clothing stems that vary in height and bear flowers with recurving sepals, the petals forming a tube from which the stigma and anthers protrude conspicuously. Of the hardy species that may be grown in favoured localities out-of-doors, *F. macrostemma* (syn. *F. magellanica*) of Chile has several varieties, notably *conica*, with carmine sepals and purple tube; *corallina*, crimson and plum; *globosa*, purplish-red; *gracilis*, scarlet and purple; *pumila*, scarlet; *thomsoni*, red and purple; and *riccartoni*, crimson and purple. The flowers vary considerably in size, those of the hardy forms being smaller than the tender kinds. They may be grown in the open border or, better still, against a south wall in good well-drained loam. Fuchsias are often cut to ground-level by hard frost, but invariably produce fresh growth and bloom freely in the same year.

Propagation is by means of cuttings of half-ripened wood in late summer.

The flowering season is from June to October.

## Blanket-flower (Plate 21)

Family *COMPOSITAE*                          *Gaillardia aristata*

A native of North America and renowned for the brilliant colouring of its flowers. *G. aristata* has narrow, deeply laciniated foliage, with stems up to one and a half feet and flowers four inches across, comprising ray florets of orange-yellow and a zone of bronze-red surrounding a cone of blackish-brown. *G. a. grandiflora* is the most noteworthy and is believed to be a hybrid between *G. aristata* and *G. picta*. From this cross has arisen the many beautifully coloured garden forms of today that vary from pure yellow selfs to shades of tangerine and self-crimson and many of mixed colours. Towards the front of the border in well-drained but rich soil Gaillardias will provide a mass of brilliant colour over a long period that it will be difficult to surpass; under exceptional cultivation the flower stems have been known to

*Pl.* 21.

64

1. Lady's Ear Drops (*Fuchsia macrostemma*), p. 64.    2. Blanket-flower (*Gaillardia aristata*), p. 64.
3. Snowdrop (*Galanthus nivalis*), p. 65.    4. Goat's Rue (*Galega officinalis*), p. 65.

*Pl.* 22.                                                                                                      65
1. Giant Summer Hyacinth (*Galtonia candicans*), p. 66.   2. Cranesbill (*Geranium ibericum*), p. 66.
3. Barberton Daisy (*Gerbera jamesonii*), p. 67.   4. Avens (*Geum* var. Lady Stratheden), p. 68.

reach three feet. The Gaillardia is particularly useful as a cut flower.

Propagation is by means of division, root cuttings or from seed which will show some variation.

The flowering season is from June to October.

## Snowdrop (Plate 21)

Family *AMARYLLIDACEAE* *Galanthus* species

A lovely bulbous native of Europe and Asia Minor. The leaves are narrow and strap-shaped, and the stems, free from foliage, carry drooping flowers composed of three outer white spoon-shaped segments and three smaller inner ones that form a short corona, white and edged with green. Our native *G. nivalis* is familiar to all and is one of the most cherished of our native plants, the flowers being borne singly from January to March on stems up to nine inches; there are many forms, including *lutescens*, with a yellow edging to the corona instead of green and also a double-flowered form; the length of the outer segments is usually a little less than an inch. *G. elwesii* and *G. byzantinus* have larger flowers and reach a height of one foot. The bulbs should be planted in late summer or early autumn in well-drained soil and should be given a ground planting of one of the prostrate growing Thymes to prevent the purity of the flowers from becoming marred by mud splashes. At the front of borders, by the side of garden paths and in sparse woodlands, Snowdrops will brighten the landscape at a season when there is little else in bloom.

Propagate by offsets when lifting the bulbs.

The flowering season is from January to March.

## Goat's Rue (Plate 21)

Family *LEGUMINOSAE* *Galega officinalis*

A member of the Pea family and native to Europe and western Asia, being of herbaceous character. The foliage is pinnate and freely clothes the stems which reach a height of three to four feet, the type having small purplish pea-shaped flowers in short racemes. A hybrid group *G. × cultorum* comprises several good plants, e.g. "George Hartland", much superior to *G. officinalis*, having large racemes of lilac flowers, the young foliage showing some variation, and a white form, "Niobe". There is also a rose-coloured one known as var. *carnea*, which has also a double-flowered (*pleneflora*) form. *G. o. compacta* is a dwarf form of

5

compact habit with lilac coloured flowers. There are a number of improved forms of garden origin. In cultivation this is among the easiest of plants, growing well in any well-drained soil in full sun or partial shade where the flowers will appear freely over a long period. Support in the form of peasticks is necessary for the taller forms.

Propagation is by means of division in late summer or spring, or from seed.

The flowering season is from June to September.


## Giant Summer Hyacinth (Plate 22)

Family *LILIACEAE*                              *Galtonia candicans*

A bulbous plant of imposing appearance which, although from South Africa, is hardy in most parts of Britain. The foliage is long, narrow, strap-like and drooping, about two and a half feet in length. The flower stems are devoid of foliage, attaining a height of four or more feet and bearing at the top a raceme of twenty or more pure white, bell-shaped, drooping flowers, one and a half inches long, of perceptible fragrance. There is another species, *G. clavata*, with smaller greenish flowers, of doubtful hardiness and less attractive than the larger species. Galtonias are easily cultivated in light and well-drained soils where they will benefit from the incorporation of well-decayed manure beneath the positions where the bulbs are planted in the early spring. In heavy soils and where the winter is severe, it is wise to lift the bulbs and store under frost-proof conditions, planting out in March. An annual mulch of farm-yard manure will benefit plants that have been established in light soils for several years. Full sun is essential.

Propagate by detaching offsets when lifting and replant in spring.

The flowering season is in summer.


## Cranesbill (Plate 22)

Family *GERANIACEAE*                              *Geranium* species

A native of the meadows and woodlands of Europe and Britain, containing some that are eminently worthy of garden cultivation. The foliage is freely produced, deeply lobed and laciniated in the case of most of the species. *G. ibericum*, from the Caucasus, reaches one and a half to two feet, with erect stems bearing flowers, one inch across, of violet-blue in panicles. *G. armenum*, from the Orient, reaches two feet, with flowers one and a half inches across, deep wine-crimson in colour. *G. grandiflorum*, from the Himalayas, one to one and a half feet high, has single flowers, one and a half inches across, of a rich blue-veined purple in the best forms. *G. endressii*, from the Pyrenees, one foot high, has stems covered with brown hairs and flowers of light rose-veined deep rose. *G. pratense*, a native of Britain, reaches two and a half feet with flowers one inch across of medium blue; its form *G. p. flore-pleno* is the more desirable and is, in fact, one of the finest of all hardy Geraniums, having flowers of perfect rosette form of purple-violet colour, borne in clusters at the ends of the stems. Any well-drained garden soil will suit these easily grown plants, and full sun is preferred.

Propagate by means of division of the roots in March, root cuttings or from seed.

The flowering season is in summer over a long period.

## Barberton Daisy: Transvaal Daisy (Plate 22)

Family *COMPOSITAE*                                    *Gerbera jamesonii*

A native of South Africa and one of the most charming of the smaller perennials. The leaves are six to eight inches long and deeply lobed and are produced freely to form a rosette at the base of the plant. The flowers are somewhat reminiscent of the single Pyrethrum in form, but are more refined with narrower ray petals and the effect is of rather a cup-shaped formation. The colours are brilliant, varying from pale amber to deep orange and terra cotta tones; the stems are leafless and rise to a height of one and a half feet or taller. Gerberas are only hardy in the most favoured localities and should be grown in full sun with a southern exposure in a well-drained soil that has been well enriched with peat or leafmould. In protected positions out-of-doors they may be encouraged to survive the winter by covering with bracken during the coldest months. As cut flowers they are superbly beautiful and will last, after being cut, for a remarkably long period, far longer, in fact, than one would suppose from the fragile appearance of the flowers.

Propagation is by means of seed or by cuttings of side-growths in spring.

The flowering season is in summer.

## Avens (Plate 22)

Family *ROSACEAE*                                               *Geum* species

A genus comprising both alpine and taller forms common to temperate regions. The leaves are oblong and lobed and form a rosette from which rise slender stems, bearing single or double flowers. The most important species is *G. quellyon* (syn. *G. chiloense*), a native of Chile, known also as *G. coccineum* in error. Of its variations *grandiflorum*, with double flowers, one and a half inches across, several to a stem and reaching a height of one and a half feet, is probably responsible for the popular varieties "Mrs. Bradshaw," red, and "Lady Stratheden", yellow. *G. montanum* has flowers of rather less size, and the effective orange-flowered *G. heldreichii splendens*, reaching a height not exceeding one foot, is believed to owe its origin to this species. *G. borisii* has rich orange-scarlet flowers and continues in flower for a long period. Geums are among the easier of border perennials to cultivate and, provided they are given a position in full sun and a soil that is rich and well drained, no difficulties are to be expected in their cultivation.

Propagation is by means of seeds or division.

The flowering season is from early summer onwards intermittently.

## Bowman's Root: Indian Physic (Plate 23)

Family *ROSACEAE*                                        *Gillenia trifoliata*

A graceful perennial native to North America and one of two known species of the genus. The habit is erect, of one to two feet when the plant is established, with lobed foliage not unlike that of some Spiraeas, the stems branching into a loose panicle at the top, bearing many small white flowers. In company with other fine foliaged plants towards the front of the border or at the side of streams and small ponds this plant is most effective, lending an airy grace that is always very welcome. In the wild garden and towards the front of the shrub border the Gillenia will be well able to fend for itself, provided a little care and attention is given in the early stages of establishment. Its cultural requirements are a position in sun or in partial shade, and a moist loamy soil into which peat can be incorporated with beneficial results. The species *G. stipulata*, one to two feet, has white flowers, but is not in general cultivation.

Propagation is effected by means of seed or division.

The flowering period is in summer.

*Pl.* 23.                                                                                                68

1. Bowman's Root (*Gillenia trifoliata*), p. 68.   2. Corn Flag (*Gladiolus* hybrid), p. 69.
3. Chalk Plant (*Gypsophila paniculata*), p. 69.   4. Helen-flower (*Helenium autumnale*), p. 70.

*Pl. 24.*     69

1. Sunflower (*Helianthus decapetalus*), p. 70.    2. North American Ox-eye (*Heliopsis scabra* var. *incomparabilis*), p. 71.

3. Hellebore (*Helleborus orientalis*), p. 71.    4. Day Lily (*Hemerocallis aurantiaca*), p. 72.

## Corn Flag: Sword Lily (Plate 23)

Family *IRIDACEAE*                                    *Gladiolus* species

A genus comprising many cormous-rooted plants native to South Africa and two in Europe. The leaves are erect and sword-like and the funnel-shaped flowers are of variable size, being borne several at a time on spikes that vary considerably in height. *G. byzantinus*, from Asia Minor, reaches two feet, bearing purplish-red flowers, two or more inches across. *G. communis*, from southern Europe, reaches two feet, with flowers that vary from white to rose and purple. *G. primulinus*, from south-east Africa, is a graceful plant up to three and a half feet, with small, hooded primrose yellow flowers, known as Maid of the Mist. *G. gandavensis*, a hybrid between the scarlet, yellow-spotted *G. psittacinus* and *G. cardinalis*, also scarlet with a white blotch on lower segments, and *G. childsii*, another hybrid noted for its blotched flowers; both reach heights up to four feet and have given rise to the present race of richly coloured and large flowered garden varieties. *G. colvillei*, an early flowering hybrid, has medium-sized flowers varying from white to shades of pink or scarlet; it is valued as a market flower for forcing. Plant *G. colvillei* in autumn and protect with bracken, also *G. byzantinus* and *G. communis*. *G. primulinus*, *G. gandavensis* and *G. childsii* are planted in March in well-drained rich soil in full sun and are lifted and stored away from frost in winter.

Propagate by cormlets and seed.

The flowering season is from June to August.

## Chalk Plant (Plate 23)

Family *CARYOPHYLLACEAE*                          *Gypsophila* species

A genus which includes hardy perennials native to Europe and Asia, showy and effective for garden display. The most important species is *G. paniculata*, sometimes known popularly as Baby's Breath, with short, narrow, strap-like leaves about three or four inches long at the base of the plant and shortening as they clothe the lower part of the very branching slender stems. The flowers are single, white and small, but produced in effective masses to a height of three feet or more. The double form *G. p. flore-pleno* and the still larger flowered "Bristol Fairy" are usually preferred and are first-class cut flowers. A double form with pink and white flowers has been named Flamingo. *G. repens* is of prostrate habit with larger white flowers, and it has a double pink form in Rosy

Veil. Gypsophila grows well in most garden soils, provided there is ample drainage. The presence of lime is desirable.

Propagation is effected, in the case of single varieties, by seed, and by grafting on stocks of the type or by cuttings in the case of the double forms.

The flowering season is during summer, over a long period.

# Helen Flower: Sneezeweed: Sneezewort (Plate 23)

Family *COMPOSITAE*                                    *Helenium* species

A genus of about thirty species native to North America and Mexico which includes annuals and perennials. Of erect growth, the leaves are lance-shaped and the flowers, several on a stem, are composed of wedge-shaped ray florets radiating from a central disc. *H. autumnale* is a tall species with varieties ranging from two to six feet and varying in colour from yellow to shades of chestnut-red. *H. a.* var. *pumilum magnificum* reaches a height of two feet with freely produced flowers of rich yellow, two inches or more across. A variation, probably originating from this species, is Moerheim Beauty, mahogany-crimson. *H. bigelovii*, from California, reaches three feet with a central brown disc with yellow rays of typical form, two to three inches across. Heleniums are indispensable border plants and grow well in full sun or partial shade in any good garden soil that has been well cultivated.

Propagate by division of the roots in early autumn or spring or from seeds.

The flowering season is from July to October.

# Sunflower (Plate 24)

Family *COMPOSITAE*                                    *Helianthus* species

The genus consists of about sixty species, mostly native to North America, and includes annual and perennial species. *H. decapetalus*, of variable height, has large oval-pointed foliage from three to nine inches long and stems reaching from four to six feet, branching towards the top and bearing flowers, three inches across, with light yellow ray petals. There are various double forms of garden origin, all more or less attractive. *H. rigidus* (syn. *H. scaberrimus*) is one of the best perennial forms, reaching a height of three to six or more feet, the finest forms of garden origin having huge golden yellow flowers, as much as nine inches across, centred with blackish discs. *H. orgyalis* is a very distinct species, reaching a height of seven to eight feet, with stems, heavily furnished with narrow leaves, eight to fourteen inches long, becoming very branched at the top and bearing many medium-sized yellow flowers. *H. multiflorus*, yellow, five feet tall, has nobler varieties in a double var. *flore-pleno*, and "Lodden Gold", and a huge single-flowered var. *maximus*, five to six feet. Easily grown in any well-drained garden soil of moderate fertility, the Helianthus is one of the most spectacular perennials of late summer.

Propagation is effected by division of the roots in late winter. The flowering season is from July to September.

## North American Ox-eye (Plate 24)

Family *COMPOSITAE*                          *Heliopsis* species

The genus consists of ten species, all native to North America, but two only appear to have entered our gardens. The plants, both in habit of growth and form of flower, have much in common with the Helianthus. *H. scabra* has produced many variations of garden origin, notably *incomparabilis*, with large semi-double orange-rayed flowers centred with yellow discs, the whole flower being six or more inches across, borne on stems of three to four feet; *patula*, golden yellow flowers on four-feet stems, and *zinniaeflora*, with full double flowers. There are a number of double forms of attractive appearance and useful for border planting. *H. laevis*, five feet tall, is a single-flowered yellow species. These plants will grow well in soil that has been well cultivated, enriched with manure and well drained. Valuable plants for herbaceous borders blooming, as they do, over a very long period. They associate well with late-flowering Delphiniums of the darker hues, and the shorter forms are ideal foils to the dark purple Phloxes.

Propagation is by means of division in late winter.

The flowering season is from July to September.

## Hellebore (Plate 24)

Family *RANUNCULACEAE*                      *Helleborus* species

A unique and fascinating race of plants native to parts of Europe and western Asia. The foliage is deeply divided and of varying widths, according to the species. The familiar Christmas Rose (*H. niger* var.) has large flowers of white, sometimes flushed with purple, on nine-inch stalks, and three or four inches across. It has a smaller form in *H.* var. *angustifolius* and var. *praecox* flowers much earlier in September. *H. viridis* has apple-green flowers on nine-inch stems and the Lenten Rose (*H. orientalis*), blooming in late winter, has flowers similar in size to those of *H. niger*, but varying considerably in colour from purple and plum shades to purplish-pink, blush and pure or spotted white. *H. foetidus,* called the Stinking Hellebore from the unpleasant odour of its green and purple flowers with sepals of less than an inch in length, is a native. These fascinating plants will thrive in any good garden soil in partial shade where sheltering evergreens may protect their blossoms from damage in wintry weather; the presence of leafmould in the soil is beneficial.

Propagate by division of the roots in early autumn or in spring. The flowering season is in autumn and winter.

## Day Lily (Plate 24)

Family *LILIACEAE*                                    *Hemerocallis* species

A race of colourful perennials that find their homes in Europe and Asia. The rush-like foliage is long and varies in width according to the species; the flowers are borne on branching stems, are like trumpet-shaped lilies in form and have the habit of lasting only for a day, being followed immediately by other  *H. flava* has two-feet leaves with flower-stems up to three feet, bearing many pale ochre flowers. *H. aurantiaca* reaches three feet, with six to eight bright orange flowers to each stem. *H. fulva* is about the same height, with yellow-orange flowers; there is also a double form. The Chinese *H. citrina*, four feet, has lemon-yellow flowers. The flowers vary from two inches to as much as six inches across in some of the garden hybrids, which also possess a wide colour range. By the side of streams or ponds where the roots may find the water without the plant becoming submerged, the Day Lily will grow satisfactorily as well as in the herbaceous border. A rich soil is necessary to grow them well as is also a position in full sun. Transplant in the spring just as growth begins, and allow to remain undisturbed for several years.

Propagation is by means of division in spring and from seed. The flowering season extends from June to September.

## Sweet Rocket (Plate 25)

Family *CRUCIFERAE*                                    *Hesperis matronalis*

An old-fashioned favourite and one of a genus whose species spread from the Mediterranean region to Central Asia. The leaves are oval and pointed and about three inches long. The stems branch from the base, attaining a height of two to three feet and bearing terminal spikes of pyramid shape consisting of many small four-petalled flowers rather like single Stocks. The colours vary from white to lilac and purple. The most desirable form is *H. matronalis alba plena*, the double white Sweet Rocket renowned for its fragrance. This plant has become somewhat scarce of recent years. In sun or partial shade, so long as the soil is not deficient of humus, this plant will grow well and will not fail to be a feature of charm in the gardens of cottage and mansion alike.

Propagate single-flowered forms from seed and the double-flowered ones by means of young growths, each with a piece of root, taken from established plants in the spring.

The flowering season is from June to August.

## Alum Root (Plate 25)

Family *SAXIFRAGACEAE*                    *Heuchera* species

Of this genus there are about fifty species, all natives of North America and finding their homes from Mexico to the Arctic regions. The leaves are heart-shaped, lobed and form a rosette at the base of the plant from which spring the slender flower-stems to a foot or more, bearing elegant panicles of flowers about one-eighth of an inch across. *H. sanguinea*, one to one and a half feet, is the best known with red flowers, and has various garden forms that vary from blood-red to orange-scarlet. The bigeneric hybrid *Heucherella tiarelloides* is from a cross between *H. brizoides* and *Tiarella cordifolia*, having pale pink flowers. *H. americana* is the true Alum Root with dull purplish flowers. Towards the front of the border and for cutting the Heucheras are among the most useful of plants. Any well-drained garden soil, rich in humus and in full sun, will grow them to perfection and the fleshy roots may be planted in early autumn or in March.

Propagation is by means of division of the roots when growth begins or from seed.

The flowering season is in early summer.

## Hawk-weed (Plate 25)

Family *COMPOSITAE*                    *Hieracium* species

A race of perennial herbs that are mostly native to Europe and North America. The leaves are toothed and lobed but not deeply, with flower-stems one to one and a half feet, bearing corymbs about an inch across, comprising eight to ten flower-heads. *H. aurantiacum* and *H. brunneocroceum* are the most valuable for garden purposes, having effective deep orange-red flowers. *H. pilosella*, six to twelve inches, has pale yellow flowers that are sometimes striped with purple or red on the exterior. *H. villosum*, twelve inches, has large effective golden yellow flowers fully two inches across and is the most desirable of the yellow-flowered members of the genus. Easily grown and difficult to disestablish, these plants should be used sparingly in the border, but may be employed freely where a disused brick wall requires furnishing. The fact that the plants are so frequently liable to attack by aphides has caused them to lack popularity as garden plants.

Propagate by means of seed or division in late winter.

The flowering season is from June to October.

## Plantain Lily (Plate 25)

Family *LILIACEAE*                              *Hosta* species

Natives of China and Japan, the Hostas are among those plants more renowned for their foliage than for their flowers. Until recently known as Funkia. The foliage is bold and deeply veined, varying in hue from green to glaucous and variegated tones; there is also considerable variation in size. The flowers are borne on stems from amid the foliage and are from one and a half to two inches long, being funnel-shaped, and six to twenty per stem, according to species. *H. plantaginea* reaches one and a half feet, has pure white fragrant flowers; *H. fortunei* has pale mauve or pure white flowers; *H. lancifolia* is a small species with lance-shaped leaves, narrowing at each end. *H. ventricosa* (syn. *Funkia ovata*) reaches one and a half feet and is of vigorous growth; it has also a variegated form. *H. glauca* is the most attractive of all, reaching a height of three feet with large glaucous foliage, heart-shaped and over a foot across, the flowers being creamy-lilac; *H. crispula* is notable for its handsome white-margined leaves. These plants are very confused as to nomenclature. A deep rich soil is necessary for their cultivation and they should be allowed to remain undisturbed to form large and imposing clumps.

Propagate by division in March or from seed.

The flowering season is in summer.

# Hyacinth (Plate 26)

Family *LILIACEAE*                              *Hyacinthus orientalis*

A genus of well-known bulbous-rooted plants found wild in the Mediterranean region and Asia Minor. In *H. orientalis* and its varieties the leaves are strap-shaped and the flowers are bell-shaped, an inch or more across, and borne in a dense raceme on thick stems up to a foot or more in height. The colour of the flowers can vary from white to yellow, orange, red, blue, pink and purple and are strongly scented. Hyacinths are produced very extensively in Holland where the plantations comprise pure sand into which has been introduced a liberal quantity of cow manure. Being quite hardy, Hyacinths may be grown easily in well-drained soil and are effective when planted to flower above a carpet of prostrate Thymes or Aubrietia of appropriate colouring. The time for planting is in late summer or early autumn. They are particularly well adapted for cultivation in bowls or pots and by appropriate treatment may be forced into bloom for Christmas if given the requisite temperature under the moist and humid conditions of a greenhouse.

Propagation is by means of offsets that may be induced by slitting mature bulbs across the base upwards when ripened, or from seeds.

The flowering season is in April.

# Candytuft (Plate 26)

Family *CRUCIFERAE*                                  *Iberis* species

A genus of annual and somewhat shrubby perennial species that may be found in western Asia, southern Europe and northern Africa, all hardy in Britain. The perennials are shrubby, dwarf and compact, evergreen with stems freely furnished with short, narrow strap-shaped leaves. The flowers are of irregular cruciferous form and borne in flat, round clusters an inch or more across. *I. sempervirens*, the common perennial Candytuft, has snow-white flowers on nine- to twelve-inch stems. *I. gibraltarica* is rather larger than other species with flowers of delicate lilac; it is doubtfully hardy. For the front of the border, especially where there is a rock or stone edging, these plants are pretty and effective, being easily cultivated in sun or partial shade. On the rock garden, too, they are effective if planted in bold colonies, and there are many others of minute size and very dwarf habit that are eminently suitable for such specialized cultivation.

Propagation is by means of cuttings of half-ripened growth, seeds or root division.

The flowering season is from April to July.

## Incarvillea (Plate 26)

Family *BIGNONIACEAE*                    *Incarvillea* species

A genus of showy perennials found in various parts of China and Central Asia. The foliage is elegant and fern-like, comprising many segments borne on stems sometimes a foot long. The flowers are trumpet-shaped, open at the mouth and two to three inches long, and of a similar width. *I. delavayi*, from China, carries up to twelve flowers of rosy-purple on two-feet stems *I. grandiflora*, from China, has its flowers either solitary or in pairs and of a deep rose shade. *I. lutea* has up to twenty yellow flowers, two inches across, of a pendulous habit. *I. olgae*, from Turkistan, has flowers of only one and a half inches in length and a pretty pale pink shade. In order to enjoy the fine foliage and general elegance of a well-grown plant of Incarvillea it is necessary to provide a light, sandy soil that has been enriched with decayed manure, and plant young stock from pots. The position should be warm and fully exposed to the sun, but protected from cold winds. In localities where the winter is severe, it is wise to afford some protection in the form of a bracken covering during winter.

Propagate by division of the root in late winter or from seed. The flowering season is in May and June.

## Flea-bane (Plate 26)

Family *COMPOSITAE*                    *Inula* species

A genus of showy herbaceous perennials that are native to Europe, Asia and Africa, and quite hardy in Britain. The foliage is broad, handsome and somewhat hairy, well clothing the stems. The flowers are of daisy-like form with narrow, silken ray florets, radiating from a central yellow disc. *I. glandulosa*, from the Caucasus, reaches a height of three feet with flowers fully four inches across and of a rich orange-yellow; its form var. *laciniata* has golden yellow flowers with fringed rays. *I. grandiflora*, from

1. Sweet Rocket (*Hesperis matronalis*), p. 72.    2. Alum Root (*Heuchera sanguinea*), p. 73.
3. Hawk-weed (*Hieracium aurantiacum*), p. 73.    4. Plantain Lily (*Hosta glauca*), p. 74.

Pl. 26.

1. Hyacinth (*Hyacinthus orientalis*), p. 75.
3. Incarvillea (*Incarvillea grandiflora*), p. 76.

2. Candytuft (*Iberis gibraltarica*), p. 75.
4. Flea-bane (*Inula glandulosa*), p. 76.

the Himalayas, reaches two feet with orange-yellow flowers fully five inches across and is the earliest species to flower. *I. hookeri*, Himalayas, reaches only two feet with pale yellow flowers only two inches across. An effective species from the Himalayas is *I. royleana*, with large flowers of orange-yellow and several to each stem; the black unopened buds are effective. A rich soil, a position in full sun and ample moisture during growth are essential.

Propagate by means of division of the roots in late winter, or from seeds.

The flowering season is in early summer.

## Flag (Plate 27)

Family *IRIDACEAE*                                        *Iris* species

A genus of great beauty and infinite variety, including bulbous and rhizomatous rooted species found throughout the temperate regions. The Bearded Irises, so called from the beard that appears at the top of the lower or fall petals, comprise many hundreds of brilliantly coloured garden varieties, the result of crosses between species such as *I. pumila*, *I. spuria*, *I. plicata* and others. The foliage is sword-like and the flowers, borne on two- to four-feet stems, have three upper or standard petals and three lower or fall petals, often of widely contrasting colours. *I. kaempferi*, the Japanese Water Iris, has broad, flat-headed flowers of varied shades, and *I. sibirica*, also a water lover, is rather like a miniature Flag, borne on long slender stems to four or more feet. *I. unguicularis* (syn. *I. stylosa*) is from Algeria, and has rich deep-purple-blue flowers from November to March; it needs poor, gritty soil, sun-scorched in summer. The Gladwyn (*I. foetidissima*) is noted for its brilliant orange seeds in autumn. The foregoing are all lime lovers. Of the bulbous Iris there are the Dutch, Spanish and English types with narrow rush-like foliage and two-feet stems, bearing flowers with long pedicels and two-inch segments blotched yellow; the colour of the flowers varies considerably from white to yellow and blue. *I. reticulata* suggests a miniature purple Iris of this form and blooms in February.

Propagate by division of the rhizomes in the case of Bearded Irises and by means of offsets in the case of bulbous species.

The flowering season is mainly in June, but there are a number of bulbous species that bloom in winter and early spring.

## Isatis (Plate 27)

Family *CRUCIFERAE*                                    *Isatis glauca*

A pretty and effective perennial from Asia Minor and particularly Persia. The plant is of erect and branching habit, its leaves being smooth and the flowers small and yellow, borne in a lax raceme, somewhat suggesting a yellow Gypsophila. The height when fully established may be as tall as four feet. Uncommon in gardens. In this genus is included *I. tinctoria*, at one time cultivated for the production of the blue dye known as woad used by the ancient Britons for staining their bodies. Up to the introduction of indigo in the seventeenth century, woad was the main medium for colouring cloth. Easily cultivated in well-drained garden soil and full sun where the seed is scattered freely.

Propagation is mainly by seed, which may be sown as soon as ripe.

The flowering season is in summer.

## African Corn Lily (Plate 27)

Family *IRIDACEAE*                                    *Ixia* species

An attractive and colourful race of South African bulbous plants rather like miniature Gladioli in form. The foliage is stiffly erect, sword-shaped and veined. The flowers are funnel-shaped, one inch across, opening flat in sun but closing in shade and borne on slender stems up to a foot or more. *I. maculata* has orange-yellow flowers with a dark blotch in the throat; *I. flexuosa* varies from pink to lilac; *I. speciosa* has purple and crimson flowers; *I. viridiflora* is curiously delicate and attractive, with its soft sea-green flowers centred with a shining black blotch. Ixias should be planted in a well-drained border of light, rich soil against a south wall in autumn and given protection in the form of a bracken covering. Apart from their use in sheltered borders and rock gardens, Ixias are excellent pot plants for indoor decorations, although for the flowers to open well they must be placed before a sunny window.

Propagation is by means of offsets detached at the time of planting, and these will bloom in the second year.

The flowering season is during spring.

# Ixia Lily (Plate 27)

Family *AMARYLLIDACEAE*                    *Ixiolirion* species

A genus of half-hardy attractive bulbous plants, not commonly seen in gardens, and natives of Asia, particularly Turkestan. The linear leaves are long and somewhat untidy in habit, and the flowers are borne on slender stems in umbels, and are funnel-shaped in form, having six perianth segments. Only two species are known. *I. kolpakowskianum* has tufts of grass-like leaves with white flowers suffused blue. *I. montanum* has bright lilac flowers in graceful umbels; its variety *pallasi* (syn. *tartaricum*), with lovely violet-blue flowers, being one of the best known and one of the most attractive, making an excellent cut flower. A warm and sunny aspect is necessary for cultivation in the open and a soil that is light, loamy and well drained containing a proportion of humus in the form of leafmould. Protect from autumn and winter rains in order to prevent premature growth.

Propagation is effected by means of offsets in spring or seed sown as soon as ripe.

The flowering season is in April for *I. kolpakowskianum* and in June for *I. montanum* and its forms.

# Torch Lily: Red-hot Poker (Plate 28)

Family *LILIACEAE*                         *Kniphofia* species

At one time known botanically as *Tritoma*, this genus of brilliantly coloured spiky flowers hails mostly from high altitudes in South Africa. The foliage is long and reed-like, varying from the thickness of coarse grass to an inch or more across. The flowers are borne on thick leafless stems, funnel-shaped and in dense racemes of varied size. *K. aloides*, the most familiar, was known once as *Tritoma uvaria*; the stems will attain a height of four feet, bearing racemes six inches long of bright scarlet flowers changing to yellow in the lower portions. It is a parent of many of our garden hybrids. *K. rufa* is a smaller species, reaching one and a half feet, with primrose yellow spikes tinged red at the apex. *K. galpini* is of two to three feet, with apricot-coloured flowers. *K. nelsoni*, two feet high, has bright scarlet flower spikes, sometimes suffused orange. *K. erecta* has scarlet flowers and is unique in that its flower-tubes turn upwards instead of in the orthodox downward manner. *K. corallina*, two feet, has coral-red flowers. *K. praecox*, three to seven feet, with red and yellow flowers, blooms early and is followed by *K. tuckii*, four and a half feet, scarlet and yellow, of which there are some fine varieties, notably "Gold Else", two and a half feet, yellow; "Royal Standard", three feet, yellow and scarlet, and "Russell's Gold", three feet, yellow. A rich soil in full sun is essential and planting is best carried out in April or May.

Propagate by division in the spring or from seed.

The flowering season is mainly in summer and early autumn.

## Everlasting Pea (Plate 28)

Family *LEGUMINOSAE*                              *Lathyrus* species

The herbaceous perennial species of this genus are over-shadowed by the more colourful annual Sweet Pea, but are not without merit. They are very hardy, grow freely, flower long, and of easy culture. The plants are tendril-bearing and vine-like, with sharply angled stems, pinnate leaves and showy racemes of keeled, pea-like flowers borne on stems rising from the axils. They are seen at their best climbing naturally over trellises, arbours, shrubs or tree-stumps or draping banks, low walls or bold rocks.

*L. latifolius*, the Everlasting Pea, is a native of Europe, eight to ten feet high, with reddish flowers, but has vastly improved varieties such as the white "White Pearl" and the pale pink "Blush Rose" with twelve to fifteen flowers to a stem. *L. grandiflorus* is the Two-flowered Everlasting Pea of southern Europe, so called from its habit of bearing large, rosy-purple flowers in pairs in June to July. Lord Anson's Pea (*L. magellanicus*) from the Straits of Magellan is a beautiful blue-flowered type, six to eight feet tall, blooming from June to September. *L. pubescens*, from Chile, has flowers of paler blue, and is three to five feet in height. *L. undulatus* (syn. *sibthorpii*), from the Dardanelles, carries rosy-purple flowers on two- to three-feet stems in May and June. *L. rotundifolius*, five feet, also bears June flowers of rosy-pink. Any ordinary, reasonably well-drained soil suits these plants.

Propagation is from seeds sown under glass in March, or out-doors in May; or by division of the fleshy roots in March to April.

## Mallow (Plate 28)

Family *MALVACEAE*                               *Lavatera olbia*

A shrubby perennial and native to southern Europe. The leaves are lobed and may be said to resemble the foliage of some

*Pl.* 27.

1. Flag (*Iris*), p. 77.
2. Isatis (*Isatis glauca*), p. 78.
3. African Corn Lily (*Ixia maculata*), p. 78.
4. Ixia Lily (*Ixiolirion montanum*), p. 79.

1. Torch Lily (*Kniphofia aloides*), p. 79.    2. Everlasting Pea (*Lathyrus latifolius*), p. 80.
3. Mallow (*Lavatera olbia*), p. 80.    4. Kansas Feather (*Liatris spicata*), p. 81.

maples. The stems are leafy, often reach five or six feet, and bear
a number of reddish-purple flowers, four inches across. Its form
var. *rosea* has flowers of a bright pink. Of easy culture in both
heavy and light soils, the plants are sometimes cut to ground-level
by severe frost, but break into growth in the spring and bloom
on the current season's growth. Planted with a foreground of
*Salvia virgata nemerosa*, it is particularly effective and beautiful.
It may also be introduced to the shrubbery with good effect,
flowering, as it does, when there is little in bloom among the
hardwoods.

Propagation may be effected by means of cuttings, or seeds
sown as soon as ripe.

The flowering season is in July and August.

## Kansas Feather: Button Snake Root (Plate 28)

Family *COMPOSITAE*                          *Liatris* species

A genus of showy perennials from North America, six species
of which are commonly cultivated in gardens. The plants are of
erect growth and tuberous rooted; the leaves are alternate and
narrow. The flower-heads have up to twelve flowers, half an inch
long, forming a dense spike, with the unusual habit of opening
from the apex downwards. *L. spicata* reaches four to five feet,
with leafy stems and flower-spikes of purple. *L. pycnostachya* is
the most effective species reaching up to five feet with spikes,
sometimes a foot long, of bright rosy-purple flowers. *L. scariosa*,
two to three feet, and *L. ligulistylis*, one to one and a half feet,
are smaller purple-flowering species. *L. elegans*, three to four
feet, is a white form. *L. graminifolia*, two to three feet, has rosy-
mauve flowers, and a taller var. *dubia* of the same colouring.
Easily grown in any good garden soil and also suitable for
planting on the banks of streams; should always be planted for
massed effect to enjoy their full beauty. They are also useful and
very decorative cut flowers.

Propagation is effected by means of division or from seed which
will probably show some variation among the seedlings.

The flowering season is in summer and autumn.

## Libertia (Plate 29)

Family *IRIDACEAE*                          *Libertia* various species

A little grown but attractive genus of the Iris family, and
native to Australia, New Zealand, Tasmania and Chile. The root is

6

a creeping rhizome, the foliage is reed-like and freely produced, and the flowers of lily-like beauty. *L. formosa*, from Chile, has pure white flowers of orchid-like beauty, half an inch long on two- to three-feet stems. The flowers are closely placed on the stem and may be said to resemble the double-white Rocket. *L. ixioides*, from New Zealand, has smaller flowers of white, tinged greenish-brown on the exterior on two-feet stems. *L. pulchella* attains one foot with small white flowers, and *L. grandiflora*, from New Zealand, reaches three feet with white flowers of a size nearly equalling *L. formosa*. Requiring a sunny position, the Libertias well deserve a specially prepared rich peaty soil, where they will form established clumps of considerable beauty. In severe climates winter protection is advisable.

Propagate by division of the rhizome in March or April or from seed.

The flowering season is in May and June.

## Golden-rayed Lily (Plate 29)

Family *LILIACEAE*                    *Lilium auratum*

The most beautiful of all Lilies and a native of Japan. Reaching up to six feet high the leafy stems carry up to fifteen flowers, eight to ten inches across, of a large and full star shape. The colour is white, with a mid-rib of pale yellow the whole length of each segment, spotted crimson. Its form var. *platyphyllum* is of more vigorous growth of the same colour, but not so heavily spotted; var. *rubrovittatum* is distinguished by a crimson band running the whole length of each segment, and the flowers are spotted crimson. There are many other forms, and the most desirable strain today is known as the Esperanza strain from British Columbia, particularly valuable for its freedom from disease (an unfortunate trait of bulbs imported from Japan) and vigorous growth. In a rich, peaty soil, well drained and free from unrotted animal manure, this Lily is seen to best advantage if planted among dwarf peat-loving plants such as Rhododendrons and Azaleas.

Propagate from scales, offsets or seed.

The flowering season is in late summer, but the flowers may be forced earlier under glass.

## Trumpet Lily (Plate 29)

Family *LILIACEAE* *Lilium longiflorum*

A native of China and Japan, with leafy stems up to three feet and narrow tubular pure white flowers, four to six inches long, widening at the mouth and slightly recurving; several are borne at the top of the stem; more in demand as a forcing bulb for the cut-flower market than as a garden plant. *L. brownii*, from China, is best described as a more refined flower of similar type. *L. regale*, the Regal Lily from China, carries up to eight or more tubular flowers, four to six inches long, widely open at the mouth, the interior being white, changing to sulphur in the throat and the exterior suffused purple; there is a pure white form. *L. giganteum* (now called *Cardiocrinum giganteum*), from the Himalayas, has the largest bulbs of all lilies, being six to eight inches long and up to six inches wide; the stems are thick and clothed with bright green, large rounded leaves a foot or more across, and have been known to attain twelve feet. At the apex are six to twelve drooping tubular flowers, five to six inches long, pure white suffused purple at the base. *L. candidum*, the Madonna Lily, reaches up to four feet with a dozen or more pure white flowers, about four inches long and as many wide, fragrant. *L. giganteum* and *L. candidum* require planting so that the top of the bulbs lie level with the earth's surface; the former is a lover of woodland conditions, and the latter prefers the open border. The remainder should be planted at a depth equal to three times the diameter of the bulbs in a well-drained soil rich in humus but free from fresh animal manure and shaded by some low-growing plant at the base.

Propagate by means of scales, offsets or from seed.

The flowering season is in summer.

## Turk's Cap Lily (Plate 29)

Family *LILIACEAE* *Lilium martagon*

Mostly natives of the Old World, Lilies of this group bear flowers of varying size, drooping with recurved petals, hence the popular name. *L. martagon* is the Turk's Cap Lily of Southern Europe, growing three feet high, with flowers one and a half inches across, of dull violet-rose, spotted carmine, at the base and borne in candelabra-like tiers. There are several garden forms. *L. chalcedonicum*, the Scarlet Turk's Cap, is of similar height with flowers, two to three inches diameter, of brilliant vermilion-scarlet, slightly dotted purple, from three to six on a stem. *L. testaceum* (syn. *L. excelsum*) is the result of a cross between *L. chalcedonicum* and *L. candidum*; it reaches up to six feet, with up to twelve flowers, two to three inches across, of a pretty nankeen yellow, flushed pink, and sweetly scented. *L. henryi* is a majestic plant up to eight feet with up to twenty flowers, three to four inches in diameter, forming a loose pyramidal spray, of brilliant orange, slightly spotted brown, with a green band at the base of each segment; a native of Central China. *L. tigrinum*, the Tiger Lily, a native of China and Japan, reaches up to four feet, with flowers, three to five inches across, of deep orange-red, heavily spotted purple. *L. pardalinum*, the Californian Panther Lily, grows four to six feet, with bright orange-red flowers, heavily blotched deep purple, three to four inches across, borne in loose pyramids of twenty to thirty. All have narrow, pointed foliage. Plant to a depth equal to three times the diameter of the bulb in a soil rich in humus and some low ground-covering to protect sun scorching.

Propagate by offsets, scales, stem bulbils in the case of *L. tigrinum* and from seed.

The flowering season is in summer.

## Candlestick Lily (Plate 30)

Family *LILIACEAE*                              *Lilium umbellatum*

A popular and easily grown group of garden hybrids, often known as *L. hollandicum*, with leafy stems up to three feet and up to five flowers like upturned chalices, about five inches in diameter, borne in an umbel. In the type these are of a brilliant orange-red colour, spotted purple, and suffused yellow at the centre. It has many forms such as var. *grectum*, with blood-red flowers, and var. "Golden Fleece", bright yellow. There are also others of garden origin. *L. macadatum* (syn. *L. elegans* and *L. thunbergianum*) reaches up to two feet, with orange-scarlet chalices about five inches across, spotted with purple at the base. There are several charming varieties of garden origin, varying in colour from red to shades of apricot and yellow. Plant to a depth equal to three times the diameter of the bulb, bedded in sand for drainage, among low-growing shrubs in a sunny or shaded position with leafmould mixed with the soil or used as a top mulch.

Propagate by means of scales, offsets or seed.

The flowering season is in June and July.

Pl. 29.

1. Libertia (*Libertia formosa*), p. 81.
3. Trumpet Lily (*Lilium longiflorum*), p. 83.
2. Golden-rayed Lily (*Lilium auratum*), p. 82.
4. Turk's Cap Lily (*Lilium martagon*), p. 83.

*Pl.* 30.
1. Candlestick Lily (*Lilium umbellatum*), p. 84.  2. Sea Lavender (*Limonium latifolium*), p. 85.
3. Toad-flax (*Linaria vulgaris*), p. 85.  4. Flax (*Linum perenne*), p. 86

## Sea Lavender  (Plate 30)

Family *PLUMBAGINACEAE*                    *Limonium* species

A genus of wide distribution, formerly known as *Statice*, that includes several perennial species at home near sea coasts. *L. latifolium*, from Bulgaria, has oblong-elliptical, smooth leaves, tall branching scapes, carrying panicles of small blue flowers, two to three feet tall, and has a larger flowered variety, *grandiflorum*. *L. gmelini*, from the Caucasus, has smooth ovate leaves, and one- to two-feet stems with panicles of deep purplish-blue flowers. *L. incanum*, from Siberia, is a dwarf of six to nine inches, with flowers of pink and calyces of white. *L. bellidifolium* is a European dwarf of six inches with lavender-blue flowers. *L. eximium*, from Central Asia, with rosy-lilac flowers, *L. sinense*, from China, with yellow flowers, *L. tartaricum*, from the Caucasus, and *L. vulgare*, the common Sea Lavender of our own coasts, with purple flowers, all grow about a foot high. Culture is simple, for the plants are easily established in any well-drained, light or sandy loam. They are highly effective massed, giving an appearance suggestive of dwarf Gypsophila of purple, lavender or pink. They like a sunny position.

Propagation may be done by root cuttings in early spring, by division or from seed, the last method giving rise to some variations.

The flowering season is from July to September.


## Toad-flax  (Plate 30)

Family *SCROPHULARIACEAE*                    *Linaria* species

*L. vulgaris* is a vigorous perennial of spreading habit and native to Britain. The stems are slender, branching and freely clothed with fine grass-like foliage, reaching a height of two feet with flowers like small snapdragons in form, borne in a raceme, sulphur-yellow in colour with an orange lip. A more refined species is *L. dalmatica*, from Dalmatia, three to five feet high, with glaucous foliage and rather larger flowers of bright yellow, borne on a loose spike. *L. macedonica*, with greyish-green foliage, has yellow flowers in graceful terminal racemes on three-feet stems; its form var. *speciosa* has attractive lemon-yellow flowers. It is probably to the latter two that most of the varieties of garden origin owe their parentage. Easily grown in any garden soil in full sun the plants, owing to their somewhat rampant spreading habit, need control to keep them within bounds.

Propagate by division of the root in spring, or from seed.

The flowering season is in summer.

## Flax  (Plate 30)

Family *LINACEAE*                                    *Linum* species

A genus which includes perennial species of considerable charm, native to Europe. The stems are slender and branching, clothed from the base upwards with short, narrow, pointed grassy foliage. *L. perenne* has five-petalled flowers, one and a half inches across, of lovely azure-blue, borne in profusion on branching stems up to one and a half feet; it also has a white flowered form. *L. narbonense* has similarly sized flowers of azure-blue with an effective white centre and stamens, up to two feet high. Less commonly seen are *L. monogynum*, a twelve- to eighteen-inch flowering species from New Zealand, *L. austriacum*, with rather smaller violet-coloured flowers, and *L. lewisii*, the Prairie Flax, from western America, very similar to *L. perenne*. *L. campanulatum*, twelve inches, and *L. capitatum*, six to nine inches, are yellow-flowering, and *L. salsoloides*, nine inches, has pinkly-tinged white flowers; all being European species. Easily cultivated in any open position in full sun and useful for the base of rock gardens.

Propagation is by division of the roots or from seed that may be sown where it is to flower.

The flowering season is in late spring.

## Cardinal Flower  (Plate 31)

Family *CAMPANULACEAE*                              *Lobelia* species

A genus of plants, containing some perennial species of magnificent colouring, all native to North America. *L. cardinalis*, the Cardinal Flower, is also known as the Indian Pink and is of erect growth. The leaves are narrow, oblong and pointed, clothing the stems from the base upwards. On the upper portion of the three- to four-feet stems are borne in a long spike flowers of bright cardinal-red, made up of a one-inch tube and three lower lobes, narrow and an inch or more long. *L. fulgens*, from Mexico, has rather broader lobes to its bright scarlet flowers whose rich colouring is enhanced by the rich purple of the foliage; its height is one to three feet. There are a number of attractive garden forms of both these species. *L. syphilitica* is a vigorous herb of two to three feet, with blue or purple flowers. *L. tupa*, from Chile, four to six feet, has larger and more hairy foliage than the foregoing and bears in late summer spikes of blood-red with the hooded lip turning downwards. In a sunny or partially shaded position where the soil is rich and moist these plants will grow well, especially if leafmould is added, but, being somewhat tender, it is necessary to provide protection by means of a bracken covering in winter.

Propagate by means of cuttings in the spring or from seed.

The flowering season is in late summer.

## Lupin (Plate 31)

Family *LEGUMINOSAE*                              *Lupinus polyphyllus*

This species of a North American genus is among the most important of perennials, inasmuch as it has given rise to some of the most brilliantly coloured early summer flowers. The foliage comprises five to fifteen long, narrow leaflets, four to six inches long, radiating from a short stem at the base of the plant and sometimes from the flower-stems. The flowers, borne in long spikes, three to four feet, comprise a lower portion pouch-shaped, known as the keel, and an upper petal that is recurved in the older types, but flat in the more modern strains, particularly the Russell strain. In the type the flowers were slaty-blue or a dull white, but in the varieties of garden origin the shades vary from white to yellow, orange, flame, red, bronze, pink and intermediate shades as well as lavender-blue and purple. The roots produce nodules which supply nitrogen. Requires a well-drained rich soil and a position in partial shade or full sun. *L. arboreus*, the Tree Lupin, is shrubby with shorter spikes of yellow, white or mauve. There are a number of alpine species.

Propagate by means of cuttings or from seed.

The flowering season is in June.

## Campion (Plate 31)

Family *CARYOPHYLLACEAE*                              *Lychnis species*

This colourful genus, embracing Agrostemma and Viscaria, is mostly found in Asia and sometimes in Europe. The leaves are opposite and entire, and the habit of the plant is usually erect, varying considerably in height. *L. chalcedonica*, the Jerusalem Cross, reaches a height of three feet or more, with erect stems, bearing at the apex flat heads, about three inches across, comprising many single flowers of brilliant scarlet; there is also var. *flore-pleno*, a double form, var. *alba*, a white form, and others of pink colouring. *L. viscaria*, the German Catchfly, reaches one foot, with narrow, sticky foliage and a short spike of reddish-pink flowers; there are also rose-pink and white forms, and one with double flowers that enjoys the greatest popularity, somewhat resembling a double-flowered Stock. *L. coronaria*, the Rose Campion, once known as *Agrostemma coronaria*, reaches two to three feet, has grey oval foliage and single flowers, an inch across, of rose-crimson. *L. haageana* is a hybrid with flowers, nearly two inches across, comprising notched and lobed petals that vary in colour from orange-red to scarlet; the height does not exceed one foot. *L. flos-jovis*, two and a half to three feet, has bright pink blooms. Easily grown in full sun or partial shade in any well-cultivated soil.

Propagate by means of division or from seed.

The flowering season is in June and early July.

## Loose-strife (Plate 31)

Family *PRIMULACEAE*                                    *Lysimachia* species

A genus of variable habit and comprising perennial herbs that inhabit moist places in the temperate and subtropical regions of the world. *L. nummularia* is the familiar Creeping Jenny of prostrate habit with slender stems clothed with rounded foliage and small yellow flowers; it will grow almost anywhere. *L. clethroides*, of Japan, reaches three feet, with large opposite foliage and white flowers, half an inch across, borne in a long, slender terminal spike. *L. fortunei*, from China and Japan, reaches one and a half feet, with loose spikes of yellow flowers above elegant foliage. *L. punctata*, two to three feet, is a European with large yellow flowers, tinged reddish at the base. *L. epheanerum*, three feet, is a white-flowered species from South Europe, and *L. atropurpurea*, two feet, is purple-flowered, from Greece. These are the leading species for use in gardens and are of the easiest cultivation, but prefer a damp situation to one where drought could cause damage.

Propagation is effected by division or from seed.

The flowering season is in summer.

## Purple Loose-strife (Plate 32)

Family *LYTHRACEAE* *Lythrum* species

Native to northern temperate regions, this genus contains three species that are cultivated in gardens. The foliage is long, widest at the base and pointed, and the flowers are borne in spikes. *L. salicaria* is common to Britain, and reaches three to four feet, with rosy-purple flowers. There are variations, including some with attractive rose-coloured flowers, and others of a greater depth of tone than the type. *L. virgatum* has smaller flowers of rose-purple and is native to Europe and northern Asia; there is a good garden form in Rose Queen. *L. alatum*, from North America, reaches two feet, of sub-shrubby habit with crimson-purple flowers. In any good garden soil and at the side of water these plants are attractive, especially if planted for massed effect. Those named are useful for border planting and will quickly establish themselves, remaining in the same position for many years and requiring the minimum of maintenance.

Propagate by division of the root or from seed.

The flowering season is in summer.

## Plume Poppy (Plate 32)

Family *PAPAVERACEAE* *Macleaya cordata*

A native of China and Japan and desirable as much for its elegant foliage as for its flower, *M. cordata* (syn. *Bocconia cordata*) is a tall free-growing perennial, rampant and spreading in rich soil and attaining a height of six to eight feet. The foliage is large, heart-shaped, lobed and glaucous. The small flowers are borne in feathery racemes, somewhat after the fashion of Astilbe, and are of a brownish-pink. Easily grown in any good soil, the Plume Poppy should be given ample space for development; otherwise it will tend to overcrowd other nearby plants. It is a useful subject for a specimen group, and can be grown to fine effect in the wilder parts of the garden or sparse woodland, doing well alike in full sun or partial shade. Plant in early autumn or spring, and allow to remain undisturbed for several years, when it will probably require to be lifted in order to control its vigorous growth and spreading habit.

Propagate by means of division or root cuttings.

The flowering season is in July and August.

## Musk Mallow: Poppy Mallow (Plate 32)

Family *MALVACEAE*                                   *Malva* species

A useful herbaceous perennial and native to Europe. The foliage is finely lobed and possesses the elegance of some ferns. The stems reach a height of two to three feet and are branching, bearing five-petalled flowers, one to one and a half inches across, of rose; the calyx is hairy. There is also a white-flowered form that is considered by many gardeners to be the most desirable of the species and is slightly musk-scented. These old garden plants may be seen growing wild at the side of roads and are easily cultivated in gardens, requiring no special cultivation but giving the best results in sun or partial shade. There are other species, including the beautiful dwarf *M. campanulata*, with lilac bell-shaped flowers and suitable only for the most favoured climates. The Poppy Mallow, *Callirhoë papaver*, a plant of the same species with bright pink flowers, grows well in rich sandy loam.

Propagation is by means of seed sown in cold frames in March and planted out in May.

The flowering season is in summer.

## Welsh Poppy: Himalayan Poppy (Plate 32)

Family *PAPAVERACEAE*                           *Meconopsis* species

A genus of very attractive plants, some of annual and others of perennial flowering, valuable for foliage as well as for flowers; native to Asia, and Europe in the case of one species. *M. cambrica*, the Welsh Poppy, a native of western Europe, reaches a foot high, with hairy fern-like foliage, much lobed, and pale yellow poppy-like flowers, two inches across, and is monocarpic. There is also a double-flowered form. *M. wallichii*, from the Himalayas, reaches four to six feet, with beautiful fern-like foliage and rust-coloured hairs; the flowers, about three inches across, are of satin texture, crinkled and of pale blue with orange anthers, forming an imposing spike. *M. baileyi* (syn. *betonicifolia*), the Blue Tibetan Poppy, has strap-like hairy leaves and stout stems up to three feet, bearing several brilliant peacock-blue flowers centred with orange stamens. It is perennial only if the flower-buds are removed in the first season before flowering. *M. regia* forms an elegant rosette of hairy foliage, with bright yellow flowers on stems up to four feet or more. *M. grandis*, three feet, from Sikkim, has violet- or slate-blue flowers, and *M. quintuplinervia*, one to one and a half feet, is a dainty Tibetan, with flowers of lilac-blue. These plants, except *M. cambrica* which will grow in ordinary sandy loam, require partial shade and a soil rich in peat or leafmould and well drained.

Propagate from seed.

The flowering season is in spring.

## Virginian Cowslip (Plate 33)

Family *BORAGINACEAE*               *Mertensia* species

A race of attractive perennial herbs from the temperate regions of the northern hemisphere, particularly North America. *M. virginica*, the Virginian Cowslip, has large basal leaves, elliptical or round, with terminal nodding clusters of rich bluish-purple flowers on arching stems, one to one and a half feet. It is considered the most handsome species and is an old garden plant. The foliage is smooth or hairy, according to species, with alternate leaves of varying form, the flowers being borne in a terminal raceme. *M. dahurica* reaches one foot, with slender branching stems, bearing panicles of sky-blue flowers. *M. maritima*, the Oyster Plant, a native of our British coast, reaches one foot, with oval foliage and branching stems bearing many tubular flowers, about one-third of an inch long and turquoise-blue in colour. *M. alpina* is a good dwarf from the Rockies, with blue flowers on six-inch stems. *M. sibirica*, eighteen inches, with trumpet flowers of purple tubes and blue bells, thrives in any ordinary soil and partial shade. A sandy soil rich in leafmould or peat and a position in either sun or partial shade are desirable. When once established, plants should be allowed to remain undisturbed.

Propagation is effected by means of division of the root or from seed.

The flowering season is from March to June. *M. sibirica* flowers from May to September.

## Monkey-flower (Plate 33)

Family *SCROPHULARIACEAE*             *Mimulus* species

A race which includes many moisture-loving perennial herbs noted for their brightly coloured flowers, and found chiefly in North America, but some are from Africa, Asia and Australasia. The leaves vary from oblong to lance-shaped with serrated edge. *M. luteus* can vary in height from twelve to eighteen inches with flowers comprising two upper and three lower lobes of deep yellow with dark blotches, the corolla being from one to two inches long. There are a number of variations. *M. ringens* reaches from two to four feet, with flowers that vary from violet to white in colour about one inch long with a narrow throat. *M. cardinalis* reaches one to two feet, with scarlet flowers, the upper lobes becoming reflexed. *M. moschatus* is the Musk Plant with creeping roots and stems up to six inches, bearing small pale yellow flowers lightly spotted brown. *M. guttatus*, native to Britain and North America, grows two to two and a half feet, with yellow flowers, spotted red. *M. lewisii*, twelve inches, with rose flowers, is a lovely species from north-west America. By the side of streams, in the moister parts of herbaceous borders, and in some shade, these plants are easily grown, provided there is ample leafmould in the soil.

Propagate by division, cuttings, or from seed.

The flowering season is continuous throughout the summer.

## Bee Balm: Bergamot (Plate 33)

Family *LABIATAE*                                    *Monarda* species

Natives of North America, these showy flowers are essential for herbaceous borders. The leaves are oval, lance-shaped and aromatic when crushed. The flowers are narrow, tubular and borne in dense whorls at the end of each stem. *M. didyma*, the Sweet Bergamot or Oswego Tea, and its forms are the most common in gardens, with flowers varying from deep purple to salmon-pink on two- to three-feet stems. *M. fistulosa* is the Wild Bergamot, not to be confused with the Bergamot of Europe, which is *Mentha aquatica*. It flowers later than *M. didyma* and the flowers vary in colour from purple in the type to crimson in var. *rubra* and flesh pink to lilac in var. *mollis*. *M. ramaleyi* is similar to *M. fistulosa* but hairy; reaches only two feet, having clover-red flowers. *M. bradburiana* has light purple flowers. These plants will grow in almost any soil, *M. didyma* and *M. fistulosa* being sufficiently vigorous to fend for themselves in the wild garden. *M. fistulosa* and *M. bradburiana* grow well in dry soils. All like sun.

Propagate from seed or by division.

The flowering season is in summer.

## Whorl-flower (Plate 33)

Family *DIPSACEAE*                                    *Morina* species

A genus of thistle-like plants, chiefly native to the Himalayas. The leaves are opposite or whorled, oblong and narrow and spiny.

1. Cardinal Flower (*Lobelia cardinalis*), p. 87.     2. Lupin (*Lupinus polyphyllus*), p. 87.
3. Campion (*Lychnis chalcedonica*), p. 87.     4. Loose-strife (*Lysimachia punctata*), p. 88.

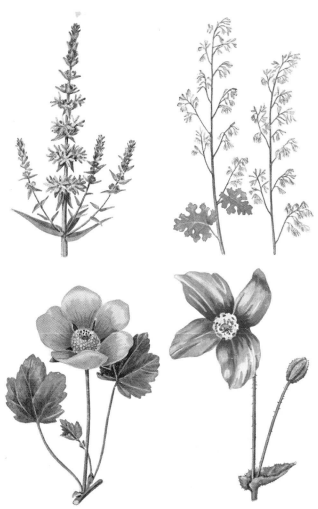

*Pl.* 32.
1. Purple Loose-strife (*Lythrum salicaria*, p. 89.    2. Plume Poppy (*Macleaya cordata*), p. 89.
3. Poppy Mallow (*Malva* species), p. 90.    4. Blue Tibetan Poppy (*Meconopsis baileyi*), p. 90.

The flowers are borne in whorls on spikes with wide bracts, leafy in appearance and occasional spines among the flowers. *M. longifolia* grows two to three feet, with leaves six inches long and an inch across and flowers that develop from white buds to pink and crimson blooms, borne in dense whorls near the end of the stem. It is known as Whorl-flower. *M. persica* is of one to two feet high, with red and white flowers and corolla tubes one and a half inches long. *M. coulteriana* is eighteen inches tall, having yellow flowers, with corolla tubes three-quarters of an inch long. *M. bulleyana* reaches two feet, with white or purple flowers. These handsome perennials grow best in deep, moist, well-drained sandy loam with partial shade.

Propagate from seed sown as soon as ripe in sandy soil, or by root division in September.

The flowering season is from June to August.

## Grape Hyacinth (Plate 34)

Family *LILIACEAE*                    *Muscari* species

A genus of attractive hardy bulbous plants of over forty species, native variously to Europe and Asia Minor. The foliage rises from the bulb and consists of narrow, linear leaves, rather fleshy and untidy in the mass. The flowers are small, of rounded shape, constricted at the mouth, and borne in close spikes; hence the name of the most popular species *M. botryoides*, meaning "like a bunch of grapes". The individual flowers are about one-third of an inch across and of a deep sky-blue shade, with six white-toothed segments; there are also pale blue and white forms, all of erect habit up to nine inches. *M. armeniacum* flowers later than most, reaches eight inches, with racemes four inches long of bright clear blue flowers with white segments. *M. racemosum*, six inches, has deep purple flowers with sprawling leaves, of vigorous growth. *M. comosum monstrosum*, eight inches, is the Feather Hyacinth and has soft violet flowers, comprising a mass of thread-like filaments that lend a feathery or fluffy aspect to them. Massed in the front of herbaceous borders, beneath deciduous shrubs and in sparse woodland, these are among the most charming of spring flowers. Plant in autumn in well-drained soil.

Propagate by division of established clumps, by offsets or seeds.

The flowering season is in spring.

# Giant Forget-me-not (Plate 34)

Family *BORAGINACEAE*            *Myosotidium nobile*

A native of the Chatham Islands off New Zealand, where it grows in the damp sand of the sea-coast. In effect this plant resembles a glorified Myosotis, with large leaves rising from the roots and winged one-seeded fruit. The plant has sometimes been known as *Cynoglossum nobile* and is often called *M. hortensis*. Its leaves are broad, semi-oval and six to nine inches long. The leafy stems grow one to two feet high, bearing at the top a flat-headed cluster up to eight inches across of dark blue flowers, paling to white at the edges and about half an inch across. This is a fine plant for the milder counties, where it will thrive in moist sandy soil, in cool, damp, sheltered borders. In more severe localities some protection in winter is necessary. During growth it should never lack moisture. It is a sun lover, but thrives in partial shade. It is worthy of a position in the rock-garden moraine.

Propagate from seed and grow the seedlings in pots until they are planted out, afterwards remaining undisturbed.

The flowering season is in early to mid-spring.

# Forget-me-not: Scorpion Grass (Plate 34)

Family *BORAGINACEAE*            *Myosotis* species

A genus of pretty perennials, which are mostly native to Europe. The leaves are alternate and entire, the flowers being a quarter of an inch or less across, divided into five lobes. *M. alpestris* (syn. *M. pyrenaica*) is the Alpine Forget-me-not; it forms a low cushion up to eight inches high, with lovely blue flowers. It has an erect form in var. *stricta*, and one with golden foliage in var. *aurea*, but the type is the most popular. *M. dissitiflora*, eight to ten inches, is long flowering, with dark sky-blue flowers from May to July, and has a white var. *alba*. *M. sylvatica*, one to two feet high, is a native with branching stems and blue flowers centred with yellow. There are also white, pink and striped forms. *M. scorpioides* (syn. *M. palustris*) is the true Forget-me-not, with slender stems, half to one and a half feet high, with bright blue, yellow-eyed flowers. It has a dwarf form var. *semperflorens*. *M. caespitosa* (syn. *M. rehsteineri*), three to six inches, forms a dense cushion of blue. *M. azorica*, six to ten inches, is blue-flowering and has a striking variety, "Imperatrice Elizabeth", with bluish-purple flowers. These plants are effective massed either as a groundwork for spring bulbs, especially Tulips, or in woodland, where they thrive exceedingly, liking a moist, gritty loam and partial shade.

Propagate from seed sown to flower the following year, or root division in October or March.

The flowering season is in spring.

## Daffodil (Plate 34)

Family *AMARYLLIDACEAE*                         *Narcissus* species

Known variously as Daffodils, Jonquils, Chalice Flowers, Lent Lilies and Chinese Sacred Lilies, the hardy bulbous perennials of this important genus come from Europe, Asia and North Africa. The leaves are narrow, linear and erect, varying in length according to species. The flowers may be borne singly or in numbers on a single stem. The larger species are now classified into sections as follows: (1) "Trumpet", in which the trumpet is as long as, or longer than, the perianth segments; (2) *Incomparabilis*, in which the cup is more than one-third but less than the length of the perianth segments; (3) *Barri*, in which the cup is less than one-third of the length of the perianth segments; (4) *Leedsii*, in which the perianth is white, and the cup white, cream or lemon; (5) Triandrus hybrids which are varieties of *N. triandrus*, with drooping trumpet and reflexed perianth; (6) *Cyclamineus* hybrids, with reflexed perianth; (7) *Jonquilla* hybrids, varieties of *N. jonquilla*, with scented flowers and short, fluted trumpets; (8) *Tazetta* hybrids, varieties of *N. tazetta*, the bunch-flowered Narcissus; (9) *Poeticus* varieties such as the Pheasant's Eye Narcissus; (10) doubles of which "Inglescombe" and "Van Sion" are typical; (11) miniature flowered species, such as *N. bulbocodium*, the Hoop Petticoat Daffodil, *N. juncifolius*, the rush-leaved Daffodil, and *N. minimus*, the Pigmy Daffodil. Daffodils may be widely used for beds and borders, but are often best when naturalized. Well-drained loamy soils are best, planting in September to October.

Propagate by offsets or from seeds.

The flowering season is from March to May.

## Catmint (Plate 35)

Family *LABIATAE*                    *Nepeta mussini* and *N. faasseni*

An aromatic herbaceous perennial native to the Caucasus and Persia. Small heart-shaped foliage, with deeply notched margin and greyish-green in hue. The flowers are tubular and small, borne in a short raceme on stems up to one and a half feet and of a light lavender-blue shade. The common catmint of gardens is *N. × faasseni*, a hybrid derived from *N. mussini* and commonly known as *N. mussini* in gardens. Other garden forms are *N. magnifica*, like a giant *N. mussini*, with deeper coloured flowers and reaching a height of two and a half feet or more, and Six Hills, which is very similar. *N. glichoma variegata* is the Ground Ivy of America and has a creeping habit; of easy cultivation and very rampant in growth if the soil is moist. *N. macrantha*, two to three feet, is a silver-blue flowering species from Siberia. The three first named are admirable for the herbaceous border, edgings to pathways and for carpeting to various bulbous subjects. They will grow well and freely in any good garden soil, preferring sun to shade. Planting may take place in early autumn or spring.

Propagate by division of the root in spring or by partly ripened tips taken as cuttings.

The flowering season is throughout the summer.

## Nerine (Plate 35)

Family *AMARYLLIDACEAE*                    *Nerine bowdenii*

The only species of this genus that may be grown out-of-doors in Britain, and a native of South Africa. The root is bulbous and the foliage is strap-shaped, slightly channelled and up to one foot long and one inch broad, developing during the winter months and going to rest in early spring. The flowers are bright rose in colour, tubular in form with open mouth and two to three inches long, borne in umbels of six to twelve, about nine inches across, on a stem of about one and a half feet. A well-drained light, sandy soil, containing well-rotted manure, and a sunny position at the base of a south wall is necessary. Planting may be carried out during the dormant period, which extends from April to August, although it may also be carried out successfully after flowering in October. Nerines flower best when they have developed a mass of bulbs that crowd together. In common with the tender kinds, *N. bowdenii* is a most decorative plant for the cool greenhouse, where it may be cultivated in pots.

Propagate by offsets or from seed. Seedlings require three years in which to develop to flowering bulbs.

The flowering season is in September or October.

33.

1. Virginian Cowslip (*Mertensia virginica*), p. 91.   2. Monkey-flower (*Mimulus luteus*), p. 91.
3. Bee Balm (*Monarda didyma*), p. 92.   4. Whorl-flower (*Morina longifolia*) p. 92.

*Pl.* 34.

1. Grape Hyacinth (*Muscari botryoides*), p. 93.  2. Giant Forget-me-not (*Myosotidium nobile*), p. 94.
3. Forget-me-not (*Myosotis alpestris*), p. 94.  4. Daffodil (*Narcissus*), p. 95.

# Evening Primrose (Plate 35)

Family *ONAGRACEAE*                          *Oenothera* species

Natives mostly of North America, the Evening Primroses are among the most charming of herbaceous flowers. As the name indicates, some species only unfold their flowers in late afternoon, but others are open during daytime. The leaves are alternate, simple or pinnate. *O. fruticosa*, known as Sun-drops, reaches one to two feet, with golden yellow flowers, about two inches across, borne on reddish branching stems. Of its forms, var. *youngii* is one of the best known, with larger foliage and two-feet stems, very branching, with bright lemon-yellow flowers. *O. missouriensis* (syn. *O. macrocarpa*) is of a trailing habit, with large flowers, often five inches across, of golden yellow. *O. speciosa* reaches two feet, with lance-shaped leaves and flowers that are white on opening, changing to delicate rose. Of dwarf habit, *O. marginata* is of similar colour to the last mentioned and reaches a foot in height. All are more or less fragrant. Useful alike for the semi-wild garden or the border, these plants require a well-drained soil and a position in sun or partial shade.

Propagate by division, seeds or cuttings taken in early spring.

The flowering season is in May in the case of *O. marginata*, and during summer for the remainder.

# Star of Bethlehem (Plate 35)

Family *LILIACEAE*                          *Ornithogalum* species

A genus of bulbous plants widely spread over the eastern hemisphere, some of considerable charm and others less distinctive. The leaves are narrow, linear, and spring from the bulb. The flowers are star-shaped and borne in corymbs. *O. arabicum* is a charming plant from southern Europe, with leaves that rise to one and a half feet and stems up to two feet, bearing clusters of cream-coloured flowers up to an inch across with bright yellow anthers, but needs shelter and winter protection. *O. nutans* is one of the hardiest species, with pendulous white flowers, green on the exterior, borne in a loose raceme on one-foot stems; there is a larger form in var. *Boucheanum*. *O. pyramidale* is also hardy and easily grown, with pure white flowers, striped green, on one and a half feet stems. *O. pyrenaicum* varies from greenish-yellow to greenish-white in colour and reaches two feet. *O. umbellatum* is the common Star of Bethlehem that has become naturalized

7

in parts of Britain; the narrow leaves, about a foot long, each have a white stripe along the centre, the green-striped white flowers being borne in an umbel on six-inch stems and opening from noon for about four hours. The hardy kinds grow in any well-drained soil and are fine for massed effect. The tender *O. arabicum* should be lifted and stored during winter and planted in March.

Propagate by offsets.

The flowering season is from May to July.

## Great Oriental Bell-flower (Plate 36)

Family *CAMPANULACEAE*                    *Ostrowskia magnifica*

Closely allied to Campanula and a native plant of eastern Bokhara. A stately plant, reaching from four to five feet high, with smooth stem and leaves produced in whorls, of ovate form, toothed and six inches long. The flowers are four or more inches across, with short lobes and of a colour of varying tints of lilac or white. The fleshy roots will reach a depth of two feet, making a deep sandy soil necessary for successful cultivation, the introduction of humus in the form of peat or leafmould being essential. Full sun is preferable to partial shade. After flowering, the plants quickly become dormant, and it is necessary to protect from rain for the remainder of the summer and in autumn. About February the protective covering may be removed and rain allowed to stimulate new growth. This is one of the loveliest of all herbaceous perennials.

Propagate from root cuttings, top cuttings in spring or seed sown as soon as ripe. Seedlings require three or four years to reach maturity.

The flowering season is in June.

## Paeony (Plate 36)

Family *RANUNCULACEAE*                        *Paeonia* species

A genus of the most lovely of all hardy plants, comprising herbaceous or shrubby species of Asiatic origin and many garden varieties. The leaves are elegant in form, being alternate and pinnately compound or dissected. The flowers vary in size and may be of single or double form. *P. officinalis* is an old garden flower, with eight-inch flowers of crimson on two- to three-feet stems. *P. tenuifolia* is a lovely miniature form with feathery foliage and double crimson flowers, about three inches across, on one- to one-and-a-half-foot stems. *P. molkosewitschii* has sulphur-yellow single flowers, five inches across, on short stems. *P. lacti-flora* (syn. *P. albiflora*) is the origin of many of the beautiful garden varieties; reaches three feet with double flowers, six or more inches across. *P. lutea*, three feet, from Yunnam, and *P. wittmanniana*, two feet, from the Orient, are good yellow-flowering species. *P. browni*, one and a half feet, with dull red flowers, comes from California. *P. suffruticosa* (syn. *P. moutan*) is the Tree Paeony, three to six feet tall, with foliage finely dissected and rose flowers. Paeonies of all kinds should be planted in September or October, not later, as they draw root in autumn. A deep soil rich in humus with the addition of bone meal and a position in full sun is essential as well as ample moisture, but perfect drainage during growth.

Propagate by division in September or October, or from seed which will require six or more years to reach the flowering stage.

The flowering season is in May and June.

## Oriental Poppy (Plate 36)

Family *PAPAVERACEAE*                    *Papaver orientale*

A brilliantly coloured perennial, native to Asia Minor, and possessing the largest flowers of the genus. The leaves are deeply lobed and bristly, often six inches across. The stems are also bristly and attain heights varying from three to four feet, though some of the garden forms are of dwarfer habit. The flowers are usually of six petals, broad and overlapping, of a brilliant orange-scarlet, with a deep purple base. Varieties of garden origin vary in colour, outstanding kinds being "Perry's White", "Salmon Glow", "Cowichan", scarlet; "Lady Haig", deep red; "Mrs. Stobart", cerise-pink; "Olympia", double red; and "Lord Lambourne", orange-scarlet. These plants will grow in any good garden soil and will remain in perfect vigour if allowed to remain undisturbed for several years to form large floriferous clumps.

Propagation is effected by root cuttings and from seed.

The flowering season is in June.

## Beard Tongue (Plate 36)

Family *SCROPHULARIACEAE*                 *Penstemon* species

A genus of most attractive perennials, largely for the herbaceous border, natives of North America. *P. barbatus* (syn. *Chelone barbata*) has long and narrow lance-shaped leaves and leafy stems rising to three feet, bearing many rosy-red tubular flowers, one inch long, each with a beard on the lower lip. Its form var. *torreyi* is more robust in habit and does not possess the characteristic beard; there is also a white form. *P. campanulatus* has a free-branching habit, with one-sided racemes of rose-pink flowers, one inch long, to a height of one to two feet. *P. hirsutus* is of decumbent habit, with two-feet stems and drooping flowers of dull purple or violet. *P. ovatus* will reach two to three feet with flowers, about three-quarters of an inch long, of bright blue fading to purple, and is one of the most attractive species for gardens. *P. antirrhinoides*, one to three feet, lemon-yellow, *P. confertus*, one foot, purple and blue, and *P. glaber*, one to two feet, purple, are all worth growing. *P. hartwegii*, usually grown as a biennial, has large tubular flowers, open at the mouth and large as Foxgloves, and of a bright scarlet. This species and *P. cobaea* have been influential in the production of the many hybrid bedding varieties which are among the most brilliant of garden flowers, blooming over a long period. Sunny position and a well-drained rich loam, containing plenty of humus, are the essentials.

Propagate from cuttings or seed.

The flowering season is in summer and often into autumn.

## Winter Heliotrope (Plate 37)

Family *COMPOSITAE*                           *Petasites fragrans*

Once known as *Tussilago fragrans* and a native of the Mediterranean region. Reaching a height of about six inches with toothed leaves smooth above and hairy beneath, the plant resembles the common Coltsfoot (*Tussilago farfara*) to which it is related. The flowers are small, varying in colour from lilac to purple and are vanilla scented. An easy plant in cultivation, growing in any garden soil and more suitable for the wild than the cultivated garden. Although it grows well in shade, it is even better when given a sunny position where it will flower more freely than if overhung by trees or shrubs. It spreads rapidly by means of underground runners and should be planted where it cannot overrun choicer subjects. Its fragrant flowers are welcome for interior adornment.

Propagate by means of division or from seed.

The flowering season is in winter.

35.
1. Catmint (*Nepta mussini*), p. 95.
3. Evening Primrose (*Oenothera fruticosa*), p. 97.

2. Nerine (*Nerine bowdenii*), p. 96.
4. Star of Bethlehem (*Ornithogalum
nutans*), p. 97.

*Pl.* 36.
1. Great Oriental Bell-flower (*Ostrowskia magnifica*), p. 98.  2. Paeony (*Paeonia*), p. 98.
3. Oriental Poppy (*Papaver orientale*), p. 99.    4. Beard Tongue (*Penstemon barbatus* var. *torreyi*), p. 99.

## Flame Flower (Plate 37)

Family *POLEMONIACEAE*                              *Phlox* species

One of the most brilliantly coloured genera, native to North America, containing annual, herbaceous and alpine species. *P. paniculata* (syn. *P. decussata*) has oblong, lance-shaped leaves and many flowers, from one to two inches across in some garden forms, borne in massive pyramidal panicles on stems up to four feet high. The colour of the garden varieties varies from white to shades of pink, mauve, violet, purple, scarlet and crimson. *P. glaberrima suffruticosa* is one to two feet tall, with smaller flowers and blooming earlier, but has not attracted hybridists to the same extent as has *P. paniculata*. *P. maculata*, two feet, has purple flowers; introduced by G. Arends of Ronsdorf, it is a hybrid between *P. paniculata* and *P. divaricata*, the latter a dwarf alpine species: the height is one to two feet and the flowers are mostly of purple shades, lacking somewhat in distinction when compared with their more colourful cousins. A deep, rich, gritty soil, well drained and sunny, is necessary for Phlox to grow really well, although partial shade is advantageous for those of orange tones that tend to burn in the sun.

Propagate from root cuttings, top cuttings or seed.

The flowering season is from late June until September.

## Cape Fig-wort (Plate 37)

Family *SCROPHULARIACEAE*                         *Phygelius capensis*

A brilliantly coloured perennial from South Africa, eminently suitable for use in herbaceous borders. The leaves are oval and lance-shaped and finely toothed, clothing the stems as far as the flowers. The flowers are funnel-shaped, about two inches long and are borne in candelabra fashion on stems up to three feet; the colour is orange-scarlet. Its form var. *coccinea* is of a much more brilliant hue and makes a most attractive plant. In severe winters the plant is sometimes cut to ground-level, but develops new growth which carries its flowers in the same year. It is particularly suitable for hot, dry sandy soils, where it thrives and flowers freely and effectively, provided it enjoys ample sunshine. In localities where winters are severe it should be grown against a south wall and given winter protection in the form of a covering of bracken or leaves.

Propagate from cuttings taken of partly ripened wood in August or from seeds, or root division in March or April.

The flowering season is in July and August.

## Winter Cherry: Chinese Lantern (Plate 37)

Family *SOLANACEAE* *Physalis* species

A race of annual and perennial plants, mostly from America but some from Europe and Asia. The leaves are rounded, serrated at the edge and pointed. *P. alkekengi*, known as Winter Cherry, Chinese Lantern, Bladder Herb and Strawberry Tomato, is from southern Europe. It reaches a height of one to two feet, with white flowers and yellow anthers, followed by red cherry-like fruit enclosed in orange-red calyces of lantern-like appearance. *P. francheti* is similar to the foregoing species but has larger calyces, two inches in diameter, and reaches one and a half to two and a half feet. It has been described as annual and biennial, but has proved to be truly perennial and quickly makes a large clump. *P. bunyardi* is a fine hybrid form, growing three feet tall. These plants are of little garden value, their main merit being their usefulness for winter adornment after the stems have been cut and dried, as the calyces retain their bright colour and are useful for mixing with other dried or everlasting flowers. Will grow anywhere in drained soil.

Propagate by division or from seed.

The flowering season is in summer and the calyces colour in late summer and autumn.

## Red-ink Plant: Virginian Poke (Plate 38)

Family *PHYTOLACCACEAE* *Phytolacca americana*

Also known as *P. decandra*, this herbaceous perennial is common in the eastern regions of North America. The leaves are oval or lance-shaped. The flowers are borne on bracted pedicels on a cylindrical spike up to ten feet high, and are white, becoming suffused with green or purple. The flowers are followed by rather flat purple berries closely packed on the stem, and these, when crushed, exude a reddish liquid which has earned for it its common name. It is also known as Blood Root and Virginian Poke. There is also a variegated form with the leaves light green in colour, shaded rose and margined white. The roots are poisonous, as are also the seeds. Of bushy habit and reaching only three feet, *P. icosandra* has foliage similar to that of the Hydrangea; the flowers are creamy-white, borne in long spikes and are followed by black berries forming a cob like that of Indian Corn. Easily grown in any soil, these plants are rather more fitted for the wild garden than the flower border. They are excellent subjects for sparse woodland, where they may easily be naturalized.

Propagate by division of the fleshy roots or from seed.

The flowering season is in summer.

## Balloon-flower (Plate 38)

Family *CAMPANULACEAE*      *Platycodon grandiflorum*

Also known as the Japanese or Chinese Bell-flower, this is a valuable border plant from China and Japan with a number of attractive forms. The leaves are lance-shaped, smooth and irregularly toothed. The flowers are not unlike those of *Campanula persicifolia* but open more flatly, are three inches across and deep blue in colour. The height is one foot. It is the inflated bud that gives the plant its popular name. There are various forms in var. *album*, white; var. *autumnale*, a late-flowering form; var. *japonicum*, stronger and more free-flowering than the type; var. *mariesii*, only six to nine inches high, with flowers varying from deep to pale blue or white. In cultivation a well-drained light soil is necessary, the roots tending to decay in heavy soils. Plant in spring in preference to autumn.

Propagate from seed, cuttings of young shoots or by division. The latter method is difficult owing to the fleshy nature of the roots.

The flowering season is in June and July.

## May Apple: Duck Foot (Plate 38)

Family *BERBERIDACEAE*      *Podophyllum peltatum*

A species from North America and effective in flower, foliage and fruit. The leaves are a foot across and shaped somewhat like an umbrella with from five to seven lobes, dark green in colour. The flowers are cup-shaped, not unlike those of the Hellebore, cream and borne on a branch from the stem and followed by egg-shaped yellow fruit, two inches long. The plant attains a height of twelve to fifteen inches. *P. emodi*, one foot tall, has three- to five-lobed foliage of an effective bronze shade in early spring, with flowers that vary in colour from white to rose; the fruit is coral red in colour, egg-shaped and two inches long; a native of the Himalayas. Easily grown in deep rich soil containing peat or leafmould and partial shade. *P. emodi* prefers rather more moist conditions than *P. peltatum*. Both are suitable for association with ericaceous plants and require situations protected from cold winds.

Propagation is by division or from seed.

The flowering season is in May.

## Jacob's Ladder (Plate 38)

Family *POLEMONIACEAE*                         *Polemonium* species

*P. caeruleum* from the copses and margins of European streams is the old-fashioned species to which the genus owes its popular name from the manner in which the leaflets are arranged on the stem to suggest a ladder. It is also called Greek Valerian. The plant reaches two feet and bears a short panicle of blue, drooping, bell-shaped flowers, an inch across. The finest form is *P. humile* (syn. *P. richardsonii*) from North America, with bell-shaped flowers of brilliant blue and white anthers. Its var. *pulchellum* has smaller flowers that vary in tone from white to violet and lavender. *P. reptans*, a native of North America, is six inches high, with light blue flowers, half an inch across, borne in a cluster. One of the finest is *P. confertum* from western North America, six to eight inches, with honey-scented bell-flowers up to an inch across and of a deep blue colour. A position in partial shade and a deep rich soil is necessary to grow these plants to perfection and, when established, they may remain for many years without disturbance.

Propagate by division or from seed.

The flowering season is in spring.

## Solomon's Seal (Plate 39)

Family *LILIACEAE*                         *Polygonatum* species

A genus comprising about sixty species, well distributed over the temperate regions of the northern hemisphere. Of graceful habit, a number are worthy additions to the flower border. *P. multiflorum* has gracefully arching stems up to three feet high, the exterior clothed its entire length with elegant oblong leaves, four or five inches long, beneath which hang the drooping, tubular flowers of white, about an inch long. It is a native of Europe and Asia. Better is the hybrid (*P.* × *hybridum*) of this and *P. odoratum* (*P. officinale*). *P. biflorum*, one to three feet, is of similar height and finds its home amid the wooded Canadian hillsides. It has the characteristic gracefully arching habit and bears its greenish-white flowers, two or three in a cluster, in the leaf axils. *P. verticillatum* carries its leaves in whorls, with flowers of greenish-white borne in bunches of three in the leaf axils; they are followed by red fruit. In the herbaceous border or naturalized in woodland, companioning such plants as Dicentra and members of the Primula family where the soil is deep and rich in humus, these plants will thrive.

Propagate by division or from seed.

The flowering season is in spring.

## Knotweed (Plate 39)

Family *POLYGONACEAE* *Polygonum* species

A genus that has herbaceous plants that are widely spread from the tropics to arctic regions, of species that vary from rampant weeds, fit only for the wild garden, to dainty gems that may be used to adorn rock gardens. *P. baldschuanicum*, from Bokhara, Central Asia, is a rampant climber of twenty to thirty feet, with heart-shaped foliage similar to that of the Convolvulus and sprays of feathery white flowers in late summer. *P. amplexicaule*, from the Himalayas, the Mountain Fleece, is of tufted habit with heart-shaped foliage and stems rising to three feet, bearing clustered spikes of bright rosy-red flowers, a quarter of an inch in diameter. Its variety *speciosum* has flowers of an effective claret colour. *P. vaccinifolium* is a trailer, also from the Himalayas, with growths a foot long with small half-inch leaves and racemes of rosy-red flowers, rather less than a quarter of an inch across. Any good garden soil that is rich in humus and not subject to drought will grow these plants satisfactorily.

Propagate by division or from seed.

The flowering season is in late summer.

## Cinquefoil (Plate 39)

Family *ROSACEAE* *Potentilla* species

A genus comprising both shrubby and herbaceous perennials of eminent value as garden plants. The foliage is elegant and strongly resembles that of the strawberry, although in many species it is more finely divided. The hybrids have a long season of flowering and comprise many brilliant colours inherited from the species that were their parents. *P. argyrophylla* has erect stems, two to three feet high, with yellow flowers an inch across, borne on long pedicels. It is a native of the Himalayas, and has been hybridized with, it is believed, *P. atrosanguinea*, purple, *P. nepalensis*, rosy-purple, and *P. villosa*, golden yellow. The garden hybrids include varieties with double as well as single flowers in form like those of the strawberry, but with a colour variation that ranges from white and yellow to shades of buff, salmon, clear rose and scarlet. Easily grown in well-drained sandy soil in full sun.

Propagate by division or from seed.

The flowering season extends throughout the summer.


## Polyanthus  (Plate 39)

Family *PRIMULACEAE*                                 *Primula* species

One of the most important genera of perennial herbs, containing many choice subjects for rock garden, flower border and woodland, native to Europe and Asia, being very widely distributed. Of the many hundreds of species, there are certain ones that are common to gardens. *P. acaulis* (syn. *P. vulgaris*) is the well-known European Primrose, with oblong crinkled leaves that form a rosette from which appear on slender stems flowers an inch or more across of yellow, purple or blue, each with a yellow centre. The Polyanthus Primrose, *P. variabilis* (syn. *P. polyantha*) is of garden origin resulting from crosses between *P. acaulis* and other species, and bears its flowers in clusters on erect stems up to a foot high. There are many fine florists' strains and some with double flowers. *P. juliae* is like a smaller *P. acaulis* in flower, purple in colour, with small oval foliage. *P. japonica* and *P. pulverulenta* bear their flowers, of a great variation in colour, in majestic candelabra fashion, tier upon tier, and love the moist banks of pond or stream. *P. auricula* is an old florist's flower, and the named varieties, both show and alpine, are best grown in pots in a frame or cold greenhouse where the lovely purple, red, yellow, grey and green edged forms are a delight to the eye. There are some excellent strains which may be grown from seed in partially shaded positions where there is ample humus. Space forbids mention of the many other charmers of this genus that may be found in the catalogues of alpine specialists.

Propagate by division or from seed.

The flowering season is in spring.

## Lung-wort (Plate 40)

Family *BORAGINACEAE*                              *Pulmonaria* species

Perennials with creeping roots and natives of Europe and Asia;
allied to Mertensia. *P. saccharata* reaches one foot, with oval
leaves springing from the root and tubular flowers of pink.
*P. angustifolia*, the Blue Cowslip, twelve inches, does not occur
in England, but is found in Europe and has blue and pink flowers.
The English species is *P. longifolia*. *P. officinalis*, the English
Lung-wort or Sage of Bethlehem, has red flowers, changing to
violet with age, and green foliage that is effectively spotted white,
and grows a foot in height. *P. montana*, from Central Europe,
has violet flowers. Among those of garden origin, *P. maweana* is
very pretty with its rich indigo-blue flowers. Easily cultivated in
light soil, rich in humus, the Lung-worts are charming associates
for the Primroses and grow well under the same open woodland
conditions at the base of deciduous trees planted in bold groups,
or masses at the edge of a copse.

Propagate by division or from seed.

The flowering season is in April and May.

## Pyrethrum (Plate 40)

Family *COMPOSITAE*                                  *Pyrethrum roseum*

Known to botanists as *Chrysanthemum coccineum*, but among
gardeners under the above name, this valuable herbaceous perennial is a native of Persia and the Caucasus. The foliage is finely
cut and fern-like in appearance, forming a thick mass from which
rise stems, clothed sparsely with foliage, to a height of two to
three feet, bearing flowers two inches or more across of white, red,
rose or lilac shades. The species is rarely seen, having long given
place to the many fine varieties of garden origin that comprise
both double and single flowered varieties ranging through pink,
salmon, scarlet, crimson and wine-red tones. The single-flowered
sorts are effectively centred with an orange, yellow or cream disc.
For masses in the herbaceous border and for cutting, this plant
is most valuable, and great quantities are grown annually for the
flower market. *P. uliginosum* is a tall white-flowered plant, very
like a Michaelmas Daisy in appearance and flowering in September. Easily grown in any well-drained soil rich in humus, but
dislikes drought conditions, moisture at all times during growth
being essential.

Propagate by division before or immediately after flowering,
or from seed. The flowering season is in June.

## Crowfoot (Plate 40)

Family *RANUNCULACEAE*                    *Ranunculus* species

A genus of several hundred species found throughout the world. *R. asiaticus*, Turban Buttercup, is an old garden favourite of a foot high with elegantly cut foliage and double yellow flowers, one and a half inches across. In cultivated varieties there is a wide range of showy colours, being white, scarlet and various combinations of colour in one flower. From this species come the garden varieties known as Turkish, with orange, yellow or purple flowers; Persian, with double and single flowers of every shade except blue. This is a species with tuberous roots, comprising claw-like fangs that are placed facing downwards when planting. *R. aconitifolius flore-pleno*, known as Fair Maids of France, reaches one and a half to two feet, is herbaceous in habit and is densely covered with small white flowers of rosette-like form on short branching stems. *R. acris flore-pleno*, the Batchelor's Button, will attain two feet, with button-like rosettes of rich yellow. *R. amplexicaulis*, six to twelve inches high, has single flowers of white, an inch across, with yellow stamens. *R. lyallii*, from New Zealand, is a gem with waxy white flowers, two to three inches across, like those of *Anemone japonica*, centred with yellow stamens and borne on two- to three-feet stems. It requires alpine garden conditions. The tuberous-rooted kinds demand a sandy soil, rich in humus and moist during growth. Except *R. lyallii*, the remaining species are of easy cultivation in any well-drained soil containing humus.

Propagate tuberous-rooted species by offsets and the remainder by division.

The period of flowering is from April to September, according to species.

## Rogers' Bronze-leaf (Plate 40)

Family *SAXIFRAGACEAE*                    *Rodgersia* species

A genus of plants renowned alike for ornamental foliage and attractive flowers; natives of China and Japan. *R. podophylla* has five-lobed leaves, toothed and spreading from a thick erect stalk, the lobes being about ten inches long and six inches across the widest portion, of a light green shade in spring, changing to a bronze tint as it matures. The flowers are small, cream and are borne in branching panicles a foot long, rather reminiscent of those of the Astilbe; the height of the plant is three feet when

Pl. 37.                                                                  108

1. Winter Heliotrope (*Petasites fragrans*), p. 100.   2. Flame Flower (*Phlox paniculata*), p. 101.
3. Cape Fig-wort (*Phygelius capensis*), p. 101.   4. Winter Cherry (*Physalis alkekengi*), p. 102.

*Pl.* 38.

1. Red-ink Plant (*Phytolacca americana*), p. 102.  2. Balloon-flower (*Platycodon grandiflorum*), p. 103.
3. May Apple (*Podophyllum peltatum*), p. 103.  4. Jacob's Ladder (*Polemonium humile*), p. 10

established. *R. pinnata*, two to three feet, has similar foliage, the lobes about eight inches long, and the flowers red; there is also a form with white flowers. *R. aesculifolia*, two to three feet, with bronze foliage and rosy-white flowers, and *R. tabularis*, three feet, with bright green foliage and creamy-white flowers, are good Chinese species. These are the most usual species to be found in British gardens and require to be grown under woodland conditions with ample leafmould or peat in the soil and very moist conditions during growth. By the side of ponds both species are very effective, and in small gardens can be used where the gigantic Gunnera would be out of proportion.

Propagate by means of root cuttings or seed.

The flowering season is in early summer.

## Californian Tree Poppy (Plate 41)

Family *PAPAVERACEAE*                    *Romneya* species

Distinct and beautiful plants, native to California and hardy in most parts of Britain. *R. coulteri* is the best-known species, with elegantly cut poppy-like leaves, glaucose green and about four inches long. The fragrant flowers are like large single white Poppies, about six inches across, with a bunch of yellow anthers at the centre; it will reach a height of five to six feet under good cultivation. *R. trichocalyx* is very similar but less tall. *R. hybrida* has flowers almost identical with those of the foregoing, but is the freest flowering of the genus and the most satisfactory for gardens. A sunny sheltered position at the base of a south wall, where the soil is well drained and some protection may be given in severe winters, is ideal. The soil must be well drained and moderately rich in humus. Once established, the plants will not transplant satisfactorily and should be allowed to remain undisturbed. Plant from pots in spring.

Propagate by root cuttings or from seed.

The flowering season is from June to September.

## Roscoea (Plate 41)

Family *SCITAMINEAE*                    *Roscoea purpurea*

A native of the Himalayas and useful for striking a novel note in the flower border, though better accommodated in the rock garden. The roots are tuberous, somewhat spindle-shaped, with leafy stems up to one foot, the leaves being lance-shaped, six to eight inches long. The flowers are borne in clusters, having an elongated tubular calyx and a corolla with an erect upper segment and spreading lower segments, both pale purple or lilac in colour and about one and a half inches long. There is a colour variation in the variety *sikkimensis*. *R. cautleoides*, from China, is a dwarf of nine to twelve inches, bearing pale yellow flowers in summer. The species are hardy in the milder counties of Britain and thrive in a sandy loam enriched with leafmould or well-decayed farmyard manure. The roots are planted six inches deep and should be encased in sand. Effective in the rock garden or in woodland where nearby evergreen shrubs can afford protection.

Propagate by division of roots in spring, or from seed.

The flowering season is summer to autumn.

## Cone-flower (Plate 41)

Family *COMPOSITAE*                                    *Rudbeckia* species

A race of handsome herbaceous perennials from North America and common in gardens. The leaves are alternate, with the blades much divided in some species and undivided in others. The flowers are usually terminal on stems and comprise yellow rays that radiate from a central conspicuous cone. *R. californica* reaches five or six feet, with leaves a foot long and lobed, the yellow rays of the flowers, about two inches long, surrounding a brown cone. *R. nitida* reaches four feet, with oval, pointed leaves and yellow drooping flowers similar in size to the foregoing. *R. maxima* has slightly larger rays of deep yellow radiating from an elongated dark brown central cone; the foliage is smooth and glaucous. *R. newmannii* (syn. *R. speciosa*) is more dwarf and reaches only two to three feet high, with deep yellow rays one and a half inches long, radiating from a small black cone. *R. grandiflora*, three feet, has yellow rays about a purplish cone, and *R. laciniata*, three to six feet, is a noteworthy yellow, with a very good double variety known as "Golden Glow". All are easily cultivated in ordinary, rich, well-drained soil in full sun.

Propagate by division or from seed.

The flowering season is in late summer.

## Sage (Plate 41)

Family *LABIATAE*                                        *Salvia* species

A genus, including herbaceous or shrubby perennials, of great charm, some hardy and others tender, native to most temperate and subtropical regions, particularly in the mountains of tropical

America. Famous for the brilliance of its large gentian blue flowers, *S. patens*, from Mexico, is an old garden favourite of one and a half to two feet, with arrow-shaped foliage and the hooded flowers typical of the Sage family; requires protection in winter. *S. superba* (*S. virgata nemorosa*), from southern Europe, a hardy herbaceous perennial, is a leafy plant of three feet, with broad cordate leaves and spikes of many small purple sage-like flowers up to an inch long, with bronze leafy bracts. *S. pratensis*, the Meadow Sage native to Britain, is also hardy, reaching three feet, with toothed cordate leaves and violet flowers an inch long; its variety *tenori*, with deep blue flowers, is the most desirable for garden planting. *S. uliginosa*, from South America, is hardy and reaches three to five feet, with four-inch lance-shaped toothed foliage and terminal racemes of brilliant blue flowers, three-quarters of an inch long. *S. splendens* is the popular scarlet bedding Sage up to two feet with rounded, pointed foliage and racemes of many scarlet flowers; it needs house protection in winter. *S. pitcheri* (syn. *S. azura grandiflora*), three feet, is Mexican, with soft sky-blue flowers, and *S. turkestanica*, of uncertain origin, has lovely rosy-mauve flowers with coloured bracts on three-feet stems, but is monocarpic. These comprise the most usually grown herbaceous forms, although there are many others. Any good well-drained soil and a position in full sun will ensure satisfactory results.

Propagate by division, cuttings and seed.

The flowering season is in summer.

## Blood-root (Plate 42)

Family *PAPAVERACEAE*           *Sanguinaria canadensis*

A plant native to the woodlands of the eastern states of North America and possessing a number of forms. Glaucous cordate one-inch broad leaves rise to about six inches high, usually singly, from the rootstock, which is about half an inch thick and fleshy. The flowers, borne singly on eight-inch scapes, appear a little before the leaves and consist of up to twelve petals, each flower being about two inches across, blush-white in colour, with a centre of yellow stamens. Delights in a light, sandy, well-drained loam or peat, in full sun or partial shade, provided there is ample moisture at the roots. Excellent for naturalizing in short grass. Best planted in August after the leaves have ripened, it being important not to keep the roots long out of the earth, and thereafter left undisturbed. There is a glorified form in var.

*major*, and another with numerous narrow petals known as var. *plena*.

Propagate by division of the stems after the foliage has withered or from seed.

The flowering season is in spring.

## Soap-wort (Plate 42)

Family *CARYOPHYLLACEAE*                     *Saponaria officinalis flore-pleno*

A genus of the Pink family, comprising both annual and perennial herbs, a number being useful for the adornment of rock gardens and flower borders, inhabiting principally the Mediterranean region. *S. officinalis flore-pleno* is a pretty native plant, known as "Bouncing Bet", reaching two feet with lance-shaped leaves clothing the stems in clusters and rose-pink flowers about one-inch or more across borne in a compact truss at the top portion of the stems, rather like *Phlox paniculata*. There is an attractive double form with pink or white flowers that is preferable to the type. There are various other forms, showing slight variation in the depth of colour and mostly with double flowers. Will grow in any well-drained soil in full sun or partial shade, and well able to fend for itself under wild garden conditions when well established. Useful for contrasting with *Scabiosa caucasica* and other perennials with light blue or lavender flowers.

Propagate by division in the spring.

The flowering season is from July to September

## Scabious: Pincushion Flower (Plate 42)

Family *DIPSACEAE*                     *Scabiosa caucasica*

The Caucasian Scabious is, as the name implies, a native of the Caucasus and is the finest of the perennial species for the flower border. The plant comprises a dense tuft of foliage, the upper portions of the leaves being cut and divided. The flowers, borne on stems up to two feet high, are three to four inches across and comprise broad ray petals of lavender-blue radiating from a cushion-like centre. The many garden varieties have superseded the type, having larger flowers that range in colour from white to lavender-blue, mauve and deep blue. *S. columbaria* is similar in all respects but colour, which is an attractive mauve-pink, and the plant lacks the robust character of the Siberian species. Well-drained medium to light loam, rich in humus, is necessary, and

olomon's Seal (*Polygonatum multiflorum*), p. 104.  2. Knotweed (*Polygonum amplexicaule*), p. 105.
Cinquefoil (*Potentilla nepalensis*), p. 105.       4. Polyanthus (*Primula variabilis*), p. 106.

it is essential to dress the ground above the roots with lime regularly in spring and autumn.

Propagate by division, cuttings or from seed.

The flowering season is from early summer until autumn.

## Squill: Bluebell (Plate 42)

Family *LILIACEAE*                                    *Scilla* species

A race of pretty bulbous plants, comprising about eighty species indigenous to the temperate regions of Europe, Asia and Africa. *S. hispanica* (syn. *S. campanulata*, *S. patula*) is the Spanish Squill, with narrow strap-shaped leaves up to an inch broad, and blue bell-shaped flowers in slender racemes on one and a half feet stems; lovely plant to associate with *Narcissus gracilis*. *S. peruviana*, the Cuban Lily, a native of Algeria, has lilac-blue star-shaped flowers in dense conical clusters, sometimes six inches across. *S. siberica*, the well-known Siberian Squill, reaches up to six inches with starry bell-shaped flowers that vary from pale to deep blue with a central line of dark blue to each segment; there is also a pure white form. *S. nutans* is the common Bluebell of English woodland and is too well known to need description. There are a number of other species, all more or less attractive. Easily grown in rich, well drained sandy soil in sun or partial shade. All are quite hardy, except *S. peruviana*, which needs some slight winter protection in severe localities. Effective for naturalizing in bold drifts in short grass.

Propagate by offsets or from seed.

The flowering season is in February or March for *S siberica*, and in May and June for the others mentioned.

## Stonecrop (Plate 43)

Family *CRASSULACEAE*                          *Sedum spectabile*

A race of succulents, mainly used in rock gardens but containing this one species from Japan that is suitable for the flower border. The leaves are rounded, fleshy, glaucous and two inches or more across. The flowers are about half an inch across, bright pink in colour and are borne in flat clustered heads, up to six inches across, on one-and-a-half-feet stems. There is a white-flowered variety not often seen, and a number of forms with deeper coloured flowers among which Brilliant, of garden origin, is the finest. One with variegated foliage is also reported. Var. *atropurpureum* has red flowers, and var. *maximum* purple foliage. This

8

plant will thrive, like most succulents, in the hottest and driest of soils as well as in shade, and the foliage alone is an attractive foil to the brighter coloured perennials. When in bloom the flowers possess some attraction that cause them to receive the constant attention of butterflies.

Propagate by offsets and from seed.

The flowering season is in late summer.

## Ragwort (Plate 43)

Family *COMPOSITAE*                    *Senecio* species

The genus *Senecio* is one of the largest, having over one thousand species scattered over the world. Few are of garden value, but two are admissible to the flower border. *S. pulcher*, from Argentina and Uruguay, is a distinctive perennial with oblong foliage, six to nine inches in length, and stems two to four feet high, with flowers comprising many reddish-purple rays around a yellow disc, with a spread of about three inches across. *S. clivorum*, botanically classed as *Ligularia clivorum*, is the better known plant in British gardens, with large round foliage up to one and a half feet across and stems up to four feet, bearing heads of orange-yellow flowers, four inches across. These are both moisture-loving plants and thrive on the banks of streams or ponds, where they develop to huge proportions and make impressive features; perfectly hardy.

Propagate by division or from seed. *S. pulcher* may be increased by root cuttings.

The flowering season is in August and September.

## Greek Mallow (Plate 43)

Family *MALVACEAE*                    *Sidalcea* species

Natives of western North America and perennials of effective use for flower gardens. The plants freely produce palmately lobed or divided leaves from which rise slender stems bearing terminal racemes of various coloured flowers. *S. candida* reaches three feet, with bluntly lobed foliage and white flowers, three-quarters of an inch across. Notable varieties are "Crimson Glow", three feet; and "Rose Queen", four to five feet, with rich rose flowers. *S. malvaeflora* reaches two to three feet, with lobed foliage and many-flowered racemes of lilac flowers, one and and quarter inches across. Of its various forms var. *atropurpurea* has purple flowers and var. *listeri* is satin-pink. There are a number of varieties of

1. Californian Tree Poppy (*Romneya coulteri*), p. 109.   2. Roscoea (*Roscoea purpurea*), p. 109.
3. Cone-flower (*Rudbeckia maxima*), p. 110.                4. Sage (*Salvia* species), p. 110.

*Pl.* 42.
1. Blood-root (*Sanguinaria canadensis*), p. 111.

2. Soap-wort (*Saponaria officinalis flor pleno*) p. 112.

3. Scabious (*Scabiosa caucasica*), p. 112.

4. Squill (*Scilla sibirica*), p. 11.

great value in the flower garden. *S. spicata*, three feet, is a late-flowering species of rosy-purple. Easily grown in any good garden soil in full sun or partial shade, but a better perennial in light soils than in heavy.

Propagate by division of the root and from seed.

The flowering season is in July and August.

## False Spikenard (Plate 43)

Family *LILIACEAE*                               *Smilacina* species

A genus of about twenty hardy perennial species of which only a few have been brought into cultivation. The plants throw up rich green foliage of parallel-veined, lily-of-the-valley-like leaves and feathery heads of white Spiraea-like flowers. The hardiest species are natives of North America, and include *S. racemosa*, the False Spikenard, which has pale green lanceolate leaves, three to six inches long, and loose sprays of fragrant white blossoms, followed by rosy-purple berries, on two-and-a-half-feet stems; *S. stellata*, the Star-flowered Lily-of-the-Valley, with similar leaves and racemes of white flowers on two-feet stems; and *S. trifolia*, which has oblong lance-shaped leaves, and simple panicles of white flowers of ten to twelve inches high. Perhaps the most striking species is *S. oleracea*, which comes from Sikkim, and bears magnificent white flower-heads from among tender green foliage, but it is somewhat slow to establish and is all too seldom seen. All these handsome plants are best managed by not being disturbed too often. They succeed best in light, deep, humus-rich soils and moist, but not wet, situations, with at least partial shade, in moist woodlands, shrubberies or borders. They are propagated by the division of the roots in mild weather between October and March.

The flowering season is May or early June.

## Golden Rod (Plate 44)

Family *COMPOSITAE*                              *Solidago* species

A genus with natives of North America and Europe that are mainstays of the late summer flower border. The plants are erect in habit with stems well clothed with leaves of oval, pointed character and heads of yellow feathery panicles, comprising many small flowers on arching stems, in effect not unlike a yellow Astilbe. The species vary considerably from the tall *S. canadensis* with its panicles borne on four- to six-feet stems to *S. brachy-stachys*, a dwarfish carpeter, six to nine inches high. *S. virgaurea*, the native Golden Rod, two to three feet, with dense terminal heads, is the origin of a number of garden varieties, notably *ballardi*, rich golden yellow; "Golden Wings", the finest of all; *nana*, a dwarf of eighteen inches; "Goldstrahl", "Mimosa" and "Sunset". *S. odora*, not generally known in gardens, has a scent similar to Anise. All may be grown easily in any good garden soil in full sun or semi-shade, and are useful as foils to the tall and dwarf blue and purple Michaelmas Daisies, *Lobelia cardinalis* and the later flowering Kniphofias.

Propagate by division and from seed.

The flowering season is in late summer.

## Lamb's Ear (Plate 44)

Family *LABIATAE*                                    *stachys* species

Known also as Betony and Woundwort, this genus is widely distributed over the temperate regions of the world, although a few are found in tropical climates. *S. coccinea*, two feet, is a scarlet-flowered species from Mexico; *S. corsica*, a minute dwarf of one inch, with cream and pink flowers, from Sardinia and Corsica. *S. officinalis*, the Betony, reaches three feet, with ovate leaves, four or five inches long, and small purple flowers, borne in a dense spike. *S. grandiflora* (syn. *Betonica grandiflora*) has violet flowers about an inch long, borne in spikes on one foot stems; it has a form var. *robusta* that reaches one and a half feet with rose flowers, and var. *superba* is an improvement on the type. *S. lanata* is the Lamb's Ear, reaching up to one foot and forming a mass of grey woolly elliptical-leafed foliage and short spikes of purple-pink flowers on woolly spikes; the most favoured for flower borders. Easily grown in any well-drained soil and particularly suitable for hot, dry soils.

Propagate by division or from seed.

The flowering season is in summer.

## Stenanthium (Plate 44)

Family *LILIACEAE*                          *Stenanthium robustum*

A noble and imposing bulbous plant found in moist situations in parts of North America. The plant attains a height of four to five feet, when well grown, with narrow leaves freely clothing the

Pl. 43.

1. Stonecrop (*Sedum spectabile*), p. 113.      2. Ragwort (*Senecio* species), p. 114.
3. Greek Mallow (*Sidalcea candida*), p. 114.      4. False Spikenard (*Smilacina racemosa*), p. 115.

1. Golden Rod (*Solidago canadensis*), p. 115.    2. Lamb's Ear (*Stachys lanata*), p. 116.
3. Stenanthium (*Stenanthium robustum*), p. 116.    4. Winter Daffodil (*Sternbergia lutea*), p. 117.

stems, each being often a foot long. The flower spike consists of a dense panicle of spreading or upright habit, bearing many small flowers of cream or greenish-white rather reminiscent of some Astilbes. *S. occidentale* is seldom seen in gardens and reaches only two feet with nodding, purplish flowers of Campanulate form. *S. angustifolium*, two to three feet, has greenish-yellow flowers. A well-drained but moist soil is necessary for this plant, and it is well to incorporate plenty of peat in order to retain moisture. A position in partial shade or in full sun is suitable. *S. robustum* also makes a most decorative pot plant.

Propagate by means of offsets or from seed.

The flowering season is in late summer.

## Winter Daffodil (Plate 44)

Family *AMARYLLIDACEAE*                    *Sternbergia lutea*

A bulbous plant, native to the Mediterranean region, Syria and Persia. It is believed to be the Lily-of-the-Field referred to in the New Testament, and has been in cultivation in Britain for more than three centuries. The tubular flowers are rather more than two inches in length, bright yellow and in shape rather like a crocus; they do not rise above the leaves, which are narrow and strap-shaped, about a foot long and half an inch wide. There are various forms, comprising var. *major*, with more substantial foliage and larger flowers, var. *sicula* with large flowers and narrow-pointed foliage and var. *angustifolia* with flowers smaller than the type and narrow leaves. Very effective when grown in bold masses in short turf and at the front of shrubberies. Easily grown in any well-drained, gritty soil. Plant three inches deep.

Propagate by means of offsets or from seed.

Flowering season is in September and October.

## Stokes' Aster (Plate 45)

Family *COMPOSITAE*                    *Stokesia cyanea*

One of the most desirable of composites from North America, and resembling a Michaelmas Daisy. The leaves are oblong and lance-shaped, up to eight inches long, with flowers somewhat between a Michaelmas Daisy and *Centaurea montana* in form and of a lovely lavender-blue colour, four inches or more across, on two-feet stems, and borne in clustered heads. Var. *superba*, introduced to Britain in 1932, is a glorification of the type and considered to be the most desirable form for gardens; it reaches three feet. There are variations in var. *alba*, with white flowers, var. *caerulea*, blue; var. *lilacina*, lilac; var. *lutea*, yellow; and var. *rosea*, pink; none of these appear to be in circulation in Britain. May be grown in rich, well-drained soil in a warm sunny position. It is also an excellent pot plant.

Propagate by division or from seed.

The flowering season is in late September and October.

## Germander (Plate 45)

Family *LABIATAE*                              *Teucrium* species

A genus of hardy herbaceous species and a tender shrub, widely scattered over the warm and temperate regions of the earth. *T. chaemaedrys* is a dwarf perennial of Europe, with ovate, toothed leaves, three-quarters of an inch long, and flowers three-quarters of an inch long, of purple or rose, spotted red or white in loose whorls on twelve-inch spikes. *T. flavum* is herbaceous, reaches two feet, with thick, ovate and hairy leaves and yellow flowers in irregular leafy spikes. *T. scorodonia* is one foot high, also with yellow flowers, one-third of an inch long in five-inch racemes. There are a number of others, not of outstanding merit, but like those named useful for planting in difficult positions where draughts and lack of sunlight make it impossible to grow much of anything else. Any ordinary well-drained garden soil will grow them quite easily.

Propagate by cuttings, in the case of shrubby kinds, and by division or from seed where the habit is herbaceous.

The flowering season is in summer.

## Meadow Rue (Plate 45)

Family *RANUNCULACEAE*                         *Thalictrum* species

A race of fine foliaged herbaceous plants, native to northern temperate regions and eminently suitable for flower borders. *T. minus adiantifolium* is attractive mainly for its foliage that resembles a miniature Maidenhair Fern up to one foot, the greenish-white flowers being insignificant from the point of view of garden effect. *T. majus adiantifolium* is similar but grows to four feet. *T. aquilegiaefolium* reaches three feet, with larger foliage similar to that of the Aquilegia, and flowers borne in elegant heads where the purple or pink stamens are numerous and conspicuous, giving an attractive fluffy appearance; there are various improved garden forms. *T. chelidoni*, Himalayas, six inches, is dwarf, with branched stems bearing large purple flowers. *T. delavayi*, China, reaches three feet, with lilac-purple sepals. *T. dipterocarpum*, often held to be a form of *T. delavayi*, is a gem with slender branching stems up to five feet or more, bearing flowers, about a quarter of an inch across, comprising violet sepals centred with yellow filaments. In cultivation *T. dipterocarpum* is confused with *T. delavayi*. Hewitt's double is an attractive double form of more vigorous growth. *T. flavum* is a vigorous species with many pale yellow-stamened flowers borne on branching four-feet stems. Easily grown in any good garden soil that is well drained, rich in humus and in full sun or partial shade.

Propagate by division or from seed.

The flowering season is from June to August.

## Thermopsis (Plate 45)

Family *LEGUMINOSAE*                    *Thermopsis montana*

Of the eighteen species found in North America and in Asia this is the most common in gardens. In general habit this may easily be mistaken for some species of Lupin. The leaves are three-parted, spreading and resemble those of the Lupin, and the flower-stems reach two feet, bearing pea-shaped flowers of bright yellow in terminal racemes. Other species are *T. caroliniana*, four to five feet, with golden yellow flowers, and *T. fabacea*, two to three feet, a native of Siberia, with yellow flowers. These plants will grow in any well-drained soil in full sun or partial shade. Being deep-rooted, they can endure long periods of drought better than most herbaceous perennials. Useful for planting in the flower border or naturalizing in bold drifts in the wild garden or in association with flowering shrubs where they are particularly effective when used as foils to blue-flowered genera.

Propagate by means of seed.

The flowering season is in June and July.

## Thyme (Plate 46)

Family *LABIATAE*                    *Thymus* species

A genus of over a hundred species, mostly native to temperate regions, particularly of the Mediterranean. Of the dwarf creeping species, *T. serpyllum*, six inches, with its small, green ovate foliage, about half an inch long, and purple flowers, a quarter of an inch long, is one of the best known. It has various forms, viz.

var. *albus*, white; var. *argenteus*, silver variegated foliage; var. *aureus*, yellow variegated foliage; var. *cinereus*, lilac flowers; var. *coccineus*, crimson flowers and of taller habit than type; var. *lanuginosus*, greyish-green pubescent foliage; and a number of others, including some of garden origin: all have aromatic foliage. The Lemon-scented Thyme (*T. citriodorus*), six to nine inches, with small leaves, lemon-scented, and pink flowers, has silver variegated and golden variegated varieties. The Thymes are easily grown in any well-drained soil, in the crevices between paving-stones and particularly effective when used as carpeters for early spring-flowering bulbous subjects.

Propagate by division, layering, cuttings or from seed.

The flowering season is from June to September.

## Foam-flower  (Plate 46)

Family *SAXIFRAGACEAE*                    *Tiarella cordifolia*

The best of this North American and Asiatic genus for gardens. The leaves are heart-shaped, lobed and toothed, being about four inches across. The flowers are a quarter of an inch across, white to rose in colour and borne in a simple raceme of twelve inches, rather like a Heuchera in form and of a light and feathery character. In autumn the foliage assumes attractive and brilliant ruddy tints that give to the plant its greatest feature. It has a number of forms such as var. *purpurea*, with purple flowers; var. *major*, rosy-salmon to ruby flowers; var. *marmorata*, maroon flowers and bronze to purplish-green foliage attractively marbled with purple. *T. polyphylla*, eighteen inches, is a white-flowering species from the Himalayas, and *T. unifoliata*, two feet, from North America, has creamy-white flowers. Delightful plants for shaded positions where their attractively coloured autumn foliage may be seen to advantage with the lighter green and glaucous foliage of other plants. May be naturalized in the wild garden in leafy soil.

Propagate by division, side growths and from seed.

The flowering season is in June and July.

## Tiger-flower: Tiger Iris  (Plate 46)

Family *IRIDACEAE*                         *Tigridia pavonia*

A half-hardy bulbous plant from Mexico, renowned for the brilliancy of its flowers. The stems are forked and leafy, rising one to two feet, the plaited leaves being from nine to fifteen inches long. The flowers consist of three outer segments and three short inner ones with a violet base, changing to scarlet at the tips of the outer segments; it is the central zone of yellow blotched with purple that gives the flower its name. There are many beautiful and richly coloured forms, including var. *alba*, white with purple spotted centre; var. *aurea*, yellow with mottled centre; var. *conchiflora*, yellow with purple blotched centre; var. *grandiflora*, a large-flowered form of the type; and a number of others, all more or less colourful and desirable. The individual flowers last only a day, but are followed by others. May be grown in full sun, in well-drained rich soil. Plant in late March, five inches deep, and, if necessary, protect from late frosts by a light covering of bracken or broom branches. Lift as soon as the foliage ripens in late summer, ripen the bulbs and store away from frost during autumn and winter. Requires the same treatment as for Gladioli, and ample moisture during growth.

Propagate by means of offsets or from seed.

The flowering season is in summer.

## Pick-a-back Plant (Plate 46)

Family *SAXIFRAGACEAE* *Tolmiea menziesii*

The only known species of the genus and found in the forests of California. Rather reminiscent of a Tiarella in general character with lobed and toothed leaves, rising from a scaly rhizome and about three and a half inches across. The flowers are about a quarter of an inch long and are borne in long racemes to a height of one to two feet. The colour of the flowers is green and a pleasing contrast to more gaudy colours. For successful cultivation a cool and shaded spot is necessary, and it may be grown under the shelter of some evergreen where it is shaded from the sun, or in sparse woodland where the leafy nature of the soil suits it admirably. Plant in early autumn or in spring.

Propagation is effected by adventitious buds that are produced at the tips of the petioles, or by root division in early spring.

The flowering season is in April.

## Spider-wort (Plate 47)

Family *COMMELINACEAE* *Tradescantia virginiana*

A genus containing both hardy and tender species, *T. virginiana* being the most favoured for gardens and a native of North America. It was named for John Tradescant, gardener to

Charles I. The leaves are produced freely and are narrow and arching, forming a generous tuft from which the leaf-clad flower-stems rise to a height of one to two feet, carrying umbels of several flowers, one to two inches across, and of an attractive violet-blue colour that varies in depth. There are various forms, such as var. *alba*, white; var. *atrosanguinea*, dark red; var. *caerulea plena*, double-flowered violet-blue; var. *coccinea*, bright red; var. *violacea*, purple-blue to violet. There are also a number of worthy garden forms of which "J. C. Weguelin", of clear lavender-blue, and "Leonora" of rich violet-blue, are first class. A most accommodating plant in cultivation, thriving under dry as well as wet conditions and in sun or shade.

Propagate by division or from seed.

The flowering season is from June until autumn.

## Toad Lily (Plate 47)

Family *LILIACEAE*           *Tricyrtis* species

A genus comprising about nine species, native to Japan, some of which are suitable for the flower garden. *T. hirta* is the most usually seen with stems of two to three feet, covered with soft white down, the leaves being alternate, broad at the base and tapering and clasping the stems. The flowers appear up to fifteen on each stem and are borne in the leaf axils, about one inch long and white spotted with purple. Its form var. *nigra* has black spots, and there is also a variegated form with leaves edged white. *T. macropoda* reaches three feet, with oblong leaves and has pale purple spotted blackish-purple flowers in a loose corymb. *T. pilosa* is taller and will attain four feet, with white flowers marked with large purple spots. The yellow, unspotted *T. flava* with yellow flowers does not appear to be known in Europe. Will thrive in a leafy soil or where there is peat and a position in partial shade. Unsuitable for chalk or clay soils.

Propagate by division or from seed.

The flowering season is from June to August.

## Wood Lily (Plate 47)

Family *LILIACEAE*           *Trillium* species

Natives of the woodlands of North America and among the most charming of plants. The plants comprise a thick, short rootstock with stems bearing three broad leaves in whorled formation at the top of the stems above which appear singly three-petalled flowers of varying colour according to the species. *T. grandiflorum*, Wake Robin, is the best known with three-inch flowers of white, changing to rosy-purple with age, on one- to one-and-a-half-feet stems. *T. undulatum* (syn. *T. erythrocarpum*) has white flowers veined purple, up to one a half inches across. *T. sessile* reaches only one foot, with two-inch flowers of purple and green, curiously attractive, and has two forms, viz. var. *album*, white; var. *rubrum*, with reddish-purple flowers. To grow these plants satisfactorily they must be given a position in woodland where there is a good depth of black leaf soil for the roots to delve into and ample shade from the hot rays of the sun. Deep planting is essential. Unsuitable for the flower border, where the hot sun will scorch the roots and cause irretrievable damage. Excellent among low ferns.

Propagate by seed.

The flowering season is in May.

## Triptilion (Plate 47)

Family *COMPOSITAE*                              *Triptilion spinosum*

A plant that was at one time grown in Britain, practically lost to cultivation, and reintroduced recently from seed sent from Chile. The leaves are hairy and of fine lance-shaped formation, up to an inch in length and clothing the whole of the stem, which rises to two feet. The flowers are small, five-petalled and of a rich, deep blue, borne in a close corymb. It has tuberous roots and requires a warm sandy soil rich in leafmould. Its hardiness is questionable except in mild localities, and until it has been cultivated more widely its general reaction to the climate of Britain cannot be stated.

Propagation has been from seed, but can probably be effected by division of the rhizome.

The flowering season is in July.

## Globe-flower (Plate 48)

Family *RANUNCULACEAE*                            *Trollius* species

Natives of the north temperate zone, where they inhabit moist or swampy places. The roots are thick and fibrous and the leaves are palmately lobed or divided. The stems are leafy, of variable stature, according to species, and bear up to fifteen sepals with numerous stamens in the centre. *T. europaeus* reaches one and a half to two feet, with lemon-yellow flowers, two inches across.

*T. asiaticus* is of similar height with orange flowers. These two have been used to produce the many fine varieties of garden origin noted for their large, full flowers of rich and varied colouring, often with effectively contrasting centres. *T. excelsior*, two feet, has large flowers of deep orange. *T. ledebouri*, from Siberia, reaches two feet, with orange flowers, and blooms after the other species. Easily grown in any deep, moist, loamy soil in partially shaded borders or by ponds or streams and a position where there is shade or moderate exposure to the sun. Excellent plants for waterside.

Propagate by division or from seed.

The flowering season is in May and June for *T. europaeus* and *T. asiaticus*, and later for *T. ledebouri*.

## Nasturtium (Plate 48)

Family *GERANIACEAE*                                    *Tropaeolum* species

A genus comprising both annual and perennial species, native to Mexico and Chile. *T. speciosum* is an attractive twining plant, up to ten feet, with leaves divided into six, and flowers, one and a half inches long, of brilliant vermilion, produced freely along the stems; one of the most attractive of all climbing plants. *T. tuberosum* is also a climber with tuberous roots, five-lobed leaves, and flowers, three-quarters of an inch long, with yellow petals and red spur; used as an article of diet in South America. *T. polyphyllum* is of climbing or trailing habit, with leaves deeply divided into about eight narrow segments; the flowers are red and yellow. There is also an orange-flowered form in var. *leichtlinii*. *T. speciosum* needs to be planted on the northern side of an evergreen hedge, such as holly, so that it enjoys a cool root run, and its growths may penetrate to the sunny side, where they will drape the evergreen foliage effectively with their brilliant flowers. The other species should be planted deeply in sandy soil in April so as to be beyond the reach of frost, and they may be lifted and stored in boxes of sand during late autumn and winter. A well-drained soil rich in humus is necessary.

Propagate by careful division of the tuberous roots or from seed.

The flowering season is from June to October.

## Tulip (Plate 48)

Family *LILIACEAE*                                         *Tulipa* species

An invaluable genus of bulbous plants, native to Europe, North Africa and many parts of Asia. The leaves are broad to narrow

45.
1. Stokes' Aster (*Stokesia cyanea*), p. 117.    2. Germander (*Teucrium chaemaedrys*), p. 118.
3. Meadow Rue (*Thalictrum dipterocarpum*), p. 118.    4. Thermopsis (*Thermopsis montana*), p. 119.

*Pl.* 46.

1. Thyme (*Thymus serpyllum*), p. 119.
3. Tiger-flower (*Tigridia pavonia*), p. 120.

2. Foam-flower (*Tiarella cordifolia*), p. 12
4. Pick-a-back Plant (*Tolmiea menziesii*), p. 12

and lanceolate, the stems mostly simple and the flowers from goblet to saucer shape. *T. gesneriana*, South Russia and Asia Minor, grows one to two feet, with black-purpled centred scarlet, white or yellow flowers, and is a parent of the florist's Tulips classed as Breeders or Selfs, Feathered, Flamed, Bizarres, Byblomens, and Roses, and the garden varieties Darwins, Rembrandts, Cottage and Parrot, in the almost infinite range of colours and shapes the many varieties now present. *T. suaveolens*, a fragrant, scarlet and orange, six-inch Tulip from the Crimea, is parent to some of the early flowering varieties. What are generally termed the Species Tulips are the wild Tulips from abroad. Outstanding kinds are *T. chrysantha*, from Persia, twelve inches, with sharply pointed golden yellow flowers; *T. clusiana*, Sicily, fifteen inches, clear white flowers; *T. eichleri*, Asia Minor, with wide grey-green leaves and large pointed scarlet buds with silvery-grey stripes on the outer petals; *T. kaufmanniana*, the Water Lily Tulip from Central Asia, twelve inches, with creamy-white flowers, striped rose on the back, and of which there are several distinguished varieties; *T. dasystemon*, Turkestan, three to six inches, with yellow, white and green flowers; and *T. praestans*, a branching Tulip of Algeria, twelve inches, with light scarlet flowers. Plant in November in well-drained sandy loam, with bone meal, in full sun.

Propagate by offsets or from seeds.

The flowering season is from March to May.

## Scarborough Lily (Plate 48)

Family *AMARYLLIDACEAE Vallota speciosa* (syn. *purpurea*)

A bulbous rooted plant from South Africa and possessed of considerable charm. It is considered to be a sub-genus of *Cyrtanthus*. The leaves are strap-shaped, bright green in colour, up to two feet in length and appear with the flowers. The flowers are funnel-shaped, about two and a half inches across the mouth, scarlet in colour, and up to nine are borne on a hollow, fleshy scape, two or three feet high. There is a white form and one, known as var. *major*, with flowers three inches or more across. Var. *minor* is smaller in every way than the type; var. *eximea* is quite distinct with four-inch flowers and white feathering at the base of the perianth segments. The best form is var. *magnifica*, with exceptionally brilliant flowers, fully five inches across and each centred with a white eye. May be grown out-of-doors in favoured climates in a light soil at the base of a south wall.

Although in parts of the western counties Vallota may come through the winter without harm, it is usually safest to lift and store under glass during the winter months.

Propagate by means of offsets.

The flowering season is in summer.

## False Hellebore (Plate 49)

Family *LILIACEAE*                          *Veratrum* species

A genus of about eighteen species in Europe, North America and Asia, four being particularly attractive for the flower garden. The best known is *V. nigrum*, with broad, ribbed foliage about a foot long and six inches across at the widest part; the flowers are maroon, bell-shaped and borne in a drooping panicle on four- to five-feet stems. *V. album*, the White False Hellebore, can attain three to four feet, with large plaited leaves, a foot long, and white flowers, suffused green, borne in dense panicles. *V. californicum* is up to six feet high, with branching panicles of greenish-white flowers. *V. viride* can reach up to six feet, with flowers of yellowish green. Best planted in a partially shaded position in a rich and well-drained soil that has been enriched with old manure. Grand plants for the semi-wild garden or the flower border, when they lend an air of novelty.

Propagate by means of division or from seed.

The flowering season is in June and July.

## Mullein (Plate 49)

Family *SCROPHULARIACEAE*                  *Verbascum* species

A genus of numerous species from Europe and the Mediterranean region. There are many that are useful for the flower garden, the following being the most usually cultivated. *V. nigrum* (syn. *V. vernale*), Britain, has long, broad leaves of felt-like texture, greyish-green in colour and well over a foot long. The stem attains three to four feet, and the upper portion consists of a number of ascending branches bearing closely together small yellow flowers, each with a purple centre. *V. chaixii*, the Nettle-leaved Mullein, has foliage six inches long, green covered with white tomentum; the flowers are yellow, with purple stamens and borne in racemes, three feet tall. There is a white form. *V. longifolium* has huge leaves, two feet long, attains four feet, and bears bright yellow flowers, an inch across, in a dense raceme. Var. *pannosum* has more woolly foliage and a larger raceme. Its

1. Spider-wort (*Tradescantia virginiana*), p. 121.    2. Toad Lily (*Tricyrtis hirta*), p. 122.
3. Wood Lily (*Trillium grandiflorum*), p. 122.    4. Triptilion (*Triptilion spinosum*), p. 123.

*Pl.* 48.
1. Globe-flower (*Trollius europaeus*), p. 123.    2. Nasturtium (*Tropaeolum speciosum*), p. 124
3. Tulip (*Tulipa kaufmanniana*), p. 124.    4. Scarborough Lily (*Vallota speciosa*), p. 125

form var. *magnificum* can reach up to seven or more feet, and is the most majestic of the Mulleins. The Common Mullein (*V. thapsiforme*) reaches five feet, with greyish-yellow woolly leaves, a foot long and one-inch yellow flowers borne in dense spikes. *V. wiedemannianum* can attain three feet, with woolly leaves, five inches long, and flowers, one and a quarter inches across, of indigo or purplish-lilac, borne in spikes. There are many beautiful garden hybrids such as "Miss Willmott", white; "Cotswold Queen", pink; *Olympicum*, yellow. Easily grown in good, well-drained soil where lime is present and with a position in full sun.

Propagate by root cuttings or from seed.

The flowering season is in June and July.

## Vervain (Plate 49)

Family *VERBENACEAE*                       *Verbena* species

A race of annual and perennial herbs, native mostly to America. *V. bonariensis*, of South American origin, reaches four feet, with long, narrow, toothed leaves, branching stems and deep lilac flowers borne closely in clusters, one and a half inches across. *V. rigida* (syn. *V. venosa*) is of dwarf habit, being at the most two feet and more often less than one and a half feet, low branching, with purple flowers in dense spikes up to three inches long. There is a white form and one with lilac flowers under var. *lilacina*. Verbenas may be grown easily in any well-drained soil that has a reasonable humus content and a position in full sun is necessary. They are hardy only in the most favoured localities, and elsewhere they must be lifted and stored during winter, and freshly propagated stock planted out when all risk of frost has passed. They are excellent alike for the flower garden and for cutting.

Propagation is effected by placing the roots in boxes of sandy compost in winter and taking cuttings of the young shoots that appear in spring. May also be raised from seed.

The flowering season is in summer.

## Speedwell: Bird's Eye (Plate 49)

Family *SCROPHULARIACEAE*                   *Veronica* species

An important genus of annual, perennial and shrubby species from Europe, America and New Zealand. Of the perennial types, eminently suitable for the flower garden, there are several attractive species and a number of varieties of garden origin.

*V. longifolia* (syn. *V. maritima*, *V. excelsa*) reaches one and a half to two feet, with lance-shaped leaves, four inches long and toothed; the flowers are small, lilac in colour and borne in a dense raceme. There is a white form and also var. *hendersoniana*, a deep blue-flowered dwarf, var. *subsessilis*, large deep-blue flowers, and var. *rosea*, pink. *V. spicata* reaches one to one and a half feet, with lance-shaped leaves, two inches long; the flowers are small, mostly blue and borne in lengthy dense racemes. Of its forms the following are important: var. *corymbosa*, pale blue on foot stems; var. *nana*, rather shorter with blue flowers; var. *rosea*, pink; var. *erica*, somewhat like pink heather; var. *rubra*, reddish-purple. *V. virginica* reaches six feet, with whorled lance-shaped leaves, six inches long and toothed, with nine-inch racemes of white or blue flowers; there is also a white form. *V. gentianoides* (syn. *V. glabra*) reaches eight to twelve inches, with pointed, oblong leaves and a long, loose raceme of dark veined pale blue flowers. Easily grown in any well-drained garden soil in full sun, or semi-shade.

Propagate by division or from seed.

The flowering season is in spring and summer.

## Periwinkle  (Plate 50)

Family *APOCYNACEAE*                                    *Vinca* species

A genus of perennial trailing plants, native to Europe and containing two species: both forms are useful for the flower garden. *V. major*, the large Periwinkle, is evergreen with leaves of a bright glossy green and heart-shaped; the five-lobed flowers, up to two inches across, are blue. There is a form with variegated foliage. *V. minor*, the lesser Periwinkle, sometimes known as Running Myrtle, is also evergreen with oblong foliage and flowers of lilac-blue, up to three-quarters of an inch across. "Bowles" variety is a form with freely produced large deep-blue flowers. There are a number of forms with variation in the colour of the flowers and some with variegated foliage. *V. herbacea* has bluish-purple flowers, an inch across, and of a less rampant habit than the two mentioned. Except the last named, which is suited for furnishing the front of the border, especially where there is a stone edging, the Periwinkles are best for providing an evergreen covering to shaded banks and the base of trees in woodland. Easily grown in any moist, well-drained soil in sun or shade.

Propagate by cuttings or from seed, or division.

The flowering season is in spring and early summer.

1. False Hellebore (*Veratrum nigrum*), p. 126.
3. Vervain (*Verbena* species), p. 127.

2. Mullein (*Verbascum nigrum*), p. 126.
4. Speedwell (*Veronica spicata*), p. 127.

*Pl.* 50.
1. Periwinkle (*Vinca major*), p. 128.  2. Pansy (*Viola cornuta*), p.
3. Bugle Lily (*Watsonia beatricis*), p. 129.  4. Californian Fuschia (*Zauschneria californica*), p.

## Pansy (Plate 50)

Family *VIOLACEAE* *Viola* species

A race of dainty and elegant herbaceous perennials that inhabit the northern and southern temperate regions of the Old and New Worlds. *V. cornuta*, the Horned Violet, has rounded foliage, toothed and of tufted habit; the flowers, two inches or less at the widest part, are violet and have a curled horn at the back of each flower. Its forms show a great variation in colour from white to yellow and purple, and it is believed that this species was used extensively by raisers when evolving the brilliantly coloured bedding Tufted Pansies or Violas. *V. gracilis* reaches about nine inches, with violet flowers. *V. pedata*, the Bird's Foot Violet, has flowers with two upper petals of deep violet and three lower ones of lilac; there is a white form. *V. odorata* is the favourite sweet-scented Violet with its many beautiful garden forms of varying shades of colour and with double and single flowers. A position in partial shade is preferable and in soil that has been enriched with a liberal quantity of leafmould or old manure, moisture with good drainage being essential to their well-being.

Propagate by means of cuttings or from seed.

The flowering season is in spring and summer.

## Bugle Lily (Plate 50)

Family *IRIDACEAE* *Watsonia* various species

A race of bulbous plants of brilliant and rich colouring from South Africa. The foliage is sword-like, similar to that of the Montbretia, and the flowers are borne in an elegant raceme, each being trumpet-shaped and varying in size. *Ardernei* reaches four feet, with lovely pure white flowers up to three inches long. *W. meriana* is three to four feet high, with bright pink flowers two inches long, each spike carrying from twelve to twenty flowers. Its var. *beatricis* is the most desirable species for garden cultivation, having three-feet stems bearing a many-flowered spike of two-inch apricot-red flowers. *W. angusta*, three to four feet, has scarlet flowers. *W. coccinea*, also scarlet-flowering, is a dwarf of twelve inches. *W. densiflora*, another twelve-inch dwarf, has rosy-red flowers. *W. rosea* (syn. *Gladiolus pyramidatus*), with rose flowers, grows three to six feet high. Given the same treatment as that required by the Gladioli, these Watsonias may be cultivated quite successfully in the flower border, provided

9

they are planted in well-drained soil that is rich in humus and fully exposed to the sun. The corms should be planted in early April and lifted in the autumn and stored where they will not be harmed by frost.

Propagate by means of offsets or from seed.

The flowering season is in summer.

## Californian Fuschia (Plate 50)

Family *ONAGRACEAE*                    *Zauschneria californica*

The most suitable species of this genus for outdoor cultivation in Britain and one of the most brilliant in flower of all perennials. A native of California, this plant is of semi-recumbent habit, reaching as high as one foot, with hairy, lance-shaped leaves, about one and a quarter inches long, with brilliant scarlet tubular flowers, two inches long, that are said to resemble Fuchsias. The form var. *splendens* is more floriferous and has flowers of larger size. Var. *microphylla* has more pleasing, narrow leaves, and var. *mexicana* is a brightly coloured kind. Plant in well-drained sandy soil, preferably in an elevated position where the growths may trail downwards. Full exposure to the sun is essential and a position where there is protection from cold winds is to be preferred. Where severe winters are the rule, it is well to cover the plant with a little bracken as a protection from frost.

Propagation is by division, cuttings or from seed.

The flowering season is in August and September.

# SECTION II
## ANNUALS and BIENNIALS
### CULTIVATION AND PROPAGATION

In this section the terms Annual and Biennial have been used in their widest sense. They have been extended to include certain subjects that, although actually perennial in their native habitat, are treated in British gardens as either annuals or biennials. Therefore the various plants described and illustrated in the following pages fall naturally into the following categories:

> Hardy Annuals.
> Hardy Biennials.
> Half-Hardy Annuals.
> Half-Hardy Perennials, treated as Annuals and/or Biennials.
> Hardy Perennials, treated as Annuals and/or Biennials.

In each instance only those that are suitable for flowering out-of-doors in Britain have been included. The selection given includes the most popular and serviceable plants, and it could have been extended considerably to include a number of less important subjects which the author, with all due deference to those who hold a contrary opinion, considers to be inferior.

#### HARDY ANNUALS

A hardy annual may be described as a plant that is raised from seed, and which matures and dies in the same year. The seed may be sown where the plants are to flower, and the seedlings thinned to appropriate distances as soon as the second pair of natural leaves appear. The time for sowing is usually in late March or early April when the sun, gaining greater strength, has warmed the soil. The seed may also be sown under glass in early February and the seedlings pricked off into boxes or pots and planted out-of-doors in May. By this method the plants will bloom a little earlier than those sown out-of-doors, but it is questionable whether the additional labour involved is worth while. Also there are certain subjects that do not transplant satisfactorily, as in the case of Larkspur, making it necessary for the first method to be employed.

Hardy annuals have few rivals in the floral world in providing a brave display of colour for a modest outlay. For a small sum it is possible to obtain a very wide and comprehensive collection that will make the garden gay from midsummer onwards. Certain plants are so prodigal in the production of seed that they scatter it as soon as ripe, and self-sown seedlings will appear in the next spring. Of such a nature is the Calendula.

Usually the seed should have been harvested from the previous season's crop, as with age germination is retarded and old seed will often prove erratic and disappointing. The ease with which young seed germinates can give a false impression regarding the plants' requirements and disappointment can occur from treating the preparation of the soil in a too casual manner. Like most plants, annuals give results according to the cultivation they receive. The soil should be prepared by deep digging and the incorporation in the top six inches of soil of a moderate amount of well-decayed farm-yard manure or granulated peat mixed with fishmeal or guano at the rate of a six-inch potful to each barrow-load of well-moistened peat. This preparation should be completed sufficiently in advance of sowing the seed to allow the soil to become reconsolidated. Seeds must never be sown immediately after digging as they may be lost as the soil settles again.

Site is important. Most annuals are sun worshippers and like a position in full sun. Where there is exposure to a strong prevailing wind the taller annuals will require some form of protection, a lattice fence, a hedge or a shrub plantation to form a wind-break.

When the seed is sown in March or early April a calm day should be chosen when there is no breeze to carry the seeds to a spot for which they were not intended. Some gardeners have a gift for distributing seed very evenly over a given area, but such skill is rather the exception than the rule, and some other method has usually to be employed by the amateur. It is a good plan to mix fine seed thoroughly with about eight times its bulk of fine sand and broadcast the whole mixture over the area to be sown. This will assist in even distribution and minimize the thinning of seedlings.

Seed sown under glass, not necessarily in heat, requires rather more care and attention. Seed-boxes, two and a half inches deep, of the standard size, or shallow pans are very suitable for the purpose. Too much emphasis cannot be laid on the importance of perfect cleanliness. Probably the finest compost for seeds is the standard John Innes formula, viz. 2 parts by bulk of sifted, good, friable loam, 1 part horticultural peat, and 1 part sharp clean sand, plus 1½ oz. superphosphate (16 per cent phosphoric acid) and ¾ oz. ground chalk or ground limestone per bushel of compost. The whole must be well mixed together, and it will be an advantage if the loam only can be sterilized before use. Sterilization of the soil ensures the best results from the seed, for it destroys all harmful bacteria, fungi, pests and other harmful organisms. This treatment will also destroy weed seeds which can prove a source of annoyance when they germinate at the same time as the annuals.

Sterilization of the soil may be done quite easily without purchasing any special apparatus. The material required is a metal container to hold water. A large saucepan is very suitable. A smaller metal container that will fit into the saucepan allowing a margin of about two inches at the side is needed, and some means of heating, a gas stove or jet being the most serviceable. The saucepan is half filled with water, which is brought to boiling-point. Into this is placed the smaller container, filled with soil, taking care that the water from the saucepan does not enter it. When the soil is heated through to 180° to 200° F. it should be kept at this temperature for 20 to 30 minutes, and then emptied on a clean surface to cool rapidly, before using for making up the compost. This should be kept in a clean place where it will not be exposed to contamination. This method will result in greater vigour in the seedlings, which should be pricked off as soon as the second pair of true leaves appear, allowing a distance of one inch between. Care in watering is necessary, and it is wiser to under-water than to over-water and risk loss from damping-off. As soon as they have become well established, the seedlings may be transferred to a cold frame and gradually hardened off. From the earliest stage it is wise to give air on every occasion the weather permits to promote sturdy growth, and the seedlings need to be near the light to avoid the development of weakly and drawn specimens. The seedlings may be planted out-of-doors in late April or early May in the positions where they are to flower.

There is a third method of growing hardy annuals. The seed may be sown in the open in late summer or early autumn with the advantage of obtaining earlier flowers of greater vigour and more floriferous habit in the following season. The risk of loss from the attacks of pests such as slugs and snails is greater, but if one of the reliable molluscides now available is used little anxiety need be felt.

It is very important to select the best time for sowing. The farther north, the earlier one must sow. Also where the soil is only of moderate fertility it will be quite safe to sow in early September, or even earlier. Where, however, the soil is rich, sowing should not be attempted before mid-October. If sown earlier the richness of the soil may cause the seedlings to make soft and sappy growth that will suffer irreparable damage during a severe winter. Too much emphasis cannot be laid on the importance of sowing the seed thinly so that the seedlings need not be transplanted before the following spring, when they can be removed to their flowering positions; it is not desirable to transplant at a period just prior to winter. Should the seedlings be too close it is better to thin out than to transplant at that season.

Throughout the whole of their growth it is important to remove all weeds as they appear so that the seedlings may have the best possible chance. It will be necessary to provide some support for the taller annuals. For those of a bushy habit, short, twiggy peasticks are the most serviceable. For those of tall and slender growth, thin bamboo canes, painted green, are suitable. These may be split if too thick.

## HARDY BIENNIALS

Biennials differ from annuals inasmuch as they mature and die in the year following the sowing of the seed. In general practice the seed should be sown as described for autumn-sown annuals, although where it is possible the seed may be sown earlier, even in June, to produce strong plants for planting out in their permanent positions by late summer or early autumn. The Wallflower, probably the most popular of all biennials, provides a good example of a plant where such early sowing is imperative if plants, sufficiently large and vigorous to provide a first-class display, are to be produced for early autumn planting.

The same precepts as those given for the general cultivation of annuals apply in the main to biennials.

## HALF-HARDY ANNUALS

These are plants, mostly from tropical or warm regions, that are unable to withstand frost, and it is not possible to plant the seedlings out-of-doors until early June. They are raised from seed sown under glass in February and treated generally as recommended for hardy annuals raised under glass at the same time. When selecting a position out-of-doors full sun is desirable, and a position with a southern aspect is distinctly advantageous, unless the plant in question is shade loving.

Certain plants, such as the Zinnia, are best grown on in pots in their seedling stage, and it is only in summers where there are long periods of sunshine that they can be relied upon to give a good account of themselves out-of-doors.

### HALF-HARDY PERENNIALS BEST TREATED AS ANNUALS

There are a number of perennials that are native to tropical regions which will bloom well in Britain if the summer is favourable. They will not, however, withstand our winters out-of-doors, and so are given the cultivation recommended for half-hardy annuals. A number may be propagated by means of cuttings as well as from seed.

### HARDY PERENNIALS BEST TREATED AS ANNUALS OR BIENNIALS

In this category are those plants that are in reality of perennial habit but are rarely satisfactory after the first flowering season. Familiar examples are the Hollyhock and Foxglove, both of which lend themselves admirably to treatment as biennials sown as soon as seed is available to produce good plants to flower in the following year. Lobelias and Antirrhinums figure largely in summer bedding schemes and for this purpose are sown under glass in February, the seedlings being pricked off into boxes and, after hardening off in a cold frame, planted out in May where they are to flower. Antirrhinums can, in fact, be propagated by means of cuttings of half-ripened shoots taken in summer, rooted in a sandy compost, wintered in a cold frame and planted out in May. This practice does not appear to enjoy the favour it did some years ago, but it serves to provide an example of another method of raising stock.

In all instances it is sheer waste of time and energy to purchase inferior strains of seed. There is so little difference between the cost of superior and inferior strains that the best is always the cheapest, and the additional cost will be more than repaid by the finer display. The Royal Horticultural Society holds periodical trials of various annuals, biennials and other plants, and it will be found to be well worth while to study the results of these trials and use them as a guide to the best varieties and strains of seed

## PLANTING FOR EFFECT

By a study of the habits of growth, height, colour and season of flowering, it is not a difficult matter to plan a border comprising the various groups of plants described to provide what may well be the most colourful feature in a garden. Most annuals bloom for a longer period than most of the hardy herbaceous perennials so that there is not the necessity to provide for the filling of gaps that follow the flowering season. There are a number of annuals that may, in fact, be used to advantage in the herbaceous perennial border to serve the double purpose of providing a pleasing mass of colour for a lengthy period and to fill a gap left by some early flowering subject. Such a system may not meet with the approval of the orthodox gardener, but it is, nevertheless, permissible on the score of garden effect.

For the front of the herbaceous perennial border most of the dwarf annuals are admirable, as are the taller ones for mid-border positions. Towards the back, Sweet Peas grown in upright columns supported by peasticks are always pleasing and Hollyhocks are essential for late summer effect, giving that height to the border in the same way as the Delphinium in June. The Shirley strain of Foxgloves is far removed from the common plant of the hedgerow. With bright and rich colours and effectively spotted throats, it provides good subjects for bold effect outdoors as well as being most useful for interior decoration. There are few finer plants than white Foxgloves for brightening woodland shadows. *Ionopsidium acaule* is the ideal hardy annual for adorning the crevices between paving-stones, to which the miniature plants provide a most effective ribbon edging. As summer wanes, there is no plant more fit for the mixed flower border than Honesty, with its silvery pods that find their autumnal foil in the orange-red bladders of Physalis.

The mere suggestion that annuals and biennials may be used for furnishing a rock garden will probably cause the purist to raise his hands in horror at the thought that anything not of a perennial nature should be permitted to invade the sanctum sanctorum of alpine genera. Yet for those who are more concerned with a show of colour rather than following an arbitrary etiquette, there are a number of dwarf plants suitable for this purpose. Annual Sedums and Mesembryanthemums may be used without question, and Meconopsis in the lower portions where there is a good leafy soil. Other plants may well include suitable forms of *Anoda, Adonis, Alyssum, Amellus, Arctotis, Baeria, Crepis, Felicia,*

*Gilia, Iberis, Linaria, Phacelia, Silene,* and suchlike. Such plants have the inestimable value of giving a long season of display, a virtue that will appeal to the vast majority of gardeners, whether it is approved by the purist or not. It is very important to sow thinly and it is better to transplant seedlings at suitable distances apart in order to provide a display in keeping with a herbaceous border where the habit of a plant is not of equal importance to its blossoms.

There is hardly a part of the garden where annuals and biennials may not be used with pleasing effect. The old-world charm of the Wallflower, whose fragrance breathes the indescribable charm of the English cottage garden in all its simple beauty; the loveliness of the Morning Glory climbing the trellis on a south wall, its azure-blue trumpets mingling perhaps with one of the pale pink climbing roses; the air-borne fragrance of Mignonette as it passes through the casement and the amazing richness of the Night Scented Stock invading a summer night; Snapdragons, finding an apparently precarious but secure roothold on some old garden wall; hedges of Sweet Peas and brilliant carpets of Marigolds, Canterbury Bells and Sweet Williams; are not these integral parts of British gardens, the like of which are not seen elsewhere?

There are no easier and few better ways of providing a long succession of cut flowers for the home than by sowing a selection of medium to long-stemmed annuals and biennials. The freedom with which the flowers are produced and the wide range of colour make them especially useful for such a purpose. By the careful cutting of the stems with a sharp knife or scissors the development of further flowers is encouraged. In order that the flower garden may not be robbed by the too prodigal cutting of flowers it is a wise plan to reserve a portion of the kitchen garden or some border in the background for use as a cut-flower plantation where they may be cut at will without an uneasy conscience for the welfare of the flower garden. For a selection of those plants suitable for cutting, the following list has been prepared:

*Alonsoa acutifolia* (syn. *myrti-folia*)
*Alonsoa warscewiczii*
*Althaea hybrida*
*Anacyclus atlanticus*
*Anchusa capensis*
*Antirrhinum majus*
*Antirrhinum maximum*

*Arctotis calendulacea*
*Arctotis stoechadifolia* (syn. *grandis*)
*Calendula officinalis*
*Campanula longestyla*
*Campanula medium*
*Centaurea cyanus*
*Centranthus macrosiphon*

F *Cheiranthus cheiri*
  *Chrysanthemum carinatum*
  *Chrysanthemum coronarium*
  *Chrysanthemum segetum*
  *Clarkia elegans*
  *Coreopsis tinctoria* (syn. *bicolor*)
  *Cynoglossum amabile*
  *Delphinium ajacis*
  *Delphinium paniculatum*
F *Dianthus barbatus*
  *Dianthus heddewigii*
  *Digitalis purpurea* (Shirley strain)
  *Dimorphotheca annua*
F *Erysimum asperum*
  *Gaillardia amblyodon*
  *Gaillardia pulchella*
  *Gerbera jamesonii*
  *Godetia grandiflora* varieties
  *Gypsophila elegans*

  *Helichrysum bracteatum*
F *Lathyrus odoratus* (Sweet Pea)
  *Linum grandiflorum*
  *Lunaria annua* (syn. *biennis*)
  *Lupinus hartwegii*
  *Myosotis sylvatica*
F *Nicotiana alata grandiflora*
  *Nigella damascena*
  *Papaver nudicaule*
F *Reseda odorata*
  *Rudbeckia bicolor*
  *Rudbeckia hirta*
  *Rudbeckia triloba*
  *Scabiosa atropurpurea* and varieties
  *Tagetes erecta*
  *Venidium fastuosum*
  *Verbena hybrida*
  *Zinnia elegans*

Those marked F are noted for fragrance.

## PROTECTION FROM INSECTS, PESTS AND DISEASES

Both annuals and perennials are subject to considerable damage from the attacks of certain insect pests. It is very desirable that the grower should have a full knowledge of how to combat them.

Where a new garden is being constructed from virgin turf, there is considerable risk for the first few years of attacks from wireworms, leatherjackets and a number of other lesser enemies. Until comparatively recently no known means of destruction was known, but it has been discovered that a light dressing of benzene hexachloride (gammexane) in powder form, given after the initial digging, spells a speedy death to these destroyers of plant life. I have used gammexane mixtures recently where the soil was freely inhabited by wireworms and leatherjackets, and it has proved a most effective means of destruction and it is quite safe to plant within a few days after applying. It is important to give just the right proportion as a dressing, and if the maker's directions are followed there will be no risk of damage to the plants.

Slugs and snails can cause havoc in a single night among young seedlings. Unless steps are taken to protect them from these pests serious loss may be sustained. If, before sowing the seed, a dressing of an anti-slug mixture is applied and lightly raked into the surface, there will be no likelihood of this trouble. The most effective mixtures are those with kamforite or naphthalene as a base. These fumigate the soil and destroy any slug or snail that may lurk therein. It is a useful precaution to dress plantations of herbaceous perennials as well as the soil for annuals and biennials with these soil fumigants. Borders of herbaceous perennials should be given a dressing just before the plants become dormant, usually in early October, for it is during the period when they lie dormant that the greatest damage is often done. Borders and nursery beds intended for annuals and biennials that have been prepared during summer should be given a dressing in early September followed by a thorough watering. It will be quite safe to sow seed or plant seedlings a week after the application has been given.

Caterpillars can be deadly if not checked as soon as they make their appearance. Fortunately control is quite a simple matter. The plants should be sprayed or dusted with a derris, nicotine or DDT insecticide. Few occurrences can be more disconcerting than an invasion of ants. They farm out aphides on plants and may disturb the roots. Ants can, however, be controlled by dusting their trails and the vicinity of their nests with a 5 per cent DDT insecticidal dust. Where the nests are found, a hole in the centre should be made with a pointed stake and a teaspoonful of calcium cyanide dropped in, and sealed in with a sod.

Greenfly and other aphides may be controlled by spraying with a liquid solution comprising 1 fluid oz. of nicotine sulphate and 4 oz. wetting compound dissolved in 10 gallons of water. Alternatively, any of the proprietary nicotine or HETP sprays will be effective, and all are quite simple to apply.

Diseases among annuals and biennials are remarkably few, and those that cause most trouble are peculiar to certain genera only.

Mildew is often found on the foliage of Delphiniums, both annual and perennial, and although not in itself a fatal disease it can cause the plant to become so unsightly as to render it useless decoratively. As soon as the first symptoms, in the form of a white mould, appear on the stems or foliage green sulphur should be applied by means of a blower specially made for such operations.

Rust on the foliage of Hollyhocks causes the plants to become unsightly, but an application of a copper fungicide as dust or liquid will prove an effective cure. Rust on Antirrhinums will cause the foliage to die if not checked and, prevention being better than cure, it is a wise plan to spray at fortnightly intervals from midsummer onwards with Bordeaux mixture in liquid form. Certain varieties are more resistant to this disease than others.

The damping-off of seedlings under glass is usually due to attacks by soil-borne fungi. In order to avoid this risk sterilized soil should always be used and the boxes of seedlings given a watering with Cheshunt Compound.

# DESCRIPTION OF SPECIES
## Pheasant's Eye (Plate 51)

Family *RANUNCULACEAE*                    *Adonis* species

Brightly coloured annuals of Syrian and European origin, hardy in Britain. The leaves are finely cut and fern-like; flowers vary in colour according to the species. *A. aestivalis* (Pheasant's Eye), has almost blood-red flowers, an inch across, with dark centres, on one-foot stems. *A. autumnalis* has scarlet flowers on twelve-inch stems. An inch or so taller is *A. flammea* with bright scarlet flowers with dark centres and a black patch on each petal where it joins the centre. The Syrian, *A. aleppica*, has brilliant scarlet flowers, two inches across, freely produced; it reaches a foot high. Among the most brilliant of annuals, the Adonis with its scarlet flowers is indispensable in the annual border. Sow seed in autumn or spring where the plants are to flower, and thin to two inches apart in spring.

Propagation is from seed.

The flowering season is early summer for *A. flammea* and *A. aestivalis*, late summer for the other two species.

## Floss-flower (Plate 51)

Family *COMPOSITAE*                    *Ageratum houstonianum*

Noted for its blue flowers, this half-hardy annual from the tropics is essential in the annual flower border. Known also as *A. mexicanum* and perhaps synonymous with *A. conyzoides*, from which it differs in having heart-shaped and not rounded leaves at the base. The leaves are small, ovate and toothed with flowers of blue or white, up to a quarter of an inch across, borne in fluffy heads with great freedom. The species is represented mostly by its garden varieties and there are dwarf forms, not exceeding six inches high, such as Little Dorrit and Little Blue Star, both with blue flowers; Swanley Blue is popular, having a taller stature with freely produced flowers of sky-blue; Blue Ball and Blue Cap have deep blue flowers and neat compact habits. Although the plant is chiefly valued as a summer bedding plant, it also makes a decorative cut flower. The seed should be sown in boxes under glass in March, the seedlings pricked off and planted out in June, six to eight inches apart, when the risk of frost is past.

Propagation is from seed.

The flowering season is from late June until Michaelmas, or later.

## Mask-flower (Plate 51)

Family *SCROPHULARIACEAE*                    *Alonsoa* species

A genus from Mexico and South America, particularly Peru, comprising a number of half-hardy annuals and at least one half-hardy perennial in cultivation. The leaves are borne in whorls and the flowers are two-lipped with a short-tubed corolla which, by the twisting of the stem, is turned upside down. The most favoured perennial is *A. warscewiczii*, from Chile, which grows one and a half to two feet and bears terminal racemes of graceful cinnabar-red flowers; it has a form *compacta* which, as the name implies, is compact and neat. Among the annuals are *A. caulialata*, with angular one-foot stems, and many scarlet flowers; *A. linifolia*, six inches taller, is of a paler hue; *A. myrtifolia* (syn. *acutifolia*), two to three feet, has scarlet-crimson flowers; and has a white variety, *alba*. *A. mutisii* is deserving of special mention for its lovely pale pink flowers, deepening at the centre, borne on one-foot stems, whilst *A. miniata*, of similar height, is of compact habit and is of a particularly brilliant scarlet. It is best to sow seed in March or April where the plants are to flower, giving cloche protection if necessary. The position must be in full sun and the soil well drained.

Propagation is from seed, or cuttings inserted in pots of sandy soil in August.

The flowering season is throughout the summer until frost.

## Hollyhock (Plate 51)

Family *MALVACEAE*                            *Althaea rosea*

An old favourite that has long been a feature of the cottage gardens of Britain, having been originally introduced from China, where it is a native. Although perennial, it is generally treated as a biennial. There are both single- and double-flowered forms, many flowers, four to five inches in diameter, being borne on substantial stems that will attain a height of six or seven feet. The colours range from white and yellow to shades of pink to scarlet, crimson and purple. Planted in groups at the back of the border, the Hollyhock lends itself to bold effect, especially if planted against a background of dark green. The foliage is large and rounded and is produced beneath the flower-spike; it is sometimes subject to rust, which is best controlled by dusting with green sulphur immediately the first symptoms appear. For successful cultivation a deep loamy soil, trenched three spits deep, is necessary and good drainage is essential.

Best treated as a biennial by sowing seed in June to produce plants that will flower in the following year.

The flowering season is in August and September.

## Sweet Alyssum (Plate 52)

Family *CRUCIFERAE*                    *Alyssum maritimum*

A native of southern Europe and sometimes found listed under *Lobularia maritima*, but best known under the above name. Actually a perennial, this species is best treated as an annual, hence its inclusion in this section. The plant, when full grown, will not exceed one foot in height with a spread of a foot across. The foliage is minute and almost entirely hidden by the freely produced white flowers, which are small and borne in lengthening racemes; it owes its popular name to its fragrance. The forms of garden origin enjoy considerable popularity, being seen in such varieties as var. *minimum*, reaching only two inches high, var. *nanum*, reaching four inches. From this latter form have been evolved varieties with white flowers that change with age to lilac or violet. The seed should be sown in March under glass, the seedlings pricked off and planted out where they are to flower when the risk of frost has passed; or outdoors in early May.

Propagation is from seed.

The flowering season is from midsummer onwards until frost.

## Love-lies-bleeding: Prince's Feather (Plate 52)

Family *AMARANTHACEAE*                    *Amaranthus* species

A genus comprising about fifty half-hardy annuals of coarse growth and native to mild and tropical countries in many parts of the world. The foliage is large, oval and pointed, and the flowers are small and numerous, forming into a drooping tassel-like raceme. The familiar Love-lies-bleeding is *A. caudatus*: two to three feet, it hails from the tropics and has drooping reddish stems, bearing purple flowers; its form var. *atropurpureus* is of a slightly deeper and richer tone; var. *viridis* is a white-flowered form similar in habit to the foregoing. Known as Joseph's Coat, *A. tricolor*, from India, has red, green and yellow foliage and drooping purple flowers. *A. hybridus* is too coarse to be of value in cultivation, but its form var. *hypochondriacus*, four to five feet, known as Prince s Feather, is favoured in gardens for its branching, erect panicles of bright red. Seed may be sown under glass with artificial heat in March, pricked off into boxes or pots when an inch or so high and planted out-of-doors in June.

Propagation is from seed.

The flowering season is from midsummer onwards.

## Amellus (Plate 52)

Family *COMPOSITAE*                                    *Amellus annuus*

An attractive half-hardy annual from South Africa and listed also as *A. strigosus* var. *willdenovii*. The leaves are two inches long, with a single tooth on each side. The flowers are not unlike some Cinerarias in form and comprise deep purplish-blue rays surrounding a dark disc, the height being about six inches. This is a most useful plant for inclusion in the annual border. It may be used as a contrast to orange, apricot or golden yellow flowers. It will usually need a position towards the front of the border owing to its dwarf stature. It is also an annual that is useful for the front of an herbaceous border as, owing to its long season of flowering, it helps to mask the gaps left by shorter lived flowers. The seed may be sown in April out-of-doors where the plants are to bloom, provided they are given the protection of cloches until late May. Alternatively, seed may be sown earlier under glass, the seedlings pricked off and planted out when risk of frost has passed.

Propagation is from seed.

The flowering season is from June until frost.

## Winged Everlasting Sand-flower (Plate 52)

Family *COMPOSITAE*                                *Ammobium alatum*

A native of Australia of perennial habit, but best treated as a half-hardy annual. Growing one and a half to two feet high, the stems are woolly and greyish-white, bearing white flowers, two inches across, each with a yellow central disc. The best form is var. *grandiflorum* with larger flowers and somewhat taller growth. The flowers are everlasting and remain white in colour if they are cut when fully grown, and hung heads downwards in

Pheasant's Eye (*Adonis aestivalis*), p. 141.
Mask Flower (*Alonsoa warscewiczii*), p. 142.

2. Floss-flower (*Ageratum houstonianum*), p. 141.
4. Hollyhock (*Althaea rosea*), p. 142.

Pl. 52.
1. Sweet Alyssum (*Alyssum maritimum*), p. 143.   2. Love-lies-bleeding (*Amaranthus cauda*
p. 143.
3. Amellus (*Amellus annuus*), p. 144.   4. Winged Everlasting Sand-flower (*Ammobium alat*
p. 144.

a cool, airy place until quite dry. Seed may be sown out-of-doors in May where the plants are to bloom and the seedlings thinned to four inches apart. The position should enjoy full exposure to the sun and the soil must be well drained. Or seed may be sown under glass in March, temperature 65° F.

Propagation is from seed.

The flowering season is from midsummer onwards.

## Anacyclus (Plate 53)

Family *COMPOSITAE*                                   *Anacyclus* species

Comprises both perennial and annual species, native to Morocco, the Mediterranean region and southern Europe. The most charming is *A. atlanticus*, a perennial up to one and a half feet high and best treated as a half-hardy annual, with white, hairy foliage of a feathery character and daisy-like flowers of white in great profusion. *A. officinarum* is an annual reaching a foot high with white flowers, an inch across, with a purple reverse. *A. radiatus* is also an annual and rather taller than the last mentioned, producing yellow flowers, one and a half inches across; it has a form var. *purpureum* with the ray florets striped purple. Seed may be sown in April where the plants are to flower and the seedlings thinned to three inches apart. A position in full sun is necessary, and the soil should be moderately rich and well drained.

Propagation is from seed.

The flowering season is from midsummer until frost.

## Pimpernel (Plate 53)

Family *PRIMULACEAE*                              *Anagallis linifolia*
                                          (syn. *A. grandiflora*)

This is a pretty perennial, best treated as half hardy. It is native to Europe and Italy, and has flax-like leaves and flowers of blue on stems of twelve inches high. *A. linifolia* var. *monelli parksii* grows six inches high, and has scarlet flowers, and var. *collina* is similar but with rose to purple flowers. *A. l.* var. *monel philipsii* is a garden variety with flowers of bright blue and a maroon centre. The species is also the parent of a number of garden varieties with flowers that vary in colour from pink to purple. They should not be confused with the native *A. tenella*, the Bog Pimpernel with rosy flowers, or the common native weed (*A. arvensis*), known as the Shepherd's or Poor Man's Weather Glass. *A. linifolia* and its

10

varieties are most delightful in hot, dry summers, and are disappointing under wet, cool conditions. They welcome a light, well-drained soil, rich in rotted organic matter, and a sunny situation. Propagate from seeds sown under glass in March, temperature 65°F., pricking off, and eventually transplanting out-of-doors where they are to flower in late May or early June, preferably massed for effect.

The flowering season is from midsummer to early autumn.

## Alkanet (Plate 53)

Family *BORAGINACEAE*                        *Anchusa capensis*

This is a South African plant, strictly biennial but treated as a hardy annual, valuable for its effective flowers and long season of blooming. The leaves are narrow and lance-shaped, being of a rough and hairy texture; the flowers are bright blue, a quarter of an inch across, with white throats but sometimes marred by a reddish staining at the margin. The plant grows one to one and a half feet. There is also a white form. The type is now superseded by a dwarfer form of garden origin known as Blue Bird, with deep, rich blue flowers borne in clusters on branching stems. Blue-flowered plants are always popular and this deserves particular attention for the freedom with which it produces its flowers and its value for providing a welcome foil to the superabundance of yellow-flowered annuals. The seed may be sown in April where the plants are to bloom. If the weather is cold, cloche protection may be given. Thin out the seedlings when large enough.

Propagation is from seed.

The flowering season is from midsummer until frost.

## Rock Jasmine (Plate 53)

Family *PRIMULACEAE*                        *Androsace* species

Natives of Europe, North America and Asia, the Androsaces are delightful plants for rock gardens, where they are entirely in harmony. *A. lactiflora* (syn. *A. coronopifolia*), a biennial from Siberia, reaches six inches, sometimes taller, with narrow lance-shaped leaves, up to two inches long, formed in a rosette; the flowers are bluish-white, about half an inch across, and borne in clusters. *A. septentrionalis* is rather taller than the foregoing with leaves only three-quarters of an inch long, forming rosettes; the flowers are white or pink, about a quarter of an inch across, and borne in umbels; its form var. *subumbellata* is of dwarfer habit.

53.                                                    146

1. Anacyclus (*Anacyclus atlanticus*), p. 145.    2. Pimpernel (*Anagallis linifolia*), p. 145.
3. Alkanet (*Anchusa capensis*), p. 146.          4. Rock Jasmine (*Androsace laciflora*), p. 146.

*Pl.* 54.

1. Anoda (*Anoda cristata*), p. 147.
2. Camomile (*Anthemis arabica*), p. 147.
3. Snapdragon (*Antirrhinum majus*), p. 148.
4. Arctotis (*Arctotis stoechadifolia*), p. 148.

*A. maxima* is very dwarf, rarely more than four inches, with white or pink flowers. *A. armeniaca* is biennial, about two inches high, with oblong lance-shaped leaves, five-eighths of an inch long, and white flowers in clusters. Although so admirable for the rock garden, the taller species are useful front-of-the-border annuals. The seed may be sown in sandy peat in a cold frame or in the positions where the plants are to flower, taking care to thin seedlings sufficiently to avoid overcrowding.

Propagation is from seed, or from cuttings of biennial kinds inserted in pots of sandy soil in the cold frame in autumn.

The flowering season is in May and June.

## Anoda (Plate 54)

Family *MALVACEAE*                                     *Anoda* species

Pretty annuals that find their home in Mexico and Central America. *A. cristata* reaches about one and a half feet, with triangular-shaped, three-lobed leaves, hairy beneath; the flowers are nearly two inches across and rose-pink to lavender, borne on long leafless stems. *A. hastata* has arrow-shaped leaves of greyish-green colour and blue- or white-coloured flowers, about one and a half inches across. *A. wrightii* is quite distinct with flowers somewhat after those of the Solanums in form, but of a bright yellow, with purple centres, the plant is of rather decumbent habit, reaching a height of six inches. *A. triangularis* reaches about one and a half feet, with triangular leaves, toothed at the base, and branching stems bearing lilac flowers, one and a half inches across. The seed should be sown in April where the plants are to bloom and the seedlings thinned to about three inches apart. The position should be of southern aspect and fully exposed to the sun; the soil should be reasonably rich and well drained.

Propagation is from seed.

The flowering season is from midsummer onwards.

## Camomile (Plate 54)

Family *COMPOSITAE*                                   *Anthemis arabica*

This is the only annual of this genus, whose perennial forms are so well known. It is a native of southern Spain and Morocco; also known as *Cladanthus arabicus*. The plant reaches one and a half feet and has leaves that are finely divided and feathery in appearance, with large flowers of golden yellow, borne singly on slender stems just above the foliage. It forms a neat, rounded plant that is valuable for contrasting with annuals of blue and purple tones such as Nigella and Cynoglossum, and it should be an ideal companion to the dwarf blue Michaelmas Daisies. The plant is quite easily grown and the seed should be sown in early April in a warm and sunny position where the soil is well drained, the seedlings being thinned out when large enough.

Propagation is from seed.

The flowering season is in late summer.

## Snapdragon (Plate 54)

Family *SCROPHULARIACEAE*                    *Antirrhinum majus*

A native of the Mediterranean region and a firm favourite in British gardens, where it is treated often as a biennial although it is, in fact, a perennial. The flowers are borne in spikes, are tubular in shape, with spreading lobes of irregular formation. The many varieties of garden origin show a considerable colour range which may extend from white, cream and shades of yellow to pink, terra-cotta, scarlet and crimson tones. There are also forms with double flowers. There is a considerable variation in height from dwarf cushion-like plants to others of two or three feet high.

Snapdragons will grow well in any ordinary soil, although the richer the medium the more satisfactory will be the results. They are great drought resisters and will grow under the driest conditions. Apart from their value in the border the dwarf and medium varieties can be grown as ornamental pot plants.

Propagation may be by seed, under glass in January to March, to flower from June to October, or in the open in late summer or early autumn to bloom the following spring, or by cuttings.

The flowering season extends from spring until well into autumn.

## Arctotis (Plate 54)

Family *COMPOSITAE*                          *Arctotis* species

Attractive and colourful South African plants of perennial habit, best treated as half-hardy annuals. Of the forty or more species known, four find particular favour in British flower gardens. All have daisy-like flowers with central discs of a dark colour. *A. stoechadifolia* (syn. *A. grandis*) is tall, growing one and a half to two feet, with a long-flowering period during which the pure white flowers, each centred with a purplish disc, rise on

Prickly Poppy (*Argemone grandiflora*), p. 149.    2. Arabian Primrose (*Arnebia cornuta*), p. 149.
Sweet Wormwood (*Artemisia annua*), p. 150.    4. Goldfields (*Baeria chrysostoma*), p. 150.

*Pl.* 56.

1. Blumenbachia (*Blumenbachia coronata*), p. 151.   2. Swan River Daisy (*Brachycome iberifolia*), p. 151.

3. Browallia (*Browallia americana*), p. 152.   4. Slipperwort (*Calceolaria integrifolia* var.), p. 1

long stems above the deeply-cut grey foliage. *A. calendulacea* (syn. *Cryptostemma calendulaceum*) produces, as the specific name implies, marigold-like flowers of bright yellow with dark centres. Of a rather prostrate habit, this plant will attain fifteen inches. *A. breviscapa* has six-inch lance-shaped cut leaves and orange-rayed flowers, two inches across, with dark centres on six-inch stems. Of a variable nature, *A. scapigera* (syn. *A. acaulis*) is of similar height, with flowers that are sometimes of brilliant orange and sometimes of a rich bronze-red; the leaves are lobed, about six inches long with white tomentum on the reverse. Raise from seed sown under glass in March and plant the seedlings out where they are to flower in late May.

Propagate from seed or from cuttings of side-shoots inserted in sandy soil in a cold frame, early summer.

The flowering season is from May to Michaelmas for all except *A. calendulacea*, which flowers from late June onwards.

## Prickly Poppy: Devil's Fig (Plate 55)

Family *PAPAVERACEAE*                    *Argemone grandiflora*

Also known as Argemony, this species is the most usually grown in flower gardens and is a native of Mexico. Best treated as a half-hardy annual, although in its native habitat it is perennial. The foliage is poppy-like and hairy, almost thorny, and has conspicuous white veins. The flowers are four inches across, creamy-white in colour, with a central bunch of orange-yellow stamens; var. *lutea* is an attractive yellow-flowered form, and both reach a height of two to three feet. One of the most attractive plants of its class, this poppy is best raised from seed sown in a warm frame, the seedlings pricked off and planted in a sunny situation, in well-drained soil and in association with the choicest denizens of the annual or perennial border.

Propagation is from seed.

The flowering period is from midsummer, continuously until frost.

## Arabian Primrose (Plate 55)

Family *BORAGINACEAE*                    *Arnebia cornuta*

One of the most attractive of annuals, not commonly grown, and a native of Turkestan. The plant grows one and a half to two feet and is related to the Prophet Flower *A.* (syn. *Macratomia*) *echioides*. The leaves are lance-shaped and hairy; the flowers are tubular and five-lobed, three-quarters of an inch across, and of

a bright yellow colour marked with five black spots which change
to maroon and disappear as the flower ages. This plant deserves
a special position of southern exposure and full sun, and a soil
that is moderately rich and well drained. The seeds are best
sown under glass in March, and the seedlings pricked off into small
pots and planted out where they are to flower in early June,
when all risk of frost has passed.

Propagation is from seed.

The flowering season is from midsummer onwards.

## Sweet Wormwood (Plate 55)

Family *COMPOSITAE*                    *Artemesia annua*

A hardy annual of a race well known for its perennial species
and native to Asia and eastern Europe. Grown more for its
decorative foliage that far exceeds the flowers in beauty. This
plant will attain six feet and is valuable for the effect of its green,
fernlike foliage that is deeply cut and aromatic; the flowers
comprise rayless heads of yellow borne in loose clusters. Other
species worth growing for elegance of foliage are *A. sacrorum*,
with white dissected foliage and reaching up to six feet, and
*A. scoparia*, with leaves divided into hair-like segments and heads
of small white flowers, in tightly packed panicles. The seed may
be sown where the plants are to grow and the seedlings thinned
to six inches apart. These are effective plants for use in the wild
or natural garden, where they blend well with the foliage of
ornamental shrubs.

Propagation is from seed.

The flowering season is in late summer.

## Goldfields (Plate 55)

Family *COMPOSITAE*                     *Baeria* species

Showy annuals from California well deserving a place in the
flower garden. *B. aristata* (syn. *B. coronaria*) has somewhat
feathery foliage and rather weak stems, six to nine inches long,
bearing golden-yellow daisy-like flowers, half an inch across.
Reaching a foot high, *B. chrysostoma* (syn. *B. gracilis*) has thread-
like leaves and branching stems bearing golden-yellow flowers, an
inch across. This species is generally known as Goldfields, and
is noted for the profusion with which it produces its flowers.
Both species are easily grown as hardy annuals by sowing the
seed where the plants are to flower, in March, and thinning to

four inches apart when the seedlings are large enough to handle.
They demand a position towards the front of the annual border,
where they may enjoy full sun and the soil must be well drained.

Propagation is from seed.

The flowering season is from midsummer onwards.

## Blumenbachia (Plate 56)

Family *LOASACEAE* *Blumenbachia* species

Half-hardy annuals, biennials and perennials, all treated as
annuals. They are natives of Argentina, Chile and Peru. The
Peruvian *B. chuquitensis* produces sprays of orange-red incurved
flowers on two-feet stems, the whole plant being covered with
spiny bristles that sting severely. *B. hieronymi*, from Argentina,
has flowers of the same incurved form comprising five white
petals around a centre of orange and yellow, borne on six-inch
stems; unhappily it, too, possesses the stinging character of the
genus. *B. coronata*, eighteen inches, is a white-flowering biennial
from Chile. *B. insignis*, a trailing annual with white flowers, is
native to Monte Video, and *B. multifida* is a native of north
Argentina, and another annual, with red flowers. Suitable plants
for the wilder parts of the garden or at the front of shrub plantations. The seed should be sown where the plants are to bloom
and the seedlings thinned to six inches apart, or more in the case
of the taller species. Full sun and well-drained soil are essential.

Propagation is from seed.

The flowering season is from midsummer onwards.

## Swan River Daisy (Plate 56)

Family *COMPOSITAE* *Brachycome iberidifolia*

A dainty and attractive half-hardy annual from West Australia. The leaves are small and narrow and the stems, of
branching habit, a foot or more in height, bearing flowers, one
inch across, rather reminiscent of a miniature Cineraria, of blue-
shaded purple. There are several forms of garden origin, with
flowers that vary in tone from blue to white and rose. Although
it is usual to sow the seeds in March where they are to bloom,
and to thin out where necessary, earlier flowers may be obtained
by sowing under glass in September, pricking four seedlings off
into four-inch pots, wintering in cold frames under dry conditions,
and planting out in April. The nature of growth being somewhat

sprawling, it is a wise plan to plant a number together so that they may find mutual support.

Propagate from seed.

The flowering season is from July to September, or a month earlier if raised in the late summer as suggested.

## Browallia  (Plate 56)

Family *SOLANACEAE*                           *Browallia* species

Tender annuals of the Nightshade family and native of Peru, *B. americana* (syn. *B. demissa* and *B. elata*) reaches about one foot with oval leaves two inches long, and tubular flowers, half an inch long and half an inch across the mouth, of blue or violet colouring borne in the leaf axils. Somewhat similar is *B. grandiflora* (syn. *B. roezlii*), two feet, with smooth green leaves and five-lobed flowers of bright sky-blue with yellow calyx tubes. Being somewhat tender and often grown as greenhouse plants, these delightful species may quite easily be grown out of doors if planted out in June from pots. Seed should be sown under glass in March, the seedlings pricked off singly into pots and nursed under glass until planted outdoors in their flowering quarters in June. They should enjoy full sun and the soil must be well drained.

Propagation is from seed.

The flowering season is from midsummer onwards.

## Slipperwort  (Plate 56)

Family *SCROPHULARIACEAE*                   *Calceolaria* species

A genus containing some half-hardy perennials and annuals native to Mexico or Chile. The large pouch-flowered hybrids are suitable only for greenhouse cultivation as pot-grown specimens, those for the open border being smaller flowered but worthy members of the genus. *C. alba*, from Chile, has linear, slightly toothed leaves about two inches long, and is of a shrubby habit; the flowers are about half an inch long and a little less across and clear white, several being borne on slender one-foot stems. *C. mexicana* is an annual and has hairy, lobed leaves and reaches a foot in height with pale yellow flowers, of a similar size to those of *C. alba*. Seed should be sown under glass in heat, 60° to 65° F., during March and the seedlings pricked off into pots or boxes and planted out in their flowering positions in late May or early June. A sheltered sunny position in well-drained, humus-rich soil should be provided for them.

Propagation is from seed or cuttings of the shrubby species.
The flowering season is from midsummer until frost.

## Pot Marigold (Plate 57)

Family *COMPOSITAE*                    *Calendula officinalis*

A native of southern Europe and an old garden favourite. The
common name owes its origin to old-time use of the flower petals
for flavouring. The leaves are hairy, coarse and oblongish. The
thick branching stems grow up to two feet, with flowers, four
inches across, of flat white-yellow to deep orange rays that tend
to close at night. The species owes its present great popularity
to the number of varieties of garden origin, with fully double
flowers such as Meteor and Orange King, and Radio with fluted
petals, that vary in tones of apricot, lemon, sulphur and golden-
yellow. One of the easiest of plants to grow, the seed may be
sown in March or April, where the plants are to bloom. As germination is free, seed should be sown sparingly, thinning seedlings
twelve inches apart. The position may be in full sun or partial
shade. Much valued as a cut flower, and may be grown for a long
season if protected by cloches in early spring and late autumn to
guard against frosts.
Propagate from seed.
The flowering season is from February to early December.

## China Aster (Plate 57)

Family *COMPOSITAE*                    *Callistephus chinensis*

One of the most popular of all annuals, being native to China
and Japan. The type has deeply lobed, hairy, ovate leaves;
branching stems of one to two and a half feet, and flowers with
ray petals surrounding a yellow central disc. The many garden
forms have flowers which range from white to shades of violet,
purple, blue and rose, often five inches or more across; but none
of yellow shades. Some of the most outstanding garden forms
are Ostrich Plumes, with quilled petals; Peony Flowered, with
incurved flowers; Comet, double flowers with loosely arranged
rays or petals; Anemone Flowered, with flat florets around a
quilled centre; Chrysanthemum Flowered, with large fully double
flowers; Leviathan, with very large double flowers; and others
with single flowers. Lilliput, a dwarf group. Plants are usually
raised from seed sown early in the year in heat, 55° to 65°F.,
pricked off into boxes of compost, and finally planted out in

May where they are to bloom, at distances of from six to nine inches, according to variety. May also be sown in cold frame or pots in windows in April. They are excellent cut flowers.

Propagate from seed.

The flowering season is from late June until Michaelmas or later, if frost is absent.

## Canterbury Bell (Plate 57)

Family *CAMPANULACEAE*                *Campanula medium*

An old-world favourite, native to southern Europe. The plant is biennial and reaches two to three feet, with leaves, up to nine inches long, radiating from the base. The flowers of the type are violet-blue, borne two or more together in long open racemes. *C. m.* var. *calycanthema* is the Cup-and-Saucer type so much associated with old English cottage gardens. There are shades of violet-blue, pink and white in both forms. From Greece we have *C. ramosissima* (syn. *C. loreyi*), reaching up to nine inches high, with saucer-shaped flowers, one inch across, of parma-violet changing to white at the base. Reaching a height of one and a half feet, *C. thyrsioides*, from the European Alps, is a somewhat hairy plant with lance-shaped leaves, up to three inches long, forming a rosette; the flowers are straw-yellow, of tubular form, rather small and borne in a close spike. The Caucasian, *C. longestyla*, forms a rosette of basal leaves, from which rise one and a half to two and a half-feet stems bearing sprays of nodding bell-shaped flowers of bluish-purple. There are also a number of alpine forms. Of those named, only *C. ramosissima* is annual, and its seed may be sown in late March where the plants are to flower, thinning to appropriate distances. The seed of the biennial types may be sown in late summer, the seedlings pricked off into nursery beds for transplanting to their flowering quarters in the following spring.

Propagation is from seed.

The flowering season is in summer.

## Cornflower (Plate 57)

Family *COMPOSITAE*                *Centaurea cyanus*

A native of Britain and Europe and one of the most popular of hardy annuals. Long narrow foliage, up to six inches long, with typical cornflower heads, borne on two to three feet stems, about one and a half inches across and of a deep blue colour in the commoner forms. The varieties of garden origin contain a wide range of colours, but the most pleasing are those of blue and pink shades. There are also double-flowered forms. *C. americana* is the Basket Flower of America, and reaches to a considerable height, sometimes five feet, with oblong leaves, about five inches long, and white, rose, pale pink or purple flowers, up to five inches across, borne singly. One of the most attractive, particularly as a cut flower, is *C. moschata*, from Persia, commonly known as Sweet Sultan. It has toothed foliage and two-feet stems bearing musk-scented heads, of rather refined thistle-like form and purple in colour; *C. m. alba* is a white, and *C. m. flava* a yellow, variety. Easily grown from seed sown in March to April out-of-doors where the plants are to flower, being thinned to four to six inches apart. A position in full sun is necessary, and well-drained moderately rich soil.

Propagation is from seed.

The flowering season is from midsummer onwards.

## Valerian (Plate 58)

Family *VALERIANACEAE*                          *Centranthus* species

Hardy annual members of this well-known genus are natives of Spain and Portugal. The most attractive species is *C. macrosiphon*, which grows one to two feet high, with oval leaves, one and a half to three inches long, glaucous and lobed or toothed, and clusters of small deep-rose tubular flowers. There is also a pure white form. *C. calcitrapa* reaches one and a half feet with divided leaves, three inches long, and terminal clusters of rose-pink flowers. These are showy plants for the front of the annual border. They are also useful to provide a long period of floral colour in the perennial border, where it is often an advantage to include suitable annuals for this purpose. The seed is best sown in late March or April, where the plants are to flower, the seedlings being thinned to avoid overcrowding. The position chosen should enjoy ample sunlight and the soil should be well drained.

Propagation is from seed.

The flowering season extends from midsummer until frost.

## Wallflower (Plate 58)

Family *CRUCIFERAE*                          *Cheiranthus cheiri*

A native of the sea cliffs, quarries and old walls of southern Europe, hence its common name. One of the best loved of plants, the Wallflower is really a perennial, but usually treated as a biennial. The leaves are lance-shaped, produced profusely, and the plant is of bushy erect habit, one to two feet high, with fragrant flowers, about an inch across, yellow or brownish-yellow in the type, but varying from off-white to pink, terra-cotta, orange, scarlet and crimson in varieties of garden origin. *C. allionii*, a native of North America, is called the Siberian Wall-flower for some curious reason, and is *Erysimum asperum* to botanists. Reaching a height of nine inches, its heads of bright orange flowers in late spring are welcome successors to the true Wallflower. There is also a pretty mauve-flowered form known as *C. linifolius* (syn. *Erysimum linifolium*). Seed should be sown in the open in July and the seedlings planted in their permanent positions by October. Fine for massed effect and one of the most fragrant of cut flowers.

Propagation is from seed.

The flowering season is from March to May for *C. cheiri* and in May and June for *C. allionii*.

## Chrysanthemum (Plate 58)

Family *COMPOSITAE*                    *Chrysanthemum* species

The annual Chrysanthemums, most favoured in gardens, are natives of Europe and North Africa. From Morocco comes the Tricolour Chrysanthemum, *C. carinatum*, with lobed leaves and two- to three-feet stems bearing large single flowers, two and a half inches across, with ray petals of white, red, purple or yellow, with a brightly coloured ring at the centre and a central disc of purple. The European and native *C. segetum* is the Corn Mari-gold, with one- to two-feet high very branching stems bearing two-inch single flowers in sprays, yellow to white in the type, but varying to canary-yellow with chocolate-coloured centres in varieties of garden origin. The Garland Chrysanthemum or Crown Daisy is *C. coronarium*, a branching annual from southern Europe, one and a half to two feet high, with single yellow and white flowers, one to one and a half inches across, set off with a cream zone at the centre. There is also a double-flowered form. As true annuals, the seeds of these species and their varieties may be sown in March or April, thinly, where the plants are to bloom, and thinned when the seedlings are large enough to a foot apart.

Propagation is from seed.

The flowering season is in late summer.

*Pl.* 58.

1. Valerian *(Centranthus macrosiphon)*, p. 155.  2. Wallflower *(Cheiranthus cheiri)*, p. 15
3. Chrysanthemum *(Chrysanthemum* species), p. 156.  4. Clarkia *(Clarkia elegans)*, p. 15

## Clarkia (Plate 58)

Family *ONAGRACEAE*                                    *Clarkia* species

A race of annuals native to California and among the most showy of garden flowers. *C. elegans* has oval leaves with stems of a ruddy glaucous hue of one and a half to four feet, if well grown, and many round flowers, half an inch or less across, that are purple in the type, white in the form var. *alba*, salmon-pink in var. *salmonea* and ranging from white to blood-red in forms of garden origin. *C. pulchella* is native to the west coast of America, from British Columbia to California. It does not exceed one and a half feet high, and has lilac-coloured flowers with the claws of the petals toothed. There is a white variety, *C. p. alba*. Easily grown in any well-drained soil in full sun, the seeds being sown in April to June where the plants are to flower. Both species and the many beautiful varieties of garden origin are valuable for providing bold masses of colour in the flower garden. There are a number with double flowers.

Propagate from seed.

The flowering season is from July to October.


## Collinsia (Plate 59)

Family *SCROPHULARIACEAE*                              *Collinsia* species

Attractive hardy annuals mostly native to western North America, including a number suitable for the flower garden. *C. bartsiaefolia* is the Seaside Collinsia, and attains a height of one foot with rather sticky stems and foliage. The leaves are narrow and oval, about an inch long; the flowers are bell-shaped and white marked with lilac or purple. There are other forms with blue, violet and pink flowers. *C. bicolor* reaches one foot with two-inch oblong, toothed leaves and flowers, an inch long, of which the upper part is white and the lower rose-purple to violet. Var. *candidissima* has pure white flowers, var. *multicolor* variegated flowers, and var. *purpurea* rich purple. *C. grandiflora*, known as Blue Lips, reaches a foot with oblong leaves, nearly two inches long, and flowers with the upper part purplish-white and the lower deep blue or violet. *C. verna* is Blue Eyed Mary, and reaches one and a half feet, with flowers half an inch long, the upper part white to purple and the lower bright blue. The seed of *C. verna* is best sown in August for flowering the following year, being given the protection of a frame until May, when they may be planted out-of-doors. The other species may be sown in late March where they are to flower, and the seedlings thinned to four inches apart. The seedlings usually bloom twelve weeks after the seed is sown.

Propagation is from seed.

The season of flowering is from midsummer onwards.

## Bindweed (Plate 59)

Family *CONVOLVULACEAE*                *Convolvulus* species

Natives of North America and the Mediterranean regions, the annual forms are to be preferred to those of perennial character for the reason that the latter often prove to be marauding weeds very difficult to control. The leaves are heart-shaped and the flowers funnel-shaped and wide open at the mouth; the habit either twining or spreading. The finest, *C. tricolor* (syn. *C. minor*), the dwarf Morning Glory from southern Europe, grows about a foot high, with three-inch diameter blue flowers, with a yellow throat margined white. There are forms with various coloured flowers, and one, considerably less charming, with white flowers. Perennials, usually treated as annuals, are *C. undulatus*, a twiner up to four feet with clusters of mid-blue flowers; *C. elongatus*, a wall plant, desirable for its small white flowers; and *C. aureus superbus*, from North America, distinct in having golden-yellow flowers on twining growths up to four or five feet. All are easily grown from seed sown in well-drained soil in full sun in March.

Propagation is from seed.

The flowering season is from June to September.

## Tickseed (Plate 59)

Family *COMPOSITAE*                *Coreopsis* species

A genus of hardy annuals native to North America and sometimes listed as *Calliopsis* and *Leptosyne*, the former often being used to differentiate the annuals from the perennials. The leaves are mostly lobed or cut and the flowers borne singly or in panicles. The most noteworthy of the annual species are the following: *C. atkinsoniana*, sometimes described as perennial, but treated as annual, two to four feet, with flowers, one and a half inches across, orange with purple shading at the base; *C. bigelovii*, reaching a foot high with flowers, one and a half inches across, of golden yellow; *C. calliopsidea*, reaching two feet, with golden-yellow flowers, three inches across; *C. coronata* (syn. *C. nuecensis*),

59.
. Collinsia (*Collinsia bicolor*), p. 157.
. Tickseed (*Coreopsis coronata*), p. 158.

2. Bindweed (*Convolvulus tricolor*), p. 158.
4. Mexican Aster (*Cosmos bipinnatus*), p. 159.

Pl. 60.
1. Hawk's Beard (*Crepis rubra*), p. 159.   2. Hound's Tongue (*Cynoglossum amabile*), p. 16
3. Thorn Apple (*Datura fastuosa*), p. 160.   4. Rocket Larkspur (*Delphinium ajacis*), p. 16

two feet, having orange-yellow flowers, with a bronze-crimson zone, two inches across; *C. drummondii*, two feet, with yellow flowers, two inches across, with a bronze-purple ring around a purple disc; and *C. tinctoria* (syn. *C. bicolor*, *C. elegans*, *C. marmorata*), three feet, has golden-yellow flowers with a crimson ring encircling a bronze-purple disc. The last has a number of garden forms varying in height from nine inches to three feet and showing colour variations, one form having red flowers and another bronze flecked with yellow. Seed may be sown where the plants are to flower and the seedlings thinned to avoid overcrowding.

Propagation is from seed.

The flowering season is from midsummer until frost.

## Mexican Aster  (Plate 59)

Family *COMPOSITAE*                              *Cosmos* species

Our present garden forms of this genus have originated from three Mexican species and are among the most colourful of hardy annuals. The handsome *C. bipinnatus* has feathery foliage divided into linear segments and flowers, rather like single dahlias, crimson in colour with yellow centres. Garden varieties vary from white to mauve and pink, and there is also a double-flowered form. The plants grow about three feet high. With rather wider foliage, *C. sulphureus* reaches three to four and a half feet, and bears large yellow, golden-centred flowers. *C. diversifolius* is a half-hardy perennial, best treated as a hardy annual, and bears flowers of crimson, with red centres on three-feet stems. It is sometimes listed as *Bidens atrosanguinea*, *B. dahlioides* and *Dahlia zimapani*. The seed may be sown under glass in February or March, and the seedlings planted out in late May. If desired, it may be sown out-of-doors in late May for flowering in late summer. All are useful as cut flowers.

Propagation is from seed.

The flowering season is from July onwards.

## Hawk's Beard  (Plate 60)

Family *COMPOSITAE*                              *Crepis* species

Hardy annuals and perennials native to Greece and Italy, which include one annual in particular, and a few others that are worthy of cultivation. The best is *C. rubra*, of branching habit, attaining a foot or less, with smooth leaves, toothed and lobed. The flowers are similar in form and size to those of the Dandelion, but red in colour. There are also forms with soft pink flowers and one that varies from white to blush. *C. virens* is a lesser beauty with flowers of yellow-tinged pink. Of a branching habit, *C. dioscoridis* has solitary flowers of yellow. The red blooms of *C. rubra* will provide a patch of brilliant colour in the annual border and the pink form is delightful in contrast with blue annual Scabious or Anchusa. The seed should be sown in late March where the plants are to flower, and the seedlings thinned to four inches apart.

Propagation is from seed.

The flowering season is from midsummer onwards.

## Hound's Tongue (Plate 60)

Family *BORAGINACEAE*                    *Cynoglossum amabile*

A perennial, usually treated as an annual, from SW. China, and a most charming plant to grow. From a basal rosette of lance-shaped and oblong leaves rise sturdy stems two feet high, bearing elegantly branched racemes of flowers, about a quarter of an inch across, of a most exquisite, soft azure blue. There is also a garden variety, under the name of Firmament, of a more compact habit with flowers of deeper blue. In effect, like glorified Forget-me-nots, these plants lend themselves to effective use in herbaceous borders, where they should be planted near to yellow Geums, pale pink Sidalceas or the brightly-coloured forms of *Alstromeria ligtu*, where they find their ideal foil. The seed may be sown in frames in March and the seedlings planted out where they are to flower. Or, if preferred, the seed may be sown in May where the plants are to bloom, choosing a sunny spot and a soil that is well drained.

Propagation is from seed.

The flowering season is from June to early September.

## Thorn Apple (Plate 60)

Family *SOLANACEAE*                            *Datura* species

Tender annuals of the Nightshade family, native to Mexico, these are among the most handsome of garden plants when well grown. *D. fastuosa* (syn. *D. cornucopia* and *D. metel*) grows up to five feet in its native habitat but rarely exceeds two feet in the open air in Britain. The leaves are oval and pointed, up to eight inches long, and the flowers are of tubular shape, wide open at the

Pink (*Dianthus sinensis* var.), p. 162.   2. Dicranostigma (*Dicranostigma franchetianum*), p. 162.
Foxglove (*Digitalis purpurea*), p. 163.   4. Cape Marigold (*Dimorphotheca aurantiaca*), p. 163.

Pl. 62.
1. Downingia (*Downingia elegans*), p. 164   **2.** Dragon's Head (*Dracocephalum moldavica*), p. 1
3. Viper's Bugloss (*Echium plantagineum*), p. 165.       4. Tassel-flower (*Emilia flammea*), p. 1

mouth, reminiscent of some Trumpet Lilies, seven inches long, white in colour, with violet shading on the exterior. There are pure white and blue forms and one, var. *huberiana*, with flowers of blue, yellow and red. There are also forms with double flowers. *D. stramonium*, the Jimson Weed, reaches two to three feet, with lobed leaves, wide at the base and pointed, eight inches long and erect flowers of white or violet, four inches long with prickly calyces. Although usually cultivated as a greenhouse plant, the species mentioned are quite successful out-of-doors if planted out in June in a sheltered but sunny position where the soil is rich and well drained. Seed should be sown under glass in heat in March; the seedlings being pricked off into pots and planted out when all risk of frost has passed.

Propagation is from seed.

The flowering season is in late summer.

## Rocket Larkspur (Plate 60)

Family *RANUNCULACEAE*                    *Delphinium ajacis*

One of the first species of these noble plants to be introduced to British gardens and a native of the Swiss Alps. Known also as the Rocket Larkspur, the foliage is finely cut and fern-like and the stems attain two or three feet, with branching spikes of five sepalled florets, of single or double form, and varying considerably in colour from white to blue, violet, purple, pink and carmine in the most recent forms of garden origin. *D. grandiflorum* (syn. *sinense*) is often cultivated as a biennial, for it is of very doubtful perennial duration. It reaches a height of two feet with very branching stems, bearing long-spurred florets of white or bright blue, an inch or more across, with small white centres sometimes shaded with blue. *D. paniculatum*, from Western North America, is of comparative recent introduction to Britain and bears its small, spurred violet-blue florets in masses on very branching racemes to a height of one and a half feet. These are the most desirable of the annual forms of this genus that is famed for the grandeur of its perennial varieties of garden origin. Annual Larkspurs do not transplant satisfactorily; it is best to sow where they are to flower in September or March and thin out when an inch or so high.

Propagate from seed.

The flowering season is from July to September.

# Pink (Plate 61)

Family *CARYOPHYLLACEAE*                    *Dianthus* species

Old garden favourites evolved from species that are native to Europe, Russia, China and Japan. *D. barbatus* is the Sweet William, an old plant of perennial habit but best treated as a biennial that is for ever appearing in some new and improved form, with broad, flat foliage and flowers of single and double form, delightfully fragrant, in large clustered heads on stems of one to two feet. The auricula-flowered form is the oldest known. There are others with flowers of salmon, scarlet and purple shades and some with parti-coloured flowers. The Indian or Chinese Pink is *D. sinensis*, native to Central Asia, and of which *D. s. heddewigii* is a most popular variety. It reaches six to nine inches and has large flowers with frilled edges with a wide colour range from white to pink, salmon and orange-scarlet, delightfully fragrant. There are some forms with double flowers. The Deptford Pink is *D. armeria*, a native of Britain, with clusters of small flowers of deep pink with fringed edges and spotted with white. Seed should be sown in April out-of-doors where the plants are to flower, and the seedlings thinned out when sufficiently developed. Seedlings may also be raised earlier under glass and pricked off into boxes for planting out in May.

Propagation is from seed, or cuttings in the case of a particularly good form of *D. barbatus*.

The flowering season is in summer.

# Dicranostigma (Plate 61)

Family *PAPAVERACEAE*        *Dicranostigma franchetianum*

Also known as *Chelidonium franchetianum*, this is a hardy annual of Chinese origin, and is related to the Poppy. The glaucous leaves are cut in the fashion typical of many of this family, and the flowers are borne on erect stems of one and a half feet. The flowers, an inch across, of a brilliant orange shade, are of broad petals of the shape associated with the Poppy family and a centre of orange stamens. This plant is one of the most attractive of annuals and deserves to be more widely known and cultivated. It is easily grown in any well-drained soil in full sun. The seeds may be sown where the plants are to flower, and the seedlings thinned when large enough to handle. It is an effective plant for contrasting with the blue forms of the annual Scabious, Purple Petunias or *Anchusa capensis*, in which it finds its ideal foil.

Propagation is from seed.

The flowering season is from midsummer onwards.

## Foxglove (Plate 61)

Family *SCROPHULARIACEAE*                    *Digitalis purpurea*

There are biennial and perennial forms of Foxglove. *D. purpurea* is a biennial, sometimes perennial, a native of western and Central Europe, including Britain, and Scandinavia. The leaves are large, ovate and downy. The flower-stems vary from two to five feet, bearing many slightly drooping tubular flowers open at the mouth, varying in colour from rose-purple in the wild form to shades of pink, salmon, cream and white, all spotted, in the cultivated strains, of which the best known is the Shirley strain. There is also a pure white unspotted form of particular beauty, and a *D. p.* var. *campanulata*, with upper flowers united to form a big, bell-shaped bloom. Growing in any soil, in full sun or in shade, the Foxglove is well adapted for the wilder parts of the garden, the white form being particularly outstanding under the dense shade cast by large forest trees. Useful also for cutting. Seed is best sown on a shady border in April outdoors, seedlings being transplanted to shady nursery beds, three inches apart, in June, and finally transferred to flowering positions in September to October.

Propagate from seed.

The flowering season is in summer.

## Cape Marigold: Star-of-the-Veldt (Plate 61)

Family *COMPOSITAE*                    *Dimorphotheca* species

A race of South African annuals and perennials, grown as half-hardy annuals, with strikingly beautiful daisy-like flowers. The most important species is *D. aurantiaca*, growing two feet, with toothed foliage and flowers of white, red, orange or yellow, opening only in sun. *D. annua* (syn. *pluvialis*) is rather taller with flowers of white, sometimes suffused with purple or yellow. This species has been crossed with *D. aurantiaca* and has produced a number of garden varieties of differing colours, comprising white, apricot, buff, orange and salmon. Twisted petals characterize

*D. sinuata*, which is, otherwise, similar to *D. aurantiaca*. The garden hybrid known as *D. calendulacea* has purple central discs with pale yellow rays. Excellent subjects for positions in the flower garden that are hot, dry and well exposed to the sun. Seed is sown out-of-doors in early April, the seedlings thinned and allowed to flower without further disturbance. May also be raised from seed sown under glass, temperature 55° to 65° F., in early spring.

Propagation is from seed.

The flowering season is in May for *D. annua* and from late June to September for the remainder.

## Downingia (Plate 62)

Family *CAMPANULACEAE*                    *Downingia* species

Includes two species native to North America which are hardy annuals and sometimes listed under *Clintonia*. Four to six inches high, *D. elegans* has oblong lance-shaped leaves, up to three-quarters of an inch long and five-petalled flowers, about a quarter of an inch across, of light blue with white lips marked greenish-yellow, borne in the leaf axils. An inch or so taller, *D. pulchella* has similar leaves, up to an inch long and flowers of deep blue with a white centre on the lower lip, splashed with white and purple. The stockiness of these annuals commends them for the rock garden, where they have a long season of flowering when many alpines have passed their best. They are also eminently suitable for the front of the flower border, providing patches of bright colour useful for contrasting with such subjects as *Ursinia*, *Tagetes* and other yellow or orange-coloured perennials of not too tall a habit of growth. Seed should be sown thinly in April where the plants are to bloom and the seedlings thinned six inches apart in June. Full sun and well-drained soil are essential.

Propagation is from seed.

The flowering season is from midsummer until frost.

## Dragon's-head (Plate 62)

Family *LABIATAE*                    *Dracocephalum* species

A genus noted mainly for its perennials but also containing a number of attractive hardy annual species native to Europe, Asia and North America. *D. moldavica*, known as Moldavian Balm, has lance-shaped toothed leaves, up to one and a half inches long, and open-mouthed tubular flowers, an inch or less across,

. 63.
1. Blush-wort (*Erythraea pulchellum*), p. 166.  2. Californian Poppy (*Eschscholtzia californica*), p. 166.
3. Spurge (*Euphorbia heterophylla*), p. 167.   4. Kingfisher Daisy (*Felicia bergeriana*), p. 167.

*Pl.* 64.                                                                                      1
  1. Blanket-flower (*Gaillardia pulchella*), p. 168.          2. Gilia (*Gilia tricolor*), p. 169.
  3. Godetia (*Godetia grandiflora*), p. 169.     4. Baby's Breath (*Gypsophila elegans*), p. 170.

of blue or white on one-and-a-half-feet stems; it is also known as *Moldavica suaveolens*. As the name suggests, *D. parviflorum* has smaller flowers of pale blue, borne in dense spikes to a height of one and a half feet. Still smaller and of less value for effect in the flower garden is *D. thymiflorum*, with pale purple flowers on fifteen-inch stems. Although not in the first rank of annuals they add somewhat to the variety of forms and are useful for their long period of flowering. Seed should be sown where the plants are to bloom, and the seedlings thinned to six inches apart. They like cool, partially shaded positions.

Propagation is from seed.

The flowering season is from midsummer onwards.

## Viper's Bugloss (Plate 62)

Family *BORAGINACEAE*                *Echium* various species

A genus of annuals, biennials and perennials, best treated as annuals, native to Europe. From the Canary Islands we have *E. callithyrsum*, reaching two to three feet, with elegant foliage and branching stems, bearing terminal sprays of purplish-blue flowers; also *E. wildpretii*, reaching three feet, and forming a white, hairy plant with lance-shaped leaves and rose-coloured flowers in terminal spikes, a most imposing species. Two outstanding species are native to southern Europe: *E. creticum*, an annual, with hairy, oblong leaves and loose spikes of deep violet flowers, one and a half to two feet, and *E. plantagineum*, a biennial, which is a hairy plant, with long lance-shaped leaves and pale blue flowers in long panicles up to three feet. Our native Blue Weed or *E. vulgare* is quite attractive, with blue and violet flowers in narrow panicles up to two and a half feet. *E. creticum* is raised from seed sown in April where the plants are to flower, in a warm and sunny situation. The biennials *E. plantagineum* and *E. vulgare* and the perennial *E. callithyrsum* should be sown in early autumn in frames, and the plants placed out in good soil in a sheltered sunny position the following May. Good for hot and dry soils.

Propagation is from seed.

The flowering season is from midsummer onwards.

## Tassel-flower (Plate 62)

Family *COMPOSITAE*                *Emilia flammea*

Also known as Flora's Paintbrush, this pretty half-hardy annual is a native of tropical America. It sometimes is listed as *Cacalia coccinea.* Reaching a height of one to one and a half feet, the plant has oval leaves and flowers, an inch across, of bright scarlet that require careful placing among other colours. It has a form var. *lutea*, with flowers of golden yellow. Of similar height, *E. sonchifolia* has toothed foliage widening from the base, and flowers in loose clusters that may vary from purple and rose to white, and about half an inch across. The soil must be rich and well drained, and the exposure sunny. Seed sown under glass in March with gentle heat will produce seedlings that will be ready for planting out in May.

Propagation is from seed.

The flowering season is from midsummer onwards.

## Blush-wort: Centaury (Plate 63)

Family *GENTIANACEAE*                              *Erythraea* species

A genus formerly known as *Centaurium*, of attractive hardy annual or perennial alpines, native to North America, Britain and Europe. *E. beyrichii* inhabits the region from Arkansas to Texas, reaching a height of four to six inches, with erect stems and pretty star-like flowers of deep pink, about an inch across. *E. pulchellum* (syn. *E. ramosissimum*) is a smaller species of similar characteristics and is particularly useful for the rock garden, where it is not considered a heresy to sow annuals; it reaches a height of six inches. *E. massoni* (syn. *E. diffusum*) is strictly perennial and comes from the Azores, reaching four inches, of tufted habit, bearing flowers of bright rose of a form similar to *Gentiana verna*. The California *E. venustum* has deep pink flowers, an inch across, with white throats spotted red. All these plants prefer a position in partial shade in a light sandy soil where leafmould has been added. In such a place the seed may be sown out-of-doors in late March and the seedlings thinned to three inches apart.

Propagation is from seed.

The flowering season is in early summer, *E. beyrichii* and *E. venustum* continuing in flower until September.

## Californian Poppy (Plate 63)

Family *PAPAVERACEAE*                          *Eschscholtzia* species

A race of hardy annuals of brilliant colouring and of Californian origin. The most important species is *E. californica*, from which have originated the horticultural varieties that enjoy so much favour today. The plant grows one to one and a half feet high, with finely cut glaucous green foliage and slender stems, bearing flowers, three inches across, that are yellow to orange in the type, but in the garden varieties vary from golden yellow to carmine, coral, vermilion, and orange-scarlet, some with double flowers. The individual flowers are short lived but soon succeeded by others. *E. caespitosa* is a pretty dwarf, six inches high, with bright yellow flowers, two inches across. *E. maritima* is of dwarf, sprawling habit, with silvery foliage and small purple-spotted pale yellow flowers. The seed should be sown in August or April, in a sunny, well-drained border where the plants are to bloom, and the seedlings thinned to four inches apart. Not suitable for a cut flower but effective in the mass.

Propagation is from seed.

The flowering season is from midsummer to Michaelmas.

## Spurge: Poinsettia  (Plate 63)

Family *EUPHORBIACEAE*                          *Euphorbia* species

Tender annuals from North America and unusual but charming plants for the flower garden. *E. heterophylla* is the Mexican Fire Plant, reaching up to two and a half feet, with narrow oval leaves, toothed and shaped like a fiddle. The true flowers are small, orange and not very showy, and the real attractiveness lies in the brightly coloured red bracts surrounding them. Known as Snow on the Mountain, *E. marginata* reaches two feet, has oval leaves, the upper ones having white margins; the flowers have white petal-like appendages and are borne in umbels. *E. nutans* has narrow oval foliage, with toothed edges, blotched and margined red. The seed should be sown under glass in March and the seedlings grown on in small pots, protected from frost and planted out in early June. The position should be in full sun and the soil of a sandy nature and well drained.

Propagation is from seed.

The season for display is from midsummer until early September.

## Kingfisher Daisy  (Plate 63)

Family *COMPOSITAE*                          *Felicia* species

An attractive race which includes biennials and perennials as well as annuals, largely native to South Africa. *F. bergeriana* is the best-known annual, with a rosette of small, rounded, hairy foliage and four- or five-inch stems, bearing flowers, similar in form and size to those of the common Field Daisy, with rays of brilliant blue and small yellow centres. *F. tenella* (syn. *fragilis*) is somewhat taller, often reaching twelve to fourteen inches, with narrow leaves, two inches long, and daisy-like flowers with rays that vary in shade from pale blue to violet, spreading from a yellow centre. *F. adfinis*, nine to twelve inches, is a branching and hairy plant with oblong leaves nearly two inches long, and pale blue flowers. There are a number of others, viz. *F. abyssinica, hyssopifolia* and *rotundifolia*, all having flowers of varying tones of blue. There are, in addition, some shrubby forms. Seed is sown thinly in well-drained pots, under glass, temperature 60° to 65°F., in February or March. The seedlings are pricked off when large enough to handle, and hardened off to plant out-of-doors in May.

Propagation is by means of seed.

The flowering season is from July to September.

## Blanket-flower (Plate 64)

Family *COMPOSITAE*                                *Gaillardia* species

These are hardy annual species of this colourful genus from North America, of which three are of particular value in the flower garden. Reaching a height of two to three feet, *G. amblyodon* is of hairy character with oblong leaves, three inches long, and flowers, two inches across, comprising bronze-red ray florets with yellow central discs. Of similar height, *G. lanceolata* has narrow leaves, rather wider towards the end, and up to three inches long, with flowers, two and a half inches across, comprising yellow ray florets with brownish-purple central discs. *G. pulchella* has four-inch oblong leaves, and flowers, two inches across, with yellow ray florets, purple at the base. There are a number of good varieties with very large flowers, such as *G. p. picta lorenziana*, a double form of many colours, and *G. p. picta albomarginata*, with ray florets bronzy-red, tipped white. Seed may be sown in February under glass, the seedlings pricked off and planted out-of-doors in late May, or it may be sown in late March where the plants are to flower and the seedlings thinned. *G. lanceolata* may be treated as a biennial and sown in late summer, protected during winter and planted out in the following spring.

Propagation is from seed.

The flowering season is from midsummer onwards.

## Gilia (Plate 64)

Family *POLEMONIACEAE* *Gilia* species

This is an attractive genus of small, free-flowering annuals, biennials and perennials, sometimes divided among several genera (see *Leptosiphon*). The annuals are hardy and mostly dwarf. Known as Bird's-Eyes, *G. tricolor* grows twelve inches tall, with foliage dissected into narrow segments and flowers of violet or lilac lobes, with the tubes orange-yellow and the throat marked with purple, borne in clusters of loose formation. There is also a pink form, a white, a rose and a violet. *G. achilleaefolia* also has the finely divided foliage with purplish-blue flowers, growing one foot high. *G. dianthoides* (syn. *Fenzlia dianthiflora*) is a pretty dwarf of four to six inches, tufted in habit with thread-like leaves and tubular flowers of lilac-pink or white, three-quarters of an inch long, in small clusters. The light blue flowers of *G. capitata* are about an inch across and are carried in clusters on eighteen- to twenty-four-inch stems. *G. coronopifolia* (syn. *G. rubra*), the Standing Cypress, is strictly a perennial but grown as a biennial in this country, and grows two feet or more with finely divided foliage and showy flowers with scarlet corolla, yellowish dotted with red inside. The seeds may be sown out-of-doors in autumn or April, where the plants are to bloom, thinning to three inches apart. They like a sunny position and ordinary soil. Short twigs are useful for support in exposed positions.

Propagation is from seed.

The flowering season is from midsummer onwards.

## Godetia (Plate 64)

Family *ONAGRACEAE* *Godetia grandiflora*

A genus of hardy annuals, related to Oenothera, that comes from California. *G. grandiflora* (syn. *Oenothera whitneyi*, *G. whitneyi*), from which our garden varieties have largely originated, has oblong leaves, up to one and a quarter inches long, and stems one to two feet high that bear flowers up to four inches across that vary in hue from white to rose red, blotched darkly at the centre. Of the varieties of garden origin var. *azaleaflora* has large double flowers of pink with crimson centre. There are others of crimson, white, salmon, cerise, rose, cream-pink; some are dwarf and do not exceed six inches in height. Varieties varying in height from fifteen inches to two feet, with both single

and double flowers in a wide range of colour are now available.
May be sown where plants are to flower in autumn or spring; or
raised from sowings under glass, temperature 55° to 65°F., in
early spring. Fine for cutting.

Propagation is from seed.

The flowering season is from late June to October.

## Baby's Breath (Plate 64)

Family *CARYOPHYLLACEAE*                    *Gypsophila elegans*

A hardy annual from the Caucasus and useful as a foil to many
of the larger flowered annuals. The leaves are lance-shaped and
the habit of the plant is free and branching up to a height of
one and a half feet, bearing on slender stems many flowers, about
a quarter of an inch across, of different colours according to the
variety. Of the forms of garden origin the following are outstanding: *G. e. alba*, with white flowers of small size; *G. e. a.
grandiflora*, with extra large flowers; *G. e. carminea*, with carmine
flowers; and *G. e. rosea*, a fine rose-pink. There is also a form with
purple flowers, foliage and stems known as Purple Queen, that
has its value in certain decorative effects. The seed should be
sown out-of-doors in April where the plants are to flower, and the
seedlings thinned to appropriate distances. A plant much valued
for cutting as well as for effect in the flower garden, where its
light and airy effect cannot fail to be welcome.

Propagation is from seed.

The flowering season is in late summer and on until frost.

## Sunflower (Plate 65)

Family *COMPOSITAE*                         *Helianthus* species

Natives of North America, some of annual duration. The
Common Sunflower of English cottage gardens is *H. annuus* that
may reach up to ten feet, with stout leafy stems topped by huge
flowers, a foot or more across, of many broad yellow petals and
a large central disc of brownish-purple. There are forms with
lemon-yellow, deep yellow and orange flowers, the last being
usually of double form. There is also a form with yellow and
green variegated foliage. Some of the garden forms are outstanding, both for the size of the flowers and their colouring,
which extends to chestnut-red; others have primrose-coloured
petals and black discs. The Cucumber Leaf Sunflower is *H.
debilis* (syn. *H. cucumerifolius*), with three-inch flowers of varied

colouring from mahogany-red to pink or purple; it reaches four feet. The Texan *H. argophyllus* is mainly noteworthy for its grey, hairy foliage and bright yellow flowers, three inches across, with purplish-brown discs. Easily grown in full sun by planting the seeds individually where the plants are to grow. The seeds are edible and may be used for poultry feed.

Propagation is from seed.

The flowering season is from August onwards.

## Everlasting-flower: Immortelle (Plate 65)

Family *COMPOSITAE*                    *Helichrysum bracteatum*

A half-hardy annual that is native to Australia. Reaching a height of two to three feet, the plant has oblong and pointed leaves, and flowers with many petals clustered and often in-curving towards a central disc. They are known as Everlasting-flowers, Straw-flowers and Immortelles. If the stems are cut when the flowers are just fully opened, and hung with the heads downwards to dry, they will retain their colour and form for a long period. There is a large-flowered form in var. *monstrosum*. The garden forms vary in colour from white to pink, purple, red and yellow. The seed is best sown under cloches in the open ground in March or, without protection, in April, and the seedlings thinned to appropriate distances. Helichrysum is probably more to be valued for its lasting qualities than as a garden plant.

Propagation is from seed.

The flowering season is from July onwards.

## Cherry Pie (Plate 65)

Family *BORAGINACEAE*                    *Heliotropium peruvianum*

A native of Peru and a tender perennial best treated as an annual in Britain. Growing between one and four feet high, the plant is shrubby with oblong lance-shaped leaves and clusters of many violet or purple flowers, famous for their pronounced vanilla scent. There is a white form and others of garden origin. The most successful method of culture consists in lifting plants from the open ground in September, wintering them in a warm greenhouse, and propagating new stock from cuttings in early spring. Seed sown early in March will produce vigorous seedlings for planting out-of-doors in a sunny and well-drained position in early June. These will provide a good display in the same summer. Also known as Heliotrope, this plant is an old garden favourite and should not be omitted from any summer bedding scheme.

Propagation is from seed or cuttings.

The flowering season is from midsummer onwards.

## Swan River Everlasting-flower (Plate 65)

Family *COMPOSITAE*                                    *Helipterum manglesii*

The most recent name for *Rhodanthe manglesii*, a native annual of Australia with everlasting flowers. The plant reaches one and a half feet, with oval leaves, and flowers, about one and a half inches across, of bright pink with yellow bracts. Var. *maculatum* has its bracts spotted with carmine. Although this is the most important species two others may be mentioned. *H. humbold-tianum* (syn. *H. sandfordii*) is of similar height with long and narrow leaves covered with white tomentum, and small heads of yellowish-green flowers in clusters. *H. roseum* (syn. *Acroclinium roseum*) reaches two feet, with fine lance-shaped leaves, and two-inch flowers of rose or white, borne singly. Best treated as half-hardy annuals, except in the most favoured climates, and sown under glass in March or April, the seedlings being pricked off and planted where they are to flower when risk of frost has passed in May or early June. If cloche protection can be afforded they may be sown where the plants are to flower.

Propagation is from seed.

The flowering season is in summer.

## Rose Mallow (Plate 66)

Family *MALVACEAE*                                       *Hibiscus* species

A genus containing hardy and half-hardy annuals from the tropics, and most attractive of their kind. Their flowers resemble those of their relation, the Hollyhock. An old garden favourite, *H. trionum* is known as the Flower-of-an-hour and is reported as growing wild in Afghanistan and Africa, and has been naturalized in North America. It attains a height of two feet, has elegantly lobed and toothed leaves and flowers of sulphur-yellow, three inches across, with purple centres that close in shadow. *H. esculentus*, known in America as Okra or Gumbo, grows six feet high, and has yellow flowers with red centres which give way to edible fruits, twelve inches long. Although strictly a perennial, *H. manihot* is a fine species, six to eight feet tall, with yellow and purple flowers, very suitable for cultivation as an annual. All

Pl. 65.
1. Sunflower (*Helianthus annuus*), p. 170.   2. Everlasting-flower (*Helichrysum bracteatum*), p. 171.
3. Cherry Pie (*Heliotropium peruvianum*), p. 171.   4. Swan River Everlasting-flower (*Helipterum manglesii*), p. 172.

*Pl.* 66.
1. Rose Mallow (*Hibiscus trionum*), p. 172.
3. Balsam (*Impatiens capensis*), p. 173.

2. Candytuft (*Iberis umbellata*), p. 173.
4. Violet Cress (*Ionopsidium acaule*), p. 174.

three species may be sown under glass, temperature 60° to 65°F., in February or March for planting out in June. Seeds of *H. trionum* may be sown outdoors in April where the plants are to flower. Ordinary soil suits, but position should be sunny.

Propagation is from seed.

The flowering season is in late summer.

## Candytuft (Plate 66)

Family *CRUCIFERAE*                    *Iberis umbellata*

A native of southern Europe and a showy dwarf annual that enjoys considerable popularity. The narrow leaves are lance-shaped and about three inches long; the stems will attain a height of nine or twelve inches, bearing flowers in clustered heads, one to two inches across, varying in colour from white to bright shades of pink, purple, red and violet. There are a number of varieties of garden origin. Unlike the foregoing, *I. affinis* has fragrant flowers of white that become suffused with lilac in ageing. The Rocket Candytuft is *I. coronaria* (syn. *amara*) and has fragrant white flowers borne in clusters that rapidly become elongated into fruit. Easily grown in well-drained soil in a sunny or partially shaded position, Candytufts are favoured for edging or massed effects in the flower garden. It is best to sow the seeds where they are to bloom in autumn for early summer flowering, in spring for summer and early autumn flowering, and, when an inch high, thin out to four inches apart.

Propagation is by means of seed.

The flowering season is from June until September.

## Balsam (Plate 66)

Family *GERANIACEAE*             *Impatiens* various species

Natives of Africa and Asia, this genus comprises both hardy and half-hardy annuals and perennials. *I. balsamina*, the old-fashioned greenhouse Balsam, is tender and at one time was grown in pots for exhibition. It may be planted out in warm weather, but is seldom seen today. The leaves are lance-shaped and the stems grow up to two and a half feet, the flowers being spurred and produced in the leaf axils, rather like miniature double Hollyhocks in form. *I. holstii* is a tender perennial best treated as a half-hardy annual by raising from seed or cuttings under glass and planting out-of-doors in early June. Under glass it attains three feet, but grows little more than a foot out-of-doors

The foliage is ovate, three to four inches long; the spurred flowers of scarlet, nearly two inches across, are on long stalks towards the tops of the stems. It has been crossed with *I. sultani* to produce a number of variations. The annual *I. capensis* has pink flowers and ruddy-hued stems, and *I. scabrida* has golden yellow flowers and requires similar culture to *I. holstii*. *I. roylei* (syn. *glandulifera*) is the old-fashioned big, coarse Balsam of gardens, of erect habit, up to five or six feet, with purple flowers. *I. amphorata* is a hardy annual from the Himalayas, growing five feet tall, with purple flowers in August. It may be sown in April outdoors where the plants are to follow. Best raised from seed sown under glass, potted on and planted out when all risk of frost has passed. Full sun and good drainage are essential.

Propagation is from seed or cuttings.

The flowering season is from June to September.

## Violet Cress (Plate 66)

Family *CRUCIFERAE*                          *Ionopsidium acaule*

A Portuguese genus of one species, being a miniature in every respect. It is also known as the Diamond Flower. The leaves are small and rounded, not more than a quarter of an inch across, and the flowers are stemless, being four-petalled, white in colour and suffused with violet, and the whole plant does not exceed three inches high or four inches across. A most useful annual for sowing between the crevices of paving where the flowers provide a very appropriate furnishing. It is also suitable for shaded or sunny positions in the rock garden, as a ribbon margin to flower-beds, and as a foreground furnishing for taller annuals. The seed should be sown in early April where the plants are to flower. Germination is usually rapid and the flowers will appear in June.

Propagation is from seed.

The flowering season is from June until autumnal frost.

## Morning Glory: Moon Creeper (Plate 67)

Family *CONVOLVULACEAE*                          *Ipomoea* species

These are mostly natives of tropical America, comprising both annuals and perennials, best treated as half-hardy annuals and among the loveliest of climbing plants, very similar in leaf and form of flower to the Convolvulus. *I. rubra caerulea* is the most favoured for outdoor cultivation with lovely clear blue flowers, four inches across at the mouth, and white in the tube, and climbs up to six feet. *I. versicolor* (syn. *Mina lobata*) will climb up to six to eight feet, with flowers that are crimson in bud, but change on opening to pale yellow. *I. quamoclit* (syn. *Quamoclit pennata*), six feet, has scarlet flowers and should be grown out-of-doors only in the warmest localities. *I. purpurea*, six to eight feet, has flowers of purple, blue or pink and sometimes produces double flowers. For the outdoor flower garden *I. rubra caerulea* is the most satisfactory and requires to be raised from seed sown early in the year under glass. The seeds are best sown at the rate of two in a four-inch pot as they do not prick off satisfactorily. Plant out against a sunny south wall or trellis in early June. The flowers open in early morning and fade by noon, hence its name.

Propagation is from seed.

The flowering season is from July to September.

## Summer Cypress (Plate 67)

Family *CHENOPODIACEAE*        *Kochia scoparia*

A European annual grown mainly as a foliage plant for summer bedding effects. The narrow linear leaves may be two inches long and the whole plant is reminiscent of a neat and compact conifer of dense pyramidal or columnar habit of two to three feet. The feathery foliage is an attractive bright yellow-green in the type, but on *K. s.* var. *trichophylla* it changes to an effective purplish red in autumn. The latter is the form most usually seen in gardens. The flowers are formed in little clusters in the axils of the leaves and have no decorative value. The seed should be sown under glass in March or April, and the seedlings grown on in pots and planted out-of-doors in late May or early June.

Propagation is from seed.

The effect of the foliage is at its full development from July to September.

## Lallemantia (Plate 67)

Family *LABIATAE*        *Lallemantia* various species

A race of annual or biennial herbs, native to western Asia and a plant of unusual character. *L. canescens* is a biennial, growing to one and a half feet, with pointed oblong leaves and bright blue and white flowers, one and a quarter inches long, with the tube longer than the calyx, borne in whorls up the leafy stem. Of similar height and habit is *L. iberica*, an annual, with soft-blue flowers. *L. peltata* is also an annual, twelve inches high, with oblong, slightly hairy leaves and blue flowers in whorls. Both annuals and biennials are most distinctive plants in the flower garden, worthy adornments of the outdoor border, and useful for interior decoration as cut flowers. The seed should be sown thinly where the plants are to bloom and thinned to about nine inches apart or a little less in the case of the dwarfer *L. peltata*. Both annuals and biennials deserve greater attention than they enjoy at present.

Propagation is from seed.

The flowering period is from midsummer until late August.

## Sweet Pea (Plate 67)

Family *LEGUMINOSAE*                          *Lathyrus odoratus*

One of the most prized of all annuals both for its charm as a decorative cut flower and its fragrance. The original species is a native of southern Europe, but it is to the many varieties of garden origin that the Sweet Pea owes its popularity. Of climbing habit, growing six to ten feet high, this species has oval and rounded foliage that varies in size according to the cultivation given. The flowers are of the familiar keeled pea shape, two or more on a stem and varying in colour from white to practically all shades except true blue and yellow. The plant climbs by means of tendrils. For ordinary garden cultivation, the seed may be sown in the late summer in pots, wintered in a cold frame and planted out in March in deeply cultivated ground that has been limed and well fed with organic manure. Peasticks or canes are necessary for support. Seed may also be sown in late March out-of-doors, spaced about six inches apart and given support. The exhibition culture of the plant is practised by specialists with remarkable results.

Propagation is from seed.

The flowering season is from midsummer onwards.

## Tree Mallow (Plate 68)

Family *MALVACEAE*                          *Lavatera* various species

A genus of hardy shrubs and showy annuals. *L. arborea*, from southern Europe, forms a shrubby plant, six to ten feet high, with large lobed leaves, and flowers, of trumpet shape, two inches across, reddish-purple veined with a deeper shade at the base in clusters. There is also a variegated form. *L. davaei* is a Portuguese shrub, up to four feet high, with clusters of violet-rose

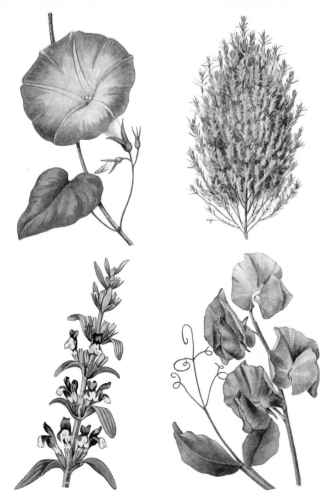

57.
orning Glory (*Ipomoea rubra caerulea*), p. 174.
allemantia (*Lallemantia canescens*), p. 175.

2. Summer Cypress (*Kochia scoparia*), p. 175.
4. Sweet Pea (*Lathyrus odoratus*), p. 176.

*Pl.* 68.
1. Tree Mallow (*Lavatera trimestris* var.), p. 176.
3. Leptosiphon (*Leptosiphon parviflorus*), p. 177.
2. Tidy-tips Flower (*Layia elegans*), p.
4. Leptosyne (*Leptosyne douglasii*), p.

flowers. *L. mauritanica*, from North Africa, is an annual of two feet, with violet flowers, shaded darker at the base. *L. trimestris* (syn. *L. rosea*) grows three to four feet, is native to southern Europe and an annual. The leaves are rounded and toothed. The flowers are borne singly, four inches across, and of a rosy-red shade. There are a number of varieties of garden origin that exceed the type in beauty, such as *alba*, a good white form, and "Loveliness", a beautiful rose. The seeds of shrubby kinds may be sown in frames in early autumn and the seedlings planted out in the following spring, or they may be sown in their flowering positions in April. The seed of the annuals may be sown out-of-doors in late March where the plants are to flower.

Propagation is from seed.

The flowering season is from midsummer onwards.

## Tidy-tips Flower (Plate 68)

Family *COMPOSITAE*                                         *Layia* species

Pretty hardy annuals, chiefly from California, of which five are known in British gardens. *L. elegans*, appropriately known as Tidy-tips on account of its neat habit, grows a foot high, with narrow leaves, three inches long, and many flowers of daisy-like form composed of three-quarter-inch rays of yellow tipped with white. It also has a pure white form. *L. caliglossa* (syn. *Callichroa douglasii*), reaches a foot high, with yellow flowers tipped glossy white. Of similar colouring and probably the most pleasing of the species, *L. chrysanthemoides* (syn. *Oxyura chrysanthemoides*) has two-inch oblong leaves and twelve-inch branching stems. Of the same colouring but of dwarfer habit, eight or nine inches high, *L. platyglossa* (syn. *Callichroa platyglossa*) has its admirers. The seed may be sown in April where the plants are to flower and the seedlings thinned as necessary.

Propagation is from seed.

The flowering season is from midsummer onwards.

## Leptosiphon (Plate 68)

Family *POLEMONIACEAE*                              *Leptosiphon* species
                                                                    (syn. *Gilia*)

Botanically, this genus is now merged with *Gilia* (q.v.), but gardeners and catalogues are somewhat resistant to the change. As this is a gardener's rather than a botanist's book, it has been thought desirable to give this group of Californian annuals

12

separate mention under their best-known name. *Leptosiphon parviflorus* (syn. *Gilia androsacea*) has finely divided leaves, grows twelve inches tall and carries salver-formed flowers, an inch long in dense heads, varying in colours of lilac, pink and white. *L. densiflorus* (syn. *Gilia densiflora*) is a dwarf of six inches with lilac flowers an inch or less long and a quarter of an inch across, and has a white flowering form, *alba*. *L. roseus* (syn. *Gilia micrantha*) is most popular for beds and borders, growing nine inches tall and having flowers of a lovely rose. The dwarf habit of these members of the *Leptosiphon* group commends them for the front of borders and beds, and they may justifiably be used to fill empty spaces in the rock garden with summer bloom. The seed is sown in autumn or spring where the plants are to flower, and the seedlings thinned three inches apart. They need a sunny position and any ordinary well-drained soil suits.

Propagation is from seed.

The flowering season is from June onwards.

## Leptosyne (Plate 68)

Family *COMPOSITAE*                              *Leptosyne* species

A genus of hardy annuals and perennials, native to California. Three annual species are worthy of mention here. *L. douglasii*, with delicately feathered foliage and yellow flowers, one and a quarter inches across, freely produced on twelve-inch stems, makes a neat and compact plant. *L. stillmanii* has large, single, golden-yellow flowers, one and a half inches across, on eighteen-inch stems. *L. calliopsidea* also bears bright yellow flowers on eighteen-inch stems in September. These hardy annuals are sown in April out-of-doors where the plants are to bloom, thinning the seedlings to appropriate distances apart when large enough to handle. They may also be sown under glass, temperature 55° to 65° F., in March, for planting out in May. A position in full sun is essential and a soil that is well drained. They are excellent dry-soil plants and withstand drought very well.

Propagation is from seed.

The flowering season is from midsummer until frost.

## Meadow Foam (Plate 69)

Family *LIMNANTHACEAE*                    *Limnanthes douglasii*

A hardy annual, native to western North America from California to Oregon. It is also known as Butter and Eggs. The

69.
Meadow Foam (*Limnanthes douglasii*), p. 178.
Toad-flax (*Linaria supina* var.), p. 180.

178
2. Sea Lavender (*Limonium suworowii*), p. 179.
4. Flax (*Linum grandiflorum*), p. 180.

plant reaches a height of twelve inches, and has finely cleft yellowish-green leaves and white, rounded flowers, with rich yellow centres, sweetly fragrant and about one inch across. An easy and useful subject to grow, unfastidious as to position or soil, doing equally well in wet or drained soils, in heavy clay or porous sand. Once grown, it tends to perpetuate itself by self-sown seedlings which form a colourful mass. There is another species, *L. alba*, with the same finely cut foliage and flowers of a pure white on six- to eight-inch stems. Seed should be sown thinly in September or April where the plants are to flower.

Propagation is from seed.

The flowering season is in late spring and early summer.


## Sea Lavender (Plate 69)

Family *PLUMBAGINACEAE*                    *Limonium* species

Formally known as Statice, the genus includes both hardy and half-hardy annuals and perennials, native to Central Asia and the Mediterranean region. The Algerian *L. bonduelli* is a half-hardy annual of one to two feet high, with long cleft foliage, up to six inches long, and winged panicles of bright yellow flowers of fibrous substance. *L. sinuata*, a perennial grown always as an annual, from the Mediterranean region, reaches one to two feet high, with similar foliage, rather longer, and winged panicles of flowers having blue calyces and yellowish-white corollas. There are a number of attractive forms with white, orange, salmon, lavender and intermediate shades. A species desirable for the production of flowers for cutting, *L. suworowii*, from Turkestan, has a rosette of eight-inch oblong, lance-shaped leaves, and eighteen-inch stems, bearing dense cylindrical spikes of rose-pink flowers with green calyces tipped with lavender. Less important species worthy of cultivation are *L. leptostachyum*, from Persia, with spikes of white flowers on six-inch stems, and *L. spicatum*, from western Asia, with cylindrical spikes of white or rose flowers. *L. leptostachyum* and *L. sinuata* may be sown out-of-doors in April where the plants are to flower. The remaining species are best treated as half-hardy annuals and sown under glass in March, and the seedlings pricked out and planted where they are to flower in late May. A sunny position and well-drained soil are essential.

Propagation is from seed.

The flowering season is in late summer.

## Toad-flax (Plate 69)

Family *SCROPHULARIACEAE*                *Linaria* species

A genus having species native to Europe, North Africa and Canada, including many annuals and perennials valuable in the flower garden. From Morocco we have *L. maroccana*, an annual of nine to twelve inches, with narrow foliage and short spikes of small flowers that are violet-rose with a speck of yellow and pointed spurs. There are many charming garden varieties, bushy and compact, that produce flowers of white, yellow, purple, lavender, pink and violet-blue. *L. heterophylla*, one to two feet, also of Morocco, has flowers mostly of straw and yellow. Important as a parent of some of the garden varieties, *L. bipartita*, from Algeria, is of erect habit of one foot high, with violet flowers, the upper portion being cut into two parts and the lower being an orange lip. There are white, red, violet, rose, yellow and purple flowered forms. Spurred flowers of yellow, pink, red, maroon and purple characterize *L. supina*, from Majorca, a half-hardy perennial, best treated as an annual and reaching nine inches. The Purple Net Toadflax is *L. reticulata*, native to Portugal, with deep purple flowers marked with orange, growing two to three feet high. *L. tristis*, twelve inches, a native of Spain, has yellow and purply-brown flowers. There are a number of other species inferior to those described. Seed may be sown in August or April where the plants are to flower, thinned to four to six inches apart. They like a sunny position and a well-drained humus-rich soil.

Propagation is from seed.

The flowering season is in early summer, and later if plants are prevented from developing seed.

## Flax (Plate 69)

Family *LINACEAE*                *Linum grandiflorum*

This Algerian species, growing a foot high, is the best annual Flax for garden purposes and has given rise to a number of garden forms. The leaves are narrow and pointed and clothe the stems; the flowers are round, five-petalled, up to one and a half inches across, and red to bluish-purple in colour with dark centres. There are a number of garden forms in var. *caeruleum*, a rather dull blue, var. *coccineum*, a good bright red, and var. *roseum*, pink. *L. usitatissimum*, eighteen inches, is the Common Flax with attractive flowers of soft blue. Seed should be sown in March out-of-doors where the plants are to flower, choosing a position

1. Large-flowered Mallow-wort (*Malope trifida*), p. 183.  2. Mallow (*Malva sylvestris* var.), p. 184.
3. Stock (*Matthiola incana* hybrid), p. 184.  4. Meconopsis (*Meconopsis integrifolia*), p. 185.

where the drainage is good and there is full exposure to the sun. To prolong the display successive sowings may be made up to early June and, if a particularly early batch of flower is desired, seed may be sown, with protection as the severity of the climate demands it, in October, for flowering in spring.

Propagation is from seed.

The flowering period is from June to September.

## Lobelia (Plate 70)

Family *CAMPANULACEAE*                                    *Lobelia* species

A widely distributed genus of hardy and half-hardy perennials, some being treated as annuals. The Edging Lobelia is *L. erinus*, from South Africa, a semi-trailing plant, six or nine inches high, with small rounded foliage and leafy stems, bearing many flowers of pale blue or violet with a white or yellow throat and about three-quarters of an inch across. It has a number of forms, some of compact habit with bright blue flowers, and others of garden origin with varying depths of colour and one with golden foliage. *L. tenuior* (syn. *L. ramosa*), from West Australia, twelve to eighteen inches, has bright blue flowers, one inch across. *L. ilicifolia*, from Australia, is of trailing habit and is best known by its garden variety, "Sapphire", which is useful alike for hanging baskets or rock gardens. The seed should be sown in a leafy compost in either autumn or spring. If in autumn, greenhouse protection during winter is necessary. The seedlings are pricked off into boxes and planted out in late May or early June. It is wise to stop the seedlings when an inch high in order to encourage bushy growth.

Propagation is from seed or cuttings.

The flowering season is from June to Michaelmas.

## Honesty (Plate 70)

Family *CRUCIFERAE*                    *Lunaria annua* (syn. *L. biennis*)

A native of Europe and of biennial habit; known also as Satin-flower, Money-flower and Moon-wort. The leaves are ovate and toothed and the stems attain a height of from two to three feet, with flowers, about half an inch across and purple in colour, borne in branching sprays. There is also a white-flowered form in var. *alba*, a crimson-flowered form in var. *atrococcinea*, and a form of garden origin with larger flowers than the type. The flowers are followed by flat, oval seed-pods, about two inches long, which, when the outer covering has been shed, reveal attractive silvery discs that are much prized, when dried, for use in winter decoration, sometimes being dyed various colours. Will grow well in any good soil in sun or partial shade, the seed being sown in the late summer for producing flowering plants for the following season. A pretty woodland plant.

Propagation is from seed.

The flowering season is in April and May.

## Lupin (Plate 70)

Family *LEGUMINOSAE*                                    *Lupinus* species

Although not comparable with the magnificent spikes produced by the modern perennial varieties of garden origin, the annual species of this genus are nevertheless possessed of a charm peculiarly their own. The leaves are digitatedly lobed like those of the perennials, and the flowers are of characteristic pea-like form. From Morocco we have *L. aureus* with short spikes of yellow flowers rising to a foot and well set off with attractive greyish frosted foliage. The various annual Lupins of garden origin have come largely from *L. hartwegii*, a Mexican species that reaches two to three feet, with flowers of blue and white in the type, and having forms that vary from white, to blue and pink shades of varying depth of colour. *L. nanus*, from California, is the dwarf blue Lupin, reaching only twelve inches, a showy compact species, of which there are forms with white and pink or white and violet bicoloured flowers. *L. hirsutus*, a Mediterranean species, reaches one and a half feet or more, and has blue and white flowers. *L. mutabilis* comes from Colombia and has flowers of white with yellow or violet standards. Its form var. *cruckshanksii* has blue flowers shaded violet and purple. Others are the Californian *L. hirsutissimus*, growing one foot high, with reddish-purple flowers; *L. densiflorus* (syn. *L. menziessii*), another native of California, two feet tall, with yellow fragrant flowers; *L. luteus*, also yellow flowering, is from South Europe, growing one to two feet; and *L. pubescens*, one and a half to three feet, has given rise to many valuable varieties of various colouring, and is native to Mexico and Guatemala. Easily raised from seed sown in March to April where the plants are to flower, thinning to nine to twelve inches apart in May. Good drought resisters.

Propagate from seed.

The flowering season is from June to September.

## Rose of Heaven: Corn Cockle (Plate 70)

Family *CARYOPHYLLACEAE*        *Lychnis coeli-rosea*

This species from the Levant is one of the gems among annuals and worthy of a place in any garden. The plant grows about twelve inches high, with linear leaves and solitary, terminal flowers, an inch across, of glowing rose and purple. Of the various forms var. *alba* and *candida*, with white flowers; var. *caerulea*, blue; var. *fimbriata*, fringed rosy purple; var. *cardinalis*, crimson; var. *kermesina*, reddish-purple; and var. *oculata*, rose with purple eye, are attractive. From this last species has originated varieties of garden origin, sometimes listed as *Viscaria oculata* with blue, carmine, white, scarlet and pink varieties. *L. githago* (syn. *Agrostemma githago*) reaches two feet or more and is the native Corn Cockle of British cornfields with purplish-red flowers and long leafy sepals. The seed should be sown in April on well-drained ground in sunny positions where the plants are to bloom, thinning to a few inches apart when the seedlings are an inch high.

Propagation is from seed.

The flowering season is from midsummer to Michaelmas.

## Large-flowered Mallow-wort (Plate 71)

Family *MALVACEAE*        Malope *trifida*

A showy annual, native to Spain, and a member of the Mallow family. The plant is a colourful addition to the flower garden. Growing two to three feet tall, the plant produces toothed, three-lobed leaves and trumpet-shaped flowers, three inches across, of rose-purple, borne singly in the leaf axils. The habit of the plant is erect, bushy and well balanced. There are a number of attractive forms, particularly var. *alba*, with white flowers; var. *grandiflora*, with very large rose-red flowers, with veins of a darker tone; var. *purpurea*, with deep purplish-red flowers; and var. *rosea*, with rose-pink flowers. *M. malacoides*, a native of South Europe, is of smaller stature, bearing rose and purple flowers on stems, one to two feet tall. Useful plants for massed effect or for adding brightness to dull parts of the garden. The seeds should be sown in April where the plants are to flower, the seedlings thinned to one or one and a half feet apart. The position should be in full sun and the soil well cultivated and perfectly drained.

Propagation is from seed.

The flowering season is from midsummer until frost.

# Mallow (Plate 71)

Family *MALVACEAE*                              *Malva* species

A showy race which includes a number of attractive annual and biennial species as well as perennials described elsewhere. They are native to Europe. Mostly of erect habit of varying height, with lobed or dissected leaves and trumpet-shaped flowers, they may all be treated as hardy annuals in Britain. The most important species for the flower garden are *M. borealis*, reaching a height of two to three feet, with pale pink flowers, half an inch across; *M. crispa*, the Curled Mallow, so called on account of its leaves, which are five- to seven-lobed, rounded and curled at the margin, the flowers being whitish and a quarter of an inch across, borne on unbranched stems, three to six feet tall; *M. nicaensis*, one and a half feet, of erect habit and with small pale blue flowers in dense clusters. The most effective is perhaps *M. sylvestris*, a biennial usually treated as an annual, three feet high, with rosy-purple flowers, over an inch across. Its best form is var. *mauritanica*, reaching four feet and having larger flowers with more pronounced stripes. Seed is best sown under glass, temperature 55° F., in March or April, and transplanted outdoors, one or one and a half feet apart, in late May or early June. The position should be in full sun and the soil well drained.

Propagation is from seed.

The flowering period is from early July onwards.


# Stock (Plate 71)

Family *CRUCIFERAE*                         *Matthiola* various species

Native to the Mediterranean region and among the most important of the annuals. *M. incana* of the Levant is the parent of the Brompton and Wallflower-leaved Stocks, a biennial of sturdy erect habit, up to two feet, with four-inch oblong leaves and terminal racemes of flowers, one inch long, varying in colour from white to blush, yellow, purple and red of delightful and pronounced fragrance. *M. annua* (syn. *Incana annua*) is the annual parent of Ten-week and Intermediate Stocks, with an equally varied colour range. From crosses made between *M. sinuata* and other species has originated the East Lothian Stocks with a range of colour equal to those named. *M. bicornis*, from Greece, is the Night Scented Stock, so called for the strong fragrance of its flowers at dusk. Of dwarf habit, this annual produces masses of small lilac-purple flowers, about three-quarters of an inch across, that close by day.

The seed of *M. incana* and varieties are sown in the open in June or July, and the plants placed in their permanent positions about Michaelmas. It is important to transplant to nursery beds as soon as the seedlings are large enough to handle, allowing ample space for development. *M. annua* and *M. sinuata* and varieties should be raised from seed sown under glass early in the year, pricked off into boxes and planted out in May.

Propagation is from seed.

The flowering season of *M. incana* is from April to July, *M. annua* from July to October, and *M. sinuata* August and September.

## Meconopsis (Plate 71)

Family *PAPAVERACEAE*                              *Meconopsis* species

A widely distributed genus containing many perennials and monocarpic species of attractive features, not the least being the elegant and hairy foliage. The biennial and annual species are mostly from the Himalayas, Tibet and western China, with one from California. Probably the most favoured of the biennials is the Tibetan Lampshade Poppy (*M. integrifolia*), with hairy leaves, smooth edged and spikes of pale yellow poppy-like flowers, six inches across, with a central mass of orange anthers on eighteen-inch stems. Another pale-yellow-flowered species is the Himalayan *M. dhwojii*, which, although not so fine as the one already described, is particularly attractive for its beautiful rosette of green leaves, elegantly cut and covered densely with bronze hairs, magnificent when seen touched with the morning dew; it will reach two feet in height. *M. aculeata*, also from the Himalayas, has flowers of medium blue with a central mass of yellow stamens and reaches two feet. From California comes the Flaming Poppy (*M. heterophylla*), producing flowers of large size, bright orange in colour, with the centre ringed with maroon; it is an annual and reaches one and a half feet. The first three species are biennial and seed may be sown in pans of peaty and sandy compost as soon as ripe, pricked off into pots and planted out in the following spring in a partially shaded position in peaty soil that is free from lime. The annual species may be sown where it is to flower and requires similar conditions.

Propagation is from seed.

The flowering season is in early summer and *M. heterophylla* will continue until September.

## Mentzelia (Plate 72)

Family *LOASACEAE*                                    *Mentzelia lindleyi*

This is more commonly known as *Bartonia aurea* and is a hardy annual native to California. The plant grows one foot tall and has felted leaves that are finely cut, and fragrant flowers about two and a half inches across with five broad overlapping petals of golden yellow, giving it the appearance of a yellow helleborus. The flowers have the curious habit of first expanding in the evening but lasting for several days. A really beautiful annual not seen as often as it deserves and excellent for association with the blue varieties of annual Scabious. *M. bartonioides*, one foot, is a yellow-flowering annual from the U.S.A., often grown as a pot plant in the cool greenhouse and also eligible for out-of-doors *M. ornata*, one foot tall, also from North America, has fragrant white flowers. The position chosen should be warm, sunny and sheltered and the soil rich but well drained. Seed may be sown in early April where the display is desired and the seedlings thinned when an inch or so high.

Propagation is from seed.

The flowering season is in late summer and early autumn.

## Fig Marigold (Plate 72)

Family *AIZOACEAE*                            *Mesembryanthemum* species

Colourful half-hardy succulents of South African origin and admirable for dry and sun-baked soils. *M. criniflorum*, growing four inches tall, has succulent leaves, about three inches long, widening from a narrow base, with a spreading habit well adapted to covering dry walls, and flowers of daisy-like form in brilliant shades of pink, red, white, yellow and orange. *M. pyropaeum* (syn. *M. tricolor*) is of similar habit with long, fleshy leaves, up to three inches long, and many flowers, up to one and a half inches across, of white, pink, purple or rose, each with dark centres. Of a hardier nature is the Ice Plant (*M. crystallinum*), with fleshy stems and of a spreading habit, comprising six-inch oval, pointed leaves and many small flowers of white or rose-pink shades; a useful wall or edging plant. Except in the mildest climates it is wisest to sow a few seeds in small pots under glass in March, grow on under protection and plant out direct from the pots into a well-drained soil that enjoys full sun in June.

Propagation is from seed.

The flowering season is from midsummer until frost.

## Michaux's Bell-flower (Plate 72)

Family *CAMPANULACEAE*                    *Michauxia campanuloides*

A rather uncommon perennial from Asia Minor, which, as the plant often fails to survive after flowering, is usually treated as a biennial. The foliage is hairy, lance-shaped and toothed and from the crown of the plant spring branching stems to heights varying between five and six feet, bearing many flowers, two inches across, with reflexing segments of white sometimes suffused with purple. *M. tchihatcheffii* is a more imposing species of some rarity with similar flowers, usually of a lavender-blue shade and borne on five- to seven-feet branching stems. Both species are lime lovers and must be given a position in full sun, but sheltered from strong winds. Perfect drainage is essential, anything in the nature of continually wet ground being fatal to their well-being. Lovely plants for contrast with the brighter coloured denizens of the flower garden. May be sown in April where they are to flower or for transplanting in July.

Propagation is from seed.

The flowering season is in July.

## Marvel of Peru (Plate 72)

Family *NYCTAGINACEAE*                    *Mirabilis jalapa*

A perennial from tropical America but, being unable to withstand winter frosts, is best treated as a half-hardy annual. The species develops into a shapely plant up to three feet, with five-lobed tubular flowers, one to two inches long, red, yellow, white and often striped and mottled. Its habit of opening in the afternoon has gained for it a further popular name of Four-o'-Clock. Rather more dwarf but resembling *M. jalapa* is *M. multiflora*, bearing clusters of rose or purple flowers, two inches long. *M. longiflora* reaches three feet with white, rose or violet flowers, four to six inches long, and *M. dichotoma*, two and a half feet high, has flowers of white heavily suffused with pink and effectively contrasting purple stamens. Seed should be sown under glass in March, and the seedlings pricked off and planted out when all risk of frost has passed. A position in full sun and a well-drained soil are essential.

Propagation is from seed.

The flowering period is from midsummer until frost.

# Nemesia (Plate 73)

Family *SCROPHULARIACEAE*          *Nemesia* species

Colourful half-hardy annuals from South Africa. *N. strumosa* is the most noteworthy species, reaching a height of one foot or more with three-inch lance-shaped leaves and two-lipped flowers, of white, yellow or purple with a bearded throat of yellow heavily spotted. There are a number of garden forms that are more attractive than the type, having flowers of more varied colours. Of the other species, *N. chamaedrifolia*, twelve inches, has pale pink flowers with spurs; *N. floribunda*, of similar height, has spurred flowers, white or pale pink in colour, on many-flowered racemes; and *N. versicolor*, about nine inches high, has spurred flowers usually two-coloured. There are also dwarf and compact forms that are invaluable for massed effect. Seed is sown in gentle heat in March, and the seedlings pricked off into boxes to be ready for planting out in May. Seed may also be sown out-of-doors in May to flower in August and September. Nemesias also are attractive pot plants if raised from seed sown in August and potted into four-inch pots at Michaelmas to flower in winter.

Propagate from seed.

The flowering season is from late June to Michaelmas.

# Californian Blue-bell (Plate 73)

Family *HYDROPHYLLACEAE*          *Nemophila* species

Charming annuals from California and North America. The flowers are bell-shaped. *N. menziesii* (syn. *N. atomaria*) is of trailing habit, with stems up to twenty inches long, four-inch lobed leaves and solitary five-petalled bell flowers, one inch across, of bright blue, changing to white at the centre. Other forms are var. *alba*, white-flowered; var. *crambeoides*, with pale blue flowers veined purple; var. *discoidalis*, with white flowers, changing to brownish-purple at the centre; and var. *marginata*, with flowers of blue, margined white. There is also a large-flowered form, var. *grandiflora*. Of other species, *N. aurita* is a twelve-inch dwarf, with purple and violet flowers; *N. maculata*, six inches, has deep blue-purple and white flowers; and *N. insignis*, known as Baby Blue Eyes in its native California, is a trailer with blue and white flowering forms. All are easily grown in a well-drained loam in a sunny, sheltered position, where the bright blue flowers contrast well with other flowers of pink or yellow. Sow in March or April where the plants are to bloom,

Nemesia (*Nemesia strumosa* var.), p. 188.   2. Californian Bluebell (*Nemophila menziesii*), p. 188.
Apple of Peru (*Nicandra physaloides*), p. 189.   4. Tobacco Plant (*Nicotiana alata* var. *grandiflora*), p. 189.

*Pl.* 74.

1. Love-in-a-mist (*Nigella damascena*), p. 190.   2. Chilian Bell-flower (*Nolana atriplicifolia*), p. 19
3. Evening Primrose (*Oenothera biennis*), p. 191.   4. Poppy (*Papaver nudicaule*), p. 19

and thin out, remembering the spread of the plant. They may be sown in autumn for spring-flowering in mild localities.

Propagate from seed.

The flowering season is from late June to September.

## Apple of Peru (Plate 73)

Family *SOLANACEAE*                              *Nicandra physaloides*

A robust annual, native to Peru and somewhat reminiscent of Physalis, its near relative. Growing one and a half to two feet high, the plant has oval, toothed leaves and bell-shaped flowers, open at the mouth, which is about an inch across, and of a pleasing pale blue shade, followed by berries enclosed singly in five-winged calyces. *N. violacea*, up to three feet, has stems of dark violet, leaves up to ten inches long with violet coloured hairs, and flowers of bell shape, violet on top and white below. May be raised from seed sown under glass, temperature 55° to 65° F., in March, for transplanting outdoors in May, or by sowing outdoors in April, in a sunny position with well-drained soil. The calyces last a long time after being cut, and are pretty in the house.

Propagation is from seed. The flowering season is summer.

## Tobacco Plant (Plate 73)

Family *SOLANACEAE*          *Nicotiana alata* var. *grandiflora*

Of these showy and fragrant perennials, best treated as half-hardy annuals, this is the best known, being a native of Brazil, and sometimes offered in seedsmen's catalogues under *N. a. affinis*. The basal leaves are wide, like those of some Mulleins, and from these rise stems three to five feet, bearing a number of tubular flowers of elegant form, widening at the mouth with five petioles that are white in the type with a reverse of pale violet. There are various forms with flowers of rose, crimson, pink, lilac and cream. Notable varieties are Crimson King, two to three feet; Crimson Border, eighteen inches; and Miniature White, eighteen inches. Cultivated both for the beauty of the flowers and for their fragrance, plants may be raised from seeds sown in gentle heat early in the year, pricked off into boxes, and planted out in late May where they are to flower. The best effects are obtained when planted in the mass near to a house window when the scent of the flowers, rather reminiscent of Jasmine, is welcome as the summer breeze wafts it through the casement. There are a number of other annual species, but this is by far the most favoured.

Propagate from seed.

The flowering season is in late summer.


## Love-in-a-Mist (Plate 74)

Family *RANUNCULACEAE*                    *Nigella damascena*

Also known as Fennel-flower and a native of south-eastern Europe. The plant owes its name to the thread-like leaves that clothe the stems in a fern-like fashion and surround the flowers. The flowers are about one and a half inches across, rounded and not unlike Cornflowers in form, being white, blue or purple in colour. The blue-flowered forms are the most desirable and the semi-double variety "Miss Jekyll" is often grown to the exclusion of others. Var. *nana* is a dwarf, useful for edgings. The Spanish species *N. hispanica* is more coarse in foliage and has flowers of blue with red stamens, up to two and a half inches across, borne singly or in pairs. There are also white and purple forms. Self-sown seedlings will germinate in autumn, withstand the winter and begin to flower as early as April. By cutting off the flowers as they fade, it is possible, in a mild autumn, to extend the flowering season until November. The normal procedure is to sow the seed outdoors in autumn or in March where the plants are to flower and allow the seedlings ample space for development. Full sun is essential and the soil must be rich in humus.

Propagation is from seed.

The normal flowering season is from June to Michaelmas.


## Chilian Bell-flower (Plate 74)

Family *CONVOLVULACEAE*                    *Nolana* various species

These are hardy annuals from Chile or Peru, and include four species valuable for the flower garden. These are of somewhat trailing habit and are reminiscent of the Convolvulus. *N. atriplicifolia* (syn. *N. grandiflora*) produces trailing stems, up to a foot long, the upper portion being streaked and spotted with purple. The leaves are spoon-shaped and about three inches long, the flowers blue and white to yellow throats, two inches across. The form var. *violacea* has flowers of a deeper tone. *N. laceolata*, from Peru, is a hairy plant up to six inches, with narrow lance-shaped

1. Zonal Pelargonium (*Pelargonium* hybrid), p. 192.    2. Petunia (*Petunia hybrida*), p. 193.
3. Phacelia (*Phacelia campanularia*), p. 193.    4. Flame-flower (*Phlox drummondii*), p. 194.

leaves and flowers similar to the foregoing. *N. paradoxa*, also of Peru, is a white-flowered species, growing twelve to eighteen inches high, and *N. tenella*, a fellow native, has trailing stems with pale blue flowers. Being an uncertain subject to transplant, it is best to sow seed sparsely in small pots under glass in March and plant out from the pots in late May, or may be sown in patches, where they are to flower, in March or April in an open, sunny position and ordinary soil. They are most attractive when planted so that they may ramble over small rocks.

Propagation is from seed.

The flowering season is from midsummer until frost.

## Evening Primrose (Plate 74)

Family *ONAGRACEAE*           *Oenothera* various species

An attractive group of hardy annuals, biennials and perennials from the Americas, with some of garden origin. Among the biennials *O. biennis*, North America, has become conspicuous since the war through its appearance on sites of buildings damaged by bombs. It grows to five feet and is a coarse plant, with lance-shaped leaves and erect branching stems, bearing yellow flowers, up to two inches across, which open late in the day. It has various forms, notably *grandiflora* and *lamarckiana* and one of garden origin named "Afterglow" with effective red calyces. Among the noteworthy annuals are the Californian *O. bistorta*, a foot high, with yellow and red, four-petalled flowers, an inch across, spotted red at the base, opening in the daytime; *O. amoena*, one to two feet, with rose and crimson flowers, also from California; *O. odorata*, one to two feet, from Chile, with yellow flowers towards evening, two inches across, fragrant, fading to red before falling, and of which there is a form with sulphur-yellow flowers; *O. drummondii*, one to two feet, a yellow-flowering native of Texas; and *O. tetraptera*, twelve inches, with white flowers, and its pink var. *rosea*, hailing from Mexico. Only six inches high, *O. trichocalyx* is described as being both biennial and perennial, but usually dies after flowering; the leaves are lance-shaped and cut like those of a Dandelion, and the flowers, up to three inches across, are white. Sow the seeds in April in a sunny, well-drained position and thin the seedlings to six inches apart, or under glass in March for early flowering.

Propagation is from seed.

The flowering season is from midsummer onwards.

## Poppy (Plate 74)

Family *PAPAVERACEAE* *Papaver* species

This popular family includes many lovely annuals with their various homes in Europe, Asia, North Africa, western North America or the Arctic regions. One of the best known is *P. nudicaule*, the Iceland Poppy, with the typical elegant foliage and leafless stems up to two feet tall, with flowers, three inches or more across of white, yellow, pink, salmon and orange. It has given rise to a number of well-known strains of garden origin, notably the Coonara, Gartref and Kelmscott, the latter having the largest flowers. *P. nudicaule* is strictly a perennial, but is best treated as an annual. The Opium Poppy is *P. somniferum*, of Europe and Asia, with smooth, greyish-green foliage, and flowers of double and single form with frilled petals, that vary from white, in the type, to red and purple in garden varieties. *P. rhoeas* is the Corn Poppy, native to Britain, with scarlet flowers, and is parent to a host of tall and dwarf, single- and double-flowered varieties, of which the Shirley Poppy is most popular. There are also the scarlet *P. californicum*, from California, the Tulip Poppy (*P. laevigatum*), two feet, with scarlet, black and white flowers; *P. glaucum*, eighteen inches, from Syria, with glaucous foliage and scarlet flowers, spotted purple at the base; and the Peacock Poppy (*P. pavonium*), eighteen inches, from Afghanistan, with scarlet and black flowers. Seed may be sown in spring or autumn where the plants are to flower.

Propagation is from seed.

The flowering season is from late June to September.

## Zonal Pelargonium (Plate 75)

Family *GERANIACEAE* *Pelargonium* (forms of garden origin)

Popularly but erroneously known as Geranium, the Zonal Pelargoniums of gardens are hybrids of the two South African species *P. zonale* and *P. inquinans*. The plants are of succulent growth and attain heights of two feet or more. The leaves are round, three to five inches across, scalloped and toothed, with a dark zone at the centre, and aromatic when crushed; the flowers are mostly single, an inch or more across and are borne in many-flowered umbels, the colours varying from orange-scarlet, pink, and salmon to white. There are some with variegated foliage known as Tricolors. These tender perennials are most popular summer bedding plants, and are easily raised from cuttings taken whenever available and rooted under glass in autumn and winter, or in the open in summer. The best plants are obtained from cuttings rooted in the autumn for planting out in the following spring when all risk of frost has passed. The site chosen must be sunny and the soil humus-rich. Seedlings raised from seed sown as soon as it is ripe, in August, will bloom in ten months if grown on under heat in a greenhouse.

Propagation is from cuttings or seed.

The flowering season is in summer.

## Petunia (Plate 75)

Family *SOLANACEAE*                                      *Petunia hybrida*

The half-hardy perennial varieties are often grown as annuals and are hybrids between the Argentine species *P. nyctaginiflora* and *P. violacea*. The stems are leafy and attain a height of a foot or more, bearing many tubular flowers, three inches or more across at the mouth, of varied colours, mostly purple, violet-blue, rose and crimson. There are a number of garden varieties with huge frilled flowers attractively veined on a self-coloured ground, usually with a deep purple blotch at the throat. Seed should be sown under glass in late January to March, care being taken to sow it thinly so as to avoid damping off. The seedlings are potted when an inch or so high, and it is important to avoid over-watering. Planting out-of-doors where the plants are to bloom may be carried out in early June when all risk of frost has passed.

Propagation is from seed, or cuttings taken in August.

The flowering season is from late June to September.

## Phacelia (Plate 75)

Family *HYDROPHYLLACEAE*               *Phacelia campanularia*

Among the numerous species of this genus, the Californian annuals are particularly favoured in flower gardens. In *P. campanularia* the leaves are ovate and toothed and the stems rise to eight inches, bearing several intense blue flowers of bell shape. *P. ciliata* has fragrant, pretty lavender-blue flowers and grows twelve inches high. *P. viscida* (syn. *Eutoca viscida*) reaches one to two feet, with small flowers of bright blue with purple or white centres, particularly attractive to bees. A deeper tone of violet-blue is seen in the large-flowered *P. parryi*, a most delightful species. *P. tanacetifolia* is distinct, having clustered heads of small lavender or blue flowers on one-and-a-half to three-feet stems. *P. whitlavia* (syn. *P. grandiflora*), one foot, is the Californian Bluebell, with blue or purple flowers and swollen corolla tubes; var. *alba* has white flowers, and var. *gloxinoides* has white flowers with blue centres. A race of plants effective in the mass and easily raised by sowing seed in April in well-drained soil, sun or partial shade, where the plants are to flower.

Propagation is from seed.

The flowering season is from late June to Michaelmas.

## Flame-flower (Plate 75)

Family *POLEMONIACEAE*       *Phlox drummondii*

This is the only annual species of this well-known genus that is grown in gardens, and it is native to Texas. The type is a plant of a foot high, of rather decumbent habit with lance-shaped leaves, three inches long, and clusters of rose-red flowers, an inch across. It is to the varieties of garden origin that the species owes its present popularity and these vary considerably in colour, including deep red, crimson, violet, yellow, white, pink and mauve in endless combinations. There is also a dwarf race known as var. *nana*, with an equally wide colour range, a pointed petal kind, var. *cuspidata*, and a large-flowered kind, var. *grandiflora*. Best treated as a half-hardy annual, the seed should be sown under glass in March, the seedlings pricked off and planted out in late May. A fairly rich, moisture-retaining soil and a position in full sun are needed. This species of Phlox is particularly valuable when used to form a carpet to such plants as roses. They may also be planted at the top of dry walls, with their stems trailing over the brick or stonework. They withstand bad weather conditions better than many other annuals.

Propagation is from seed.

The flowering season is from June to October.

## Knotweed (Plate 76)

Family *POLYGONACEAE*       *Polygonum* various species

Most of the hardy annuals of this genus are rather rampant and chiefly suitable for the wilder parts of the garden. The European species include *P. arenarium*, only six inches high, the only one suitable for the flower border. It is of rather sprawling habit and produces small cream flowers freely. Known as Lady's Thump.

*P. persicaria* grows two feet or more tall, with lance-shaped leaves, and flowers shaped like Cornflowers, of bright pink suffused with greenish-purple at the tips. *P. orientale* is the Prince's Feather and a native of Asia. It reaches four to six feet high and has broad oval leaves, ten inches long, with dense spikes of bright pink or rose flowers, six inches or more in length, of a graceful pendulous habit. There are several varieties, red, pink or white, tall or dwarf. Seeds may be sown in April where the plants are to flower, and the seedlings thinned to eighteen inches apart; or they may be sown under glass in March, temperature 65°F., for planting out in early June.

Propagation is from seed.

The flowering season is in summer.

## Sun Plant (Plate 76)

Family *PORTULACACEAE*                    *Portulaca grandiflora*

A half-hardy annual from Brazil, known as the Sun Plant or Rose Moss. Of semi-prostrate habit, the plant grows six to nine inches high. The leaves are fleshy and the flowers, borne at the ends of the stems, are an inch or more across and noted for their brilliance of colouring, which ranges from yellow to pink, scarlet, purple and crimson. There are several varieties. The plant is only suitable for a warm situation where it is fully exposed to the sun; the soil must be well drained. Like the Zinnia, the Sun Plant gives of its best in a hot and dry summer. Inasmuch as the seedlings do not transplant well, it is best to sow the seed out-of-doors where the seedlings are to flower, under cloches, in April, giving protection until early June.

Propagation is from seed.

The flowering season is from July to October.

## Mignonette (Plate 76)

Family *RESEDACEAE*                          *Reseda odorata*

For long a cherished favourite in British gardens and a native of North Africa and Egypt. The plant, familiar to all who visit gardens, is a perennial, treated as an annual. Of upright growth at first, it tends to a spreading and decumbent habit, with leafy stems and trusses of many small yellowish-white flowers of delightful and pronounced fragrance. There are a number of garden forms with flowers of red and yellow, sulphur and golden yellow and one of orange. The spikes of these garden varieties are invariably much larger than those of the type. Choose a sunny position and well-drained soil, and sow the seed out-of-doors in April, where the plants are to bloom. When a few inches high, the seedlings should be thinned to four or six inches apart. Owing to the fineness of the seeds thin sowing is necessary. Mignonette may also be sown in autumn and protected by cloches if the weather is severe. The plants will flower earlier than those sown in the spring.

Propagation is from seed.

The flowering season is from late June to Michaelmas.

## Cone-flower (Plate 76)

Family *COMPOSITAE*                    *Rudbeckia* various species

This race contains a number of distinctive perennials and also several showy annuals, native to North America. *R. bicolor* is an annual that grows one to two feet tall, with lance-shaped leaves and yellow-rayed flowers, two inches or more across, with maroon centres. It has given rise to a number of forms of garden origin, among which var. *semiplena* is a particularly outstanding semi-double-flowered form. *R. hirta*, Black-eyed Susan, is an annual or biennial of one to three feet, with golden yellow-rayed flowers, up to four inches across, deepening at the base, where they merge into purplish-brown discs, three-quarters of an inch across. Also annual or biennial, *R. triloba*, Brown-eyed Susan, reaches three to four feet, with flowers, about two inches across, of yellow with orange or bronze-purple shading at the base and black central discs. In the case of the biennials, seeds may be sown in late summer to provide plants that will flower in the following year. But it is more usual to sow them and the annual species under glass in March, the seedlings being pricked off and planted out where they are to flower in late May, or seeds may be sown where they are to flower in late April.

Propagation is from seed.

The flowering season is in late summer and early autumn.

## Painted-tongue (Plate 77)

Family *SOLANACEAE*                    *Salpiglossis sinuata*

A half-hardy annual, native to Chile, that is quite distinctive in character. The plant is of an elegant branching habit, growing two to two and a half feet tall. The leaves are oblong, and the flowers are funnel-shaped with a wide throat. There are many

1. Painted-tongue (*Salpiglossis sinuata*), p. 196.        2. Sage (*Salvia splendens*), p. 197.
3. Soap-wort (*Saponaria calabrica*), p. 198.    4. Sweet Scabious (*Scabiosa atropurpurea*), p. 198.

*Pl.* 78.

1. Butterfly-flower (*Schizanthus hybridus*), p. 199.    2. Stonecrop (*Sedum caeruleum*), p. 199.
3. Purple Ragwort (*Senecio elegans*), p. 200.    4. Catchfly (*Silene* species), p. 200.

garden strains and varieties in colours of primrose, scarlet, pink, yellow and almost blue, all attractively veined and mottled. Var. *superbissima* is non-branching and of a decided columnar character. For outdoor flowering, seed must be sown under glass, temperature 65° to 75°F., in March, the seedlings being pricked off singly into two-inch pots and planted out when large enough in early June, choosing a well-drained soil and a position in full sun. Seed may also be sown in August or September, under glass, and the seedlings grown on in pots for flowering in the following March or April.

Propagation is from seed.

The flowering season is in April and May under glass and from June to September out-of-doors.

## Sage (Plate 77)

Family *LABIATAE*                                    *Salvia* species

A favourite genus that includes annuals, biennials and perennials grown as annuals. The biennial *S. sclarea* (syn. *S. bracteata*) is the Clary, native to the Mediterranean, with broad leaves, up to nine inches long, with bracts of rose and white and bluish-white flowers, about one inch long, borne in branched racemes, and two feet tall. Its best form is var. *turkestanica*, with attractive flowers of white, heavily suffused pink. *S. horminum*, from South Europe, reaches one and a half feet with oblong leaves and lilac-purple flowers, half an inch long, borne in racemes. It is a true annual and has several varieties, mostly with richly coloured bracts. *S. columbaria* has basal leaves, over two inches long, and blue flowers, half an inch long, borne in whorls on fifteen-inch stems. The Thistle Sage (*S. carduacea*), of California, a perennial grown as an annual, is an effective plant of two feet, with spiny oblong basal leaves and one-inch flowers of bluish-purple in whorls. *S. coccinea*, two to three feet, is a North American species, bearing deep scarlet flowers in autumn; *S. farinacea*, two to three feet, from Mexico, with lavender-blue flowers; *S. patens*, two feet, also Mexican, with the loveliest Gentian blue flowers; and *S. splendens*, two to three feet, of Brazil, the Scarlet Sage, are all favourites, grown as annuals. *S. sclarea*, being biennial, is best raised from seed sown in spring, planted out in permanent positions, when the plants are large enough, to flower in the following summer. The remainder should be raised from seed sown in March where the plants are to flower, in warm sunny positions.

Propagation is from seed. The flowering season is in summer.

## Soap-wort (Plate 77)

Family *CARYOPHYLLACEAE*            *Saponaria* species

A race that includes alpine perennials and some very lovely annuals. The leaves are broad, flat and pointed and the flowers colourful and effective. The Italian *S. calabrica* (syn. *S. multiflora*) has pale rose flowers, half an inch across, borne singly in the leaf axils and forming leafy panicles of six to twelve inches high. There is a white form and varieties of garden origin with flowers of pink almost to scarlet. *S. vaccaria* (syn. *Lychnis vaccaria*) is the Cow Herb of two to three feet stature, bearing loose panicles of deep pink flowers, a quarter of an inch across. There is also a white and pale pink flowered form. The dwarfer species is useful for edging or for planting in groups at the front of a border in the flower garden. Seed may be sown in March or autumn out-of-doors where the plants are to flower, choosing a sunny position and well-drained soil, and thinning the seedlings to two to three inches apart.

Propagation is from seed.

The flowering season is in late spring and early summer.

## Sweet Scabious (Plate 77)

Family *DIPSACEAE*            *Scabiosa atropurpurea*

Known also as Mournful Widows and Pincushion Flower, this biennial is native to southern Europe. Of erect habit, the plant grows one to three feet tall, with leaves divided into oblong-toothed lobes, and flowers of purplish-rose or white and two inches across. It has a number of forms such as var. *candidissima*, white and occasionally double, var. *compacta*, a neat compact habit of growth, var. *nana* and var. *pumila*, both of more diminutive character and of dwarfer habit than the type. There are many garden forms of great attraction, varying in colour from white to shades of pink, salmon, red, purple and blue: much favoured as a decorative cut flower. Best treated as an annual. Seed may be sown where the plants are to flower out-of-doors in April and thinned to four inches apart, or for earlier flowering under glass in March, pricked off into boxes and planted out in May. The quality of the flowers is hardly comparable with that of those of the perennial *S. caucasica* varieties and, to avoid invidious comparison, should be kept apart.

Propagation is from seed.

The flowering season is from July to September.

# Butterfly-flower: Fringe-flower (Plate 78)

Family *SOLANACEAE*          *Schizanthus hybridus grandiflorus*

A Chilian genus known mostly for the race of garden forms of varied origin and grouped under *S. hybridus*. A tender annual valued as a decorative greenhouse plant, where the best specimens are developed, and also for outdoor planting. Of erect habit with dainty, fern-like foliage, forming an imposing pyramid of irregularly shaped, spreading flowers of butterfly-like form and possessing a very wide colour range. All manner of varied combinations of white, yellow, pink, salmon, mauve, apricot, violet and red make this plant one of the most colourful of annuals. Under glass the plant may reach a height of two or more feet, but is considerably smaller out-of-doors. Sow the seed in gentle heat under glass in March, prick the seedlings off into pots and, for outdoor cultivation, plant out in early June. It is wise to provide support in the form of short twiggy peasticks or thin bamboo canes to prevent plants from being blown down by high winds. Propagation is from seed.

The flowering season is in late summer.

# Stonecrop (Plate 78)

Family *CRASSULACEAE*                              *Sedum* species

The most noteworthy annuals and biennials of this genus, famed for its perennial species, are native to Asia Minor and the Mediterranean region, and hardy. The best of the Mediterranean species is *S. caeruleum* (syn. *S. azureum*), an annual, no more than three inches high, with succulent, oblong leaves, up to three-quarters of an inch long, and many star-shaped flowers, a quarter of an inch across, blue in colour, shading to white at the base. The remaining two are biennial: *S. pilosum*, four inches high, with a dense rosette of hairy, succulent foliage of particularly neat and balanced formation, and flowers, three-eighths of an inch across, of rose-pink, and *S. sempervivoides*, with a flattened rosette of leaves, oval and pointed and an inch long, and red flowers, half an inch across, with a centre of yellow stamens. The annual species should be sown in a well-drained soil and sunny position out-of-doors in March where it will form a mass of growth and many flowers, perpetuating itself thereafter from self-sown seed. The biennial species should be sown in late summer or early autumn in boxes in frames, the seedlings pricked off and planted out in the following spring.

Propagation is from seed.

The flowering season is in early summer for *S. caeruleum*, and in late spring for the two other species.

## Purple Ragwort (Plate 78)

Family *COMPOSITAE*                                    *Senecio* species

The annual species are natives of South Africa. *S. elegans* (syn. *Jacobaea elegans*), the Purple Ragwort, has sticky, hairy, oblong leaves, about three inches long, and two-feet stems, bearing loose corymbs of purple to reddish-rayed flowers with yellow central discs. There are now single and double forms of various colours from red to white. *S. multibracteatus* reaches one and a half feet, with lance-shaped leaves, about two and a half inches long, and long-stemmed corymbs bearing purple-rayed flowers with central discs of yellow. From Spain we have *S. rodriguezii*, a dwarf of only six inches or so, with lance-shaped oblong leaves, up to two inches long, of metallic green with purplish reverse, and short-rayed rose-pink flowers, about half an inch across, borne in two- to three-headed clusters. The seeds are sown outdoors in April where the plants are to flower, the seedlings being thinned to six inches apart when large enough to handle. A sunny position and a well-drained soil are suitable.

Propagation is from seed.

The flowering season is from midsummer until frost.

## Catchfly (Plate 78)

Family *CARYOPHYLLACEAE*                              *Silene* species

This genus contains some pleasing annuals and biennials. *S. pendula*, an annual from the Mediterranean region, grows six to nine inches tall, with lance-shaped, hairy leaves, and stems that sprawl outward at the base, branching upward to bear loose, pendulous racemes of flesh-pink flowers, rather less than half an inch across. It has various forms in var. *alba*, white; var. *bonnettii*, purple; var. *rosea*, bright rose, and one of compact habit, *S. armeria*, the Sweet William Catchfly, of South Europe, is one to two feet tall, with three-inch lance-shaped leaves and terminal flat-topped clusters of pink flowers, a little more than half an inch across. *S. asterias*, one to two feet, is an annual native to

Rumania and Macedonia, and has rosy-purple flowers. *S. compacta*, a biennial of Asia Minor, grows eighteen inches, with two-inch leaves, and many pink flowers in dense clusters at the ends of the upright stems; a plant of particularly pleasing and balanced habit. Seed may be sown in early autumn or spring in the positions where the plants are to flower and thinned to six inches apart; cloche protection will result in earlier blooming.

Propagation is from seed.

The flowering season is from midsummer until late summer.

## French and African Marigold (Plate 79)

Family *COMPOSITAE*                *Tagetes* species

This is a genus, native to Mexico, of half-hardy annuals of brilliant and showy colouring much in demand for summer bedding. Through having been erroneously supposed to have originated in Africa, *T. erecta* is still called the African Marigold: it is of stout and upright growth of two to three feet with pinnate foliage and solitary flower-heads, up to four inches across, made up of numerous rays of brilliant orange or yellow. The French Marigold is *T. patula*, with finely divided fern-like leaves and flowers, one and a half inches across, on one to one-and-a-half-feet stems. The flowers of the type are yellow, marked red. Those of garden varieties may vary from yellow to orange, all with red, maroon or mahogany markings. The dwarf var. *nana* is excellent for edging. *T. signata*, one to one and a half feet, has finely cut leaves and solitary yellow flowers, one inch across. There is a six-inch dwarf form in var. *pumila*. Although seed may be sown out-of-doors in April where the plants are to flower, the best flowers are produced from seedlings raised under glass from seed sown in March and planted out-of-doors in May.

Propagation is from seed.

The flowering season is from late June to September.

## Joy-weed (Plate 79)

Family *AMARANTHACEAE*    *Telanthera* (syn. *Alternanthera*)

These plants are grown for their richly coloured foliage and are natives of Brazil. Although perennial in their native habitat, they are best treated as half-hardy annuals in Britain. The most desirable forms have originated from *T. amoena*, a species with broad, lance-shaped leaves of red and orange, veined green; it reaches a height of three to six inches. Of the various forms var.

*amabilis*, with deep orange and scarlet foliage, and var. *spectabilis*, a brighter form of the type, are the most useful and may be planted out in favoured localities where there is protection from cold winds and full exposure to the sun. The soil should be rich and well drained. Very popular for carpet bedding effects or, where such sophisticated schemes are not favoured, they provide welcome foliage effect in contrast with annuals possessing flowers of a suitably contrasting colour.

Propagation is from seed or cuttings, taken in early spring and rooted in sandy compost, temperature 75°F.

The season of display is from midsummer until September.

## Yellow Garden Hawkweed (Plate 79)

Family *COMPOSITAE*          *Tolpis barbata* (syn. *Crepis barbata*)

An annual from South Europe, somewhat similar to the native Wild Hawkweed and sometimes known as the Yellow Garden Hawkweed. Reaching a height of one to two feet, the plant has leaves that are toothed and lance-shaped and long slender stems bearing double, frilled flowers, half an inch across, golden yellow in colour and of particularly neat form. Free-flowering and attractive, this is an annual that deserves wider cultivation, being easily grown from seed sown where the plants are to flower, the seedlings being thinned to six or eight inches apart. This annual should possess attraction for those who have a keen eye for something new in floral decoration, and the inclusion of these in a mixed ensemble cannot fail to add meritorious novelty.

Propagation is from seed.

The flowering period is from midsummer until frost.

## Nasturtium (Plate 79)

Family *GERANIACEAE*                    *Tropaeolum majus*

*T. majus* is strictly a perennial and native to Peru, but is cultivated in Britain as a hardy annual. It is curious how the name Nasturtium, the botanical name for Water Cress, came to be applied. The habit is climbing; the leaves are rounded and of kidney shape, being produced in great profusion; the flowers are about two and a half inches across, with nectary spurs, and are familiar enough not to need detailed description. There are now many varieties, climbing and dwarf, single and double, with a colour range varying from yellow to shades of orange, yellow, pink and red. Some varieties have variegated leaves. The Gleam varieties are notable double semi-dwarfs, and the Globe double dwarfs. Var. *nanum* is the single dwarf Tom Thumb Nasturtium of many colours and low bushy growth. The Peruvian *T. peregrinum* is the familiar Canary Creeper with yellow flowers and of self-climbing habit. Seed of *T. majus* and varieties may be sown in April outdoors in a sunny situation and not too rich soil where the plants are to flower. The seeds are used for salads. Seed of *T. peregrinum* may be sown under glass in March and planted out in May.

Propagation is from seed.

The flowering season is from July to September.

## Ursinia (Plate 80)

Family *COMPOSITAE*                 *Ursinia* species

A race of free-flowering South African annuals of half-hardy character, sometimes known as *Sphenogyne*. *U. anthemoides* has leaves that are finely cut and one and a half inches long, stems varying in height from a foot to fifteen inches and bearing daisy-like flowers of orange-yellow with a central ring of dark purple, one inch across. It has a dwarf form with orange-scarlet flowers and a maroon central ring. A dwarfer form is *U. pulchra* (syn. *Sphenogyne speciosa*), reaching only nine inches with orange flowers, spotted with bronze-purple at the base. Even dwarfer is *U. pygmaea*, of four inches, with freely produced flowers of glowing orange. The seed may be sown in boxes, under glass in March, pricked off and planted in the flowering positions in May; or it may also be sown out-of-doors in late April or early May where the plants are to flower and thinned when large enough to handle. Requires a position in full sun and well-drained soil.

Propagation is by seed.

The flowering season is from late June to Michaelmas.

## Venidium (Plate 80)

Family *COMPOSITAE*                 *Venidium* species

Annuals or half-hardy perennials from South Africa, treated in Britain as half-hardy annuals, although sometimes may be grown as perennials under glass. *V. fastuosum* has irregularly lobed furry leaves, about three inches long; the stems reach one and a half to two and a half feet and bear solitary heads of daisy-like flowers, up to four inches across, brilliant orange in colour with a brownish-purple base and black centre. There are a number of variations, all more or less attractive. *V. decurrens calendulaceum* (syn. *V. calendulaceum*) is less well known and is a somewhat hairy perennial, best treated as a half-hardy annual, with large golden-yellow daisy-like flowers, two and a half inches across, on two-feet stems, if well grown, but usually less. Seeds may be sown under glass in March, and pricked off into boxes and planted out-of-doors in their flowering positions in late May. These plants are most colourful and distinctive, highly useful for hot, sunny positions and poorish soils, where they contrast well with blue and purple-flowered subjects.

Propagation is from seed.

The flowering season is in late summer.

## Vervain (Plate 80)

Family *VERBENACEAE*                                      *Verbena* species

Hardy and half-hardy perennials, usually grown in Britain as annuals. The leaves are of a soft texture, oblong, two or three inches long, and notched; the flowers are borne on nine- to twelve-inch stems and form a broad corymb, two to three inches long, of white, yellow, pink or red colouring. *V. hybrida* is believed to be a multiple hybrid and closely related to the Chilian species *V. teucrioides*, which possibly has been used to produce the forms of garden origin. *V. canadensis* is the Clump Verbena with branching stems to one and a half feet, with heads of reddish-purple, lilac, rose or white flowers; there are improved forms of garden origin. A useful genus for massed effect and easily raised from seed sown under glass in March, and the seedlings pricked off and planted out-of-doors in May, or early June. It is also practicable to sow out-of-doors in May for flowering in late summer.

Propagation is from seed.

The flowering season is from July to September.

## Zinnia (Plate 80)

Family *COMPOSITAE*                                      *Zinnia elegans*

Known in its country of origin, Mexico, as Youth and Old Age; why, it is difficult to say. An annual of upright stiff habit with oval foliage well furnishing the stems that rise to as high as two and a half feet with daisy-like flowers, four and a half inches across, of many broad rays of purple and lilac in the type. The

French and African Marigold (*Tagetes erecta; T.
patula*), p. 201.

2. Joy-weed (*Telanthera amoena*), p. 201.

Yellow Garden Hawkweed (*Tolpis barbata*), p. 202.

4. Nasturtium (*Tropaeolum majus*), p. 202.

*Pl.* 80.

288

1. Ursinia (*Ursinia anthemoides*), p. 203.
3. Vervain (*Verbena hybrida*), p. 204.
2. Venidium (*Venidium fastuosum*), p. 203.
4. Zinnia (*Zinnia elegans*), p. 204.

type is now superseded by double-flowered varieties of garden origin, possessing an extremely wide range of colours that may vary from white to yellow, orange, scarlet, crimson and almost every conceivable shade except blue. *Z. haageana*, of tropical America, has orange-scarlet flowers of single form on twelve-inch stems. It is only in a really hot summer that Zinnias can be relied upon to give of their best in Britain. Seed may be sown in a house or cold frame in mid-March, and the seedlings potted as soon as the first pair of natural leaves appear, and planted out-of-doors in mid-May. In warm seasons seed may be sown outdoors in late April where the plants are to flower, and thinned out. Zinnias need a sunny position and a deep, humus-rich, well-drained soil, and repay one for generous watering, feeding and mulching.

Propagation is from seed.

The flowering season is from late July until autumnal frost.

# GLOSSARY

ALTERNATE: succeeding regularly on opposite sides of a branch.

ANNUAL: plants which flower and die in the same year as they are raised from seed.

ANTHER: the male organ of a flowering plant, the head of the stamen.

ARROW-SHAPED LEAF: a wide base with two pointed lobes directed downwards.

AXIL: the angle between a stem and the upper side of a leaf-stalk.

Arrow Shaped

BASAL: leaves at the base of a plant.

BIENNIAL: plants which flower in the year following that in which the seeds are sown.

BIGENERIC: a cross between two species of different genera.

BOTRYOID: like a bunch of grapes.

BRACT: a modified leaf beneath a flower.

BRACTEOLE: a diminutive bract.

BULBIL: a small bulb attached to the main bulb.

Bract

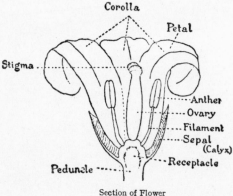

Section of Flower

Corolla · Petal · Stigma · Anther · Ovary · Filament · Sepal (Calyx) · Receptacle · Peduncle

CALYX: the cup or collection or sepals of a flower.

CAMPANULATE: bell-shaped.

CAPITULUM: a close cluster of flowers consisting of tiny florets packed together on a common platform.

CARPEL: a division of the ovary or seed vessel.

CLASPING LEAF: when a stalkless leaf encircles the stem.

CLEISTOGENE: flowers devoid of a corolla. The flowers never open, but develop into fruits by self-fertilization.

COMPOUND: a leaf broken up into several leaflets.

CONNATE: when the bases of opposite leaves are grown together.

CORDATE: heart-shaped.

CORM: a bulbous underground stem.

COROLLA: the inner whorl of the flower composed of the petals.

Connate

CORONA: the outer edge of a radiated compound flower.

CORYMB: where the cluster of flowers is brought more or less to the same level.

CRUCIFEROUS: with four petals in the form of a cross.

CYME: a shoot terminating in a flower, then sending off side branches each of which terminate in like manner.

Cyme

DECIDUOUS: plants and trees which shed their leaves in winter.

DECUMBENT: lying flat (usually with tip raised).

DIGITATE LEAF: leaflets radiating from the leaf-stalk.

DIMORPHIC: flowers that appear in two forms such as the Primrose, in which one form has a short style with anthers near the mouth of the corolla-tube, and the other form has a long style and anthers midway down the tube.

DISC: the central part of a radiate flower in which the florets are tubular.

ENTIRE LEAF: having the margin undivided.

ERICACEOUS: belonging to the heath family.

FILAMENT: the stalk-like portion of the stamen.

FLORESCENCE: the blossoming of a plant; the flowering season.

Entire leaf

FLORET: one of the small flowers in a composite blossom; a floweret.

FLORIFEROUS: bearing flowers.

FUNICLE: a small stalk by which the seed is attached to the placenta.

GENERA: the plural of *genus*.

GENUS: an assemblage of species, which all agree in one or more important structural characters.

GLAUCOUS: a sea-green colour; having a down of this colour.

HEART-SHAPED LEAF: broad, with two rounded lobes.

HYBRIDIZED: produced from two species.

HYPOGYNOUS: when petals or stamens spring from beneath the base of the ovary and are not attached to the calyx.

Heart-shaped

INFERIOR: denotes that the calyx or corolla is free from and below the ovary.

INFLORESCENCE: the arrangement of grouping of the flowers on a plant; collective blossoms.

INVOLUCRE: a series of bract-like leaves below a cluster of flowers.

Involucre

KEEL: the lowest petal of a flower, resembling the wings of a butterfly.

LACINIATED: with a fringed border.

LANCEOLATE: gradually tapering towards the tip; lance-shaped.

LATIFOLIATE: having broad leaves.

LEAFLETS: when there are several succeeding leaves on each side of a midrib; a little leaf.

LEGUMINOUS: bearing seeds which split into halves like the pea.

LINEAR: slender; a leaf that is long and very narrow with parallel sides.

LOBE: a division of a leaf.

Leaflets

14

Monocarpic:  annual plant, or one which dies after it has once borne fruit.

Moraine:  accumulation of stones in a rockery.

Nectary:  the gland of a flower which holds the nectar.

Node:  the point of juncture of leaf and stem.

Nodule:  a small knot or rounded lump.

Oblong Leaf:  twice as long as broad with both ends rounded.

Obovate:  egg-shaped with the small end at the base; inversely ovate.

Oblong leaf

Offset:  a shoot; a short runner bending up at the end to form a new plant.

Order:  a group of *genera* all of which agree in some striking particular.

Oval Leaves:  tapering to each end.

Ovary:  the seed vessel.

Ovate:  egg-shaped.

Ovula:  the seed of a plant before it is fertilized.

Oval leaves

Palmate:  in the shape of a hand.

Panicle:  when the pedicels are branched, supporting two or more flowers in a loose cluster.

Pappus:  the calyx of composite flowers: usually a whorl of bristles or silky hairs.

Pedicel:  a flower stalk supporting several flowers without footstalks.

Peduncle:  the stalk of a flower or a cluster of flowers.

Panicle

Pendent:  hanging down.

Pendulous:  hanging so as to swing.

Perennial:  rootstocks that increase and expand yearly.

Perfoliate Leaf:  when the stem passes through the base of a stalkless leaf.

Perianth:  flowers showing no distinction from calyx and corolla; the floral envelope or outer part of a flower.

Perfoliate leaf

PETALS: flower-leaves forming part of a corolla.

PETIOLE: a leaf stalk.

PINNATE: leaflets of elongate shape, forming pairs on opposite sides.

PISTIL: the seed-bearing part of a flower comprising the ovary, stigma and style.

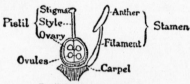

Fertilizing Organs of Flowers

PLACENTA: the part of the ovary to which the ovules are attached.

POLLEN: the fertilizing powder or male elements held by the anthers by contact of which the ovules are fertilized.

POLLINIUM: containing pollen.

PUBESCENT: hairy; downy.

RACEME: flowers arranged like a spike but with footstalks.

RADIATE: a composite flower consisting of a disc in which the florets are tubular.

RADICAL LEAVES: leaves that rise directly from the rootstock.

RAY: the outer part of a compound radiate flower.

RECEPTACLE: the fleshy head of the peduncle supporting the flower.

Raceme

RECURVED: curving outwards.

REFLEX: bent or turned back.

RHIZOME: an underground creeping stem which sends out shoots above the roots below.

ROSETTE: rose-shaped.

SCAPE: a flower stalk rising direct from the rootstock.

SEPAL: a leaf of the calyx; the outer whorl of the perianth.

SERRATED: notched on the edge like a saw.

SESSILE: leaves or flowers connected with the stem without footstalks.

SIMPLE LEAF: an undivided leaf.

SPADIX: an inflorescence where the flowers are arranged round a thick fleshy spike.

SPATHE: the large bract that envelops certain flowers before opening.

SPECIES: individual plants bearing certain characters in common.

SPIKE: bearing a number of flowers without footstalks.

SPREADING: when the petals of a flower are at right angles with the central column.

SPUR: a projection, usually the nectary.

STAMEN: the male pollen-bearing organ.

STIGMA: the organ holding the pollen grains at the top of the pistil.

STIPULES: small leaves, always in pairs at the base of a leaf-stalk.

STOLON: a trailing stem which roots and develops a new plant at intervals.

STYLE: the support for the stigma.

SUCCULENT: with fleshy foliage and stalks.

TERMINAL: flowers produced at the summit of a stem or end of a branch.

TOMENTOSE: downy or cottony.

TREFOIL: a form of leaf with three leaflets.

TUBER: thickened underground stem.

TUBERCLE: a small swelling or knob.

TUBEROUS: consisting of round fleshy tubers

UMBELS: a flat-topped cluster of flowers having their footstalks of nearly equal length and radiating outwards.

VARIEGATED: marked with different patches of colour; dappled.

VERSATILE: when the anther is so connected to the filament that it swings freely, as if balanced on a pivot.

WHORL: a ring of leaves or flowers around a stem.

ZONE: a band or girdle of colour.

Simple leaf

Spike

Stipules

Trefoil

Umbels

# INDEX TO FAMILY NAMES

# INDEX TO SPECIES

215

Printed for the Publishers by Jarrold & Sons Ltd,
Norwich and London
931.1153

Printed for the Publishers by Jarrold & Sons Ltd,
Norwich and London
931.1153